McCormack's
life in San Francisc
understandable. Th
sented in a readable

MW01278599

Scholastic Aptitude Test (SAT) scores, rankings for public schools, what to look for in private and public schools, a directory of private schools — they are all inside. The perfect guide for San Francisco and San Mateo County parents or people shopping for homes or apartments.

The **"San Francisco & San Mateo County '94"** edition of McCormack's Guides tells which months have the most rain, which the least, when to expect the fog.

Neighborhood and city profiles. Home prices, rents. Housing trends.

Hospital services and day care. Directory of major local hospitals and a directory of San Francisco and San Mateo County day-care centers.

Places to visit. Things to do. Parks, museums, recreation and entertainment for children and adults. Giants, A's schedules.

The commuting scene. Tactics to save time and sanity. SamTrans, BART, Muni, CalTrain as alternatives to driving.

Looking for work? "San Francisco & San Mateo County" tells what jobs are in demand. Salary sampler.

Vital statistics. Population, income, education by town. Republicans and Democrats. Crime, ethnic makeup, history.

Don McCormack is a former newspaper reporter, editor and columnist. Cops, courts, planning, schools, politics — he has covered them all.

Publisher and editor Don McCormack formed McCormack's Guides in 1984 to publish annual guides to California counties. A graduate of the University of California-Berkeley, McCormack joined the Contra Costa Times in 1969 and covered police, schools, politics, planning, courts and government. Later with the Richmond Independent and Berkeley Gazette, he worked as a reporter, then editor and columnist. McCormack writes a twice-monthly article for the real estate section of the San Francisco Examiner.

Co-editor and co-publisher Allen Kanda has worked as a reporter and editor for the Richmond Independent and Berkeley Gazette. A University of Washington graduate with a degree in chemical engineering, Kanda researches trends in computers, business and information technology.

To Deborah Ann: Neither blizzards nor earthquakes nor stock market crashes will silence the call of the Pacific. Best wishes!

DISCLAIMER

Indexed   ISBN 0-931299-43-8

SAN FRANCISCO & SAN MATEO COUNTY '94

Edited by Don McCormack
and Allen Kanda

3211 Elmquist Court, Martinez, CA 94553
Phone: (510) 229-3581 or Fax: (510) 228-7223

Contents

(Contents continued on Page 6)

—4—

CENTURY 21® DIRECTORY
San Francisco & San Mateo County

DALY CITY

CENTURY 21 City Center Realty, Inc.
331 E. Market St.
Daly City, CA 94014
(415) 985-0500

CENTURY 21 Herd & Co. Realtors, Inc.
100 Skyline Plaza
Daly City, CA 94015
(415) 992-4900

CENTURY 21 Imperial
2141 Junipero Serra Blvd.
Daly City, CA 94014
(415) 992-6000

CENTURY 21 Vision Realty, Inc.
207 Southgate Ave.
Daly City, CA 94015
(415) 991-2120

EAST PALO ALTO

CENTURY 21 Alpha Pacific
1926 University Ave.
East Palo Alto, CA 94303
(415) 328-6100

FOSTER CITY

CENTURY 21 Compass Alta
385 Foster City Blvd.
Foster City, CA 94404
(415) 341-2121

HALF MOON BAY

CENTURY 21 Sunset Realty
210 Main St.
Half Moon Bay, CA 94019
(415) 726-6346

PACIFICA

CENTURY 21 Bay Area Real Estate
450 Dondee Way, Suite 7
Pacifica, CA 94044
(415) 359-8300

San Francisco

San Mateo County

REDWOOD CITY

CENTURY 21 Mutual Realty
1060 El Camino Real
Redwood City, CA 94063
(415) 365-1555

SAN BRUNO

CENTURY 21 C & R Realty, Inc.
358 El Camino Real
San Bruno, CA 94066
(415) 873-3460

SAN FRANCISCO

CENTURY 21 Action Realty Service
1430 Taraval St.
San Francisco, CA 94116
(415) 566-9800

SAN FRANCISCO

CENTURY 21 Baldini Realty
4977 Mission St.
San Francisco, CA 94112
(415) 587-4212

CENTURY 21 City Properties
5812 Geary Blvd.
San Francisco, CA 94121
(415) 668-5900

CENTURY 21 Fox & Fox Realtors
100 W. Portal Ave.
San Francisco, CA 94127
(415) 665-0330

CENTURY 21 Gateway Realty
201 Granada Ave.
San Francisco, CA 94112
(415) 334-6500

CENTURY 21 Gibraltar Realty
1708 Church St.
San Francisco, CA 94131
(415) 641-1030

CENTURY 21 Tower Realty
2454 Noriega St.
San Francisco, CA 94122
(415) 564-6600

SAN MATEO

CENTURY 21 Pacific Coast Properties
155 East 5th Ave.
San Mateo, CA 94401
(415) 347-2900

SOUTH SAN FRANCISCO

CENTURY 21 Best Sellers II
3540 Callan Blvd., Suite 205
South San Francisco, CA 94080
(415) 872-1200

CENTURY 21 Towne Realty
663 El Camino Real
South San Francisco, CA 94080
(415) 583-5360

Each Office Is Independently Owned & Operated

Cover Photo:
A view of Alamo
Square Victorians
with downtown
high rises in the
background. Photo
courtesy of the
San Francisco
Convention &
Visitors Bureau.

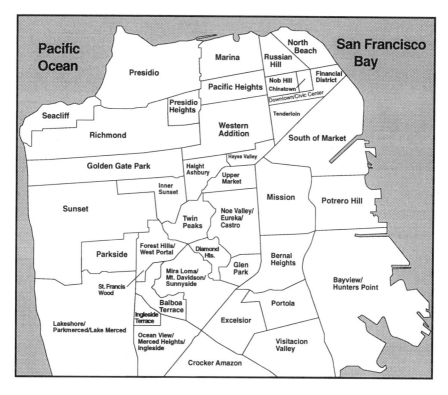

Pacific Ocean

San Francisco Bay

Presidio

Marina

North Beach

Russian Hill

Nob Hill

Financial District

Pacific Heights

Chinatown

Downtown/Civic Center

Presidio Heights

Tenderloin

Seacliff

Richmond

Western Addition

South of Market

Golden Gate Park

Haight Ashbury

Hayes Valley

Upper Market

Inner Sunset

Mission

Potrero Hill

Sunset

Twin Peaks

Noe Valley/ Eureka/ Castro

Forest Hills/ West Portal

Diamond Hts.

Parkside

Glen Park

Bernal Heights

Mira Loma/ Mt. Davidson/ Sunnyside

St. Francis Wood

Balboa Terrace

Portola

Bayview/ Hunters Point

Ingleside Terrace

Excelsior

Lakeshore/ Parkmerced/Lake Merced

Ocean View/ Merced Heights/ Ingleside

Visitacion Valley

Crocker Amazon

City & County of San Francisco

Pacific Ocean

1/San Francisco at a Glance

Population, Dimensions, History, Income, Voter Makeup, Presidential Choices, Vital Stats

SMALL IN SIZE, LARGE IN STATURE, SAN FRANCISCO covers 45 square miles and measures from east to west and from north to south about 8 miles. Every year in a traditional race known as the Bay-To-Breakers thousands run the east-west route in less than an hour, and the fastest cover the distance in about 35 minutes.

Residents, who number 752,049 (state estimate 1993), call it "The City," a conceit absentmindedly parroted by reporters. It is in fact not the largest city in the Bay Area. That honor goes to San Jose, population 822,013.

But in history, tradition, allure and power to cast spells, it is, unmistakably, The City, one of the magic places of the world. Much credit must go to nature and location.

San Francisco sits atop a peninsula. To the west is the Pacific, to the east is the Bay, on many a day filled with billowing sails, and to the north is the Golden Gate. Hills run up and down San Francisco. Delightful vistas. Golden sunrises and sunsets. In summer, the fog pours through the Golden Gate and cascades over the hills and into valleys — damp and cold (many hate it) but entrancing to behold.

San Francisco, to an extent that frequently surprises newcomers, is an intimate city. Politics are conducted with all the gusto and venom of a family feud. The electorate in important races numbers only about 200,000.

Five thousand votes is a lot in this town. This leads politicians to cultivate neighborhoods and small groups. Frank Jordan, the mayor, won by 7,616 votes.

An Immigrant's City
San Francisco has always welcomed immigrants and newcomers.

San Francisco Population vs. Other Counties

County	Male	Female	Total	*Total
Alameda	630,342	648,840	1,279,182	1,337,126
Contra Costa	393,448	410,284	803,732	855,109
Marin	114,001	116,095	230,096	241,265
Napa	54,892	55,873	110,765	116,918
San Francisco	**362,497**	**361,462**	**723,959**	**752,049**
San Mateo	320,188	329,435	649,623	680,885
Santa Clara	759,503	738,074	1,497,577	1,563,800
Solano	174,346	166,075	340,421	369,522
Sonoma	190,272	197,950	388,222	416,278

Source: 1990 Census and Demographic Research Unit of the California Dept. of Finance. *Population estimates by Dept. of Finance., Jan. 1, 1993.

The roster of recent mayors: Jordan (Irish), Agnos (Greek), Feinstein (Jewish), Moscone (Italian), Alioto (Italian) — not one descended from the Puritans, all what used to be called, hyphenated Americans (Irish-American, Italian-American, etc.).

The immigration continues. In the last decade, Asians, many of them Chinese, and Asian-Americans increased by 43 percent and Hispanics by 20 percent. Thousands of Russians are settling in San Francisco.

The 1990 census showed the makeup of the city as 47 percent White, 11 percent Black, 28 percent Asian and Pacific Islander, and 14 percent Hispanic.

In 1993, a freighter loaded with 250 illegal immigrants from China sailed unhindered through the Golden Gate and deposited its human cargo at a dock near the bridge. All were caught, almost immediately. Town was surprised.

Trends

Although San Francisco increased its population by 7 percent in the last decade, it is not expected grow dramatically and some planners predict the numbers will level and fall. The limit might be about 800,000, which would bring the City back to about where it was 40 years ago.

San Francisco is, and has been for years, built-out. The old is demolished for the new, but almost nothing is built on virgin land. In 1992, only 767 new housing units were built, a 30-year low, city hall reports.

To compensate for its lack of space, the City has purchased a good deal of its southern neighbor, San Mateo County, and uses its land for an international airport, miles of wooded watershed, a reservoir and a jail.

In population, San Francisco, which is both a city and a county, ranks 10th among California counties and fourth among its cities, surpassed by Los Angeles, San Diego and the upstart San Jose.

San Francisco's Place in Northern California

Although the acknowledged cultural and social leader in Northern California, San Francisco in many ways is out of step with the region.

Politically, Northern California votes the middle of the road, or slightly left of middle. San Francisco (joined by Alameda County) almost invariably votes liberal Democratic: McGovern, Mondale and Dukakis.

In 1991, the school district booted the Boy Scouts out of classrooms, accusing the Scouts of being homophobic because they did not welcome gay scout masters (The ban applied only to daytime programs. Scouts are free to work after hours at schools.)

City Hall recognizes gay marriages. San Francisco is second only to New York in number of gay and lesbian couples (6,816 reports the 1990 census). Condoms are available at the high schools. During the Gulf War, the board of supervisors declared San Francisco a sanctuary for conscientious objectors.

In crime, San Francisco follows a typical urban pattern: high in poor neighborhoods, medium to low in middle and rich neighborhoods. But overall, crime is probably the biggest worry of the City. Preliminary count for 1993 put violent deaths at 132, the highest tally in 17 years.

The homeless, many in number, have buttressed this image as being unsafe.

Many California school systems are struggling to educate immigrant and minority children but very few are under court order to integrate. San Francisco schools are under court order and the school system's enrollment policy infuriates many parents. (Scores are a mixed bag. Many low, many high. Private schools are plentiful and generally successful.)

San Francisco, in an important way, is an adults' town. Around the Bay Region, kids under age 18 make up about 25 percent of the population. In San Francisco, the 1990 census revealed, they account for only 16 percent (Kids under 5 years: 18,226 boys, 17,373 girls). San Francisco is a singles town, another difference from the suburbs. The Bay Area average for people-never-married (census 1990) is 31 percent, and for people now married is 51 percent. The corresponding figures for San Francisco are 42 percent and 38 percent.

Although almost every city in the Bay Region offers apartments for rent, by far the dominant form of housing in the outlying counties is the single home owned by the inhabitants (who are in hock to the bank). San Francisco has its

---

FOHHHHHG, YES; BEEP, NO

When the Coast Guard decided to replace its San Francisco foghorns with electronic beepers, a great groan went up.

The horns are soooo San Francisco, the critics said. "Unnecessary progress," a politician labeled the beepers.

Horns are back, maintained by a private group.

Ethnic Makeup of Neighborhoods

District	Population as Percent of Total				Total Population
	Asian	White	Hisp.	Black	
Bay View-Hunter's Point	21	8	9	61	27,899
Bernal Heights	20	37	35	8	23,445
Chinatown	92	6	1	1	8,263
Crocker-Amazon	44	23	30	3	17,384
Diamond Heights	17	61	11	11	7,973
Excelsior	32	28	36	3	26,638
Financial Downtown	34	54	7	5	11,724
Glen Park	9	67	20	3	4,098
Haight-Ashbury	8	72	6	13	17,262
Hayes Valley	8	50	10	30	20,734
Ingleside Terrace, Balboa Terrace	24	60	8	7	9,769
Inner Sunset	26	63	7	9	16,667
Lakeshore, Park Merced, Lake Merced	23	63	7	7	13,521
Marina	8	86	5	1	12,649
Miraloma, Mt. Davidson, Sunnyside	23	55	16	6	12,282
Mission	11	29	55	4	44,118
Nob Hill	51	44	3	2	24,892
Noe-Eureka-Castro	7	75	15	2	24,899
North Beach	46	47	4	3	12,487
Ocean View, Merced Heights, Ingleside	27	17	12	42	19,924
Pacific Heights	8	86	4	2	24,527
Parkside	37	56	6	1	6,981
Portola	39	27	23	10	17,649
Potrero Hill	10	57	13	20	9,836
Presidio Heights	18	71	4	6	9,501
Richmond	45	46	5	3	73,497
Russian Hill	45	51	3	1	18,594
Seacliff	17	78	3	1	2,457
South of Market	23	39	27	10	24,883
Sunset	45	47	6	2	67,457
Tenderloin-Civic Center	33	44	11	11	24,169
Twin Peaks	12	75	7	6	11,082
Upper Market	7	76	12	4	10,171
Visitacion Valley	43	12	14	31	17,675
Western Addition	18	42	5	34	24,420
West Portal, Forest Hills, St. Francis Wood	25	67	6	1	12,627

Source: U.S. Census, 1990. Percentages are rounded off to nearest whole number.

Average Household Income in San Francisco, Other Counties

County	1990	*1995	*2000
Alameda	$48,994	$52,300	$56,800
Contra Costa	59,432	62,200	65,800
Marin	73,412	78,600	86,400
Napa	49,911	52,000	57,300
San Francisco	**49,360**	**54,200**	**58,400**
San Mateo	63,672	67,500	73,200
Santa Clara	62,440	65,700	72,100
Solano	46,868	49,600	53,900
Sonoma	47,970	50,900	54,400

Source: Association of Bay Area Governments, *"Projections 92."* Average income per household includes wages and salaries, dividends, interest, rent and transfer payments such as Social Security or public assistance. Based on 1990 Census data, income is stated in 1990 dollars. *Projections.

homeowners but it is mainly a renting city.

Of its 332,538 housing units, 55,446 are single family, 49,784 single-family attached and 227,195 multiples (1993 state estimates).

Year in and year out Bay Area residents, in polls, place traffic congestion at the top of local problems. San Francisco, short of parking, saddled with earthquake-ruined freeways, also suffers from congestion but — and it's a big but — compared to most other counties, it comes off quite well. No matter how creaky the buses or late the trains, eight miles, after all, is eight miles, and no bridges to cross.

Despite these Differences ...

Northern Californians continue to look to San Francisco for leadership, and in ways large and small the City exerts great influence on the region.

San Francisco is the only Northern California city that seems to command enough media attention to produce in quantity state political leaders. The speaker of the Assembly and the lieutenant governor got their starts in San Francisco politics. Dianne Feinstein, U.S. senator, is a former mayor of the City.

Only a few cities in the north have shown metropolitan energy — the will and imagination to attempt and manage big projects. Modern San Francisco is often accused of resting on its laurels but the laurels are substantial and include an international airport, a high-rise downtown and financial center, and numerous civic amenities. San Francisco retains its status as a headquarters city.

In the arts and amusements — museums, plays, exhibits, operas, symphonies, restaurants, saloons and more — San Francisco remains light years ahead of what the suburbs can muster.

When you think the City is slipping, it somehow often manages to come back. San Jose said no to the Giants; San Francisco said let's try again. The Giants stayed.

In style, despite its zanies, San Francisco is the only Northern California city that can be called cosmopolitan.

Gays in San Jose and Concord and other suburban cities enjoy freedoms unthinkable 20 or 25 years ago. San Francisco, which has a large homosexual community, shamed and badgered the Bay Area into respecting the rights of homosexuals and the feelings of AIDS victims.

The West Coast has two world-class cities: Los Angeles and San Francisco. The rest — Seattle, Vancouver, San Diego — are nice but are not the stuff of myth and magic.

San Francisco Before the Europeans

Before the Europeans, there were the Indians, called Costanoans by the Spanish and Ohlones by modern historians. The Indians fished for salmon in the bay and ocean, gathered shellfish, ground acorns for meal and hunted deer, bear and other animals.

Historians estimate that about 10,000 lived between San Francisco and Monterey. Their ways were the ways of their ancestors; very little changed apparently over several thousand years. They had no contact with the great outside world and when contact was made, it destroyed them.

Nothing about the days of the Dons (the Spanish and Mexican periods) makes sense unless it is realized that they came late and came few in number.

Fierce Indians and a hostile desert discouraged exploration north from Mexico and ship explorations of the coast were rare and haphazard. Sir Francis Drake supposedly set foot in Marin County in 1579 and a Portuguese explorer likewise in 1595.

The Spanish Arrive

Not until 1769, on the eve of the American Revolution, did the Spanish (Gaspar de Portola and Junipero Serra) discover the Bay. The mission, named after St. Francis of Assisi, and the Presidio followed.

———

VOTE SPEAKS WELL OF DUMMY

Among the more bizarre matters decided by San Francisco voters in 1993 was an initiative to let a police officer work with his dummy (a puppet).

Police brass wanted to scrap the hunk of wood but the officer said "Brendan O'Smarty," the dummy, helped him to relate to people.

Cop and dummy won.

Coming & Going
(Driver's License Address Changes)

County	Moved To SF from	Moved Out of SF to	Net
Alameda	5,021	6,468	-1,447
Alpine	3	4	-1
Amador	12	21	-9
Butte	164	123	41
Calaveras	12	20	-8
Colusa	3	7	-4
Contra Costa	2,402	3,812	-1,410
Del Norte	7	7	0
El Dorado	76	102	-26
Fresno	286	226	60
Glenn	5	11	-6
Humboldt	100	102	-2
Imperial	12	13	-1
Inyo	6	5	1
Kern	122	80	42
Kings	29	29	0
Lake	43	108	-65
Lassen	13	5	8
Los Angeles	4,153	2,918	1,235
Madera	28	23	5
Marin	1,778	3,113	-1,335
Mariposa	9	12	-3
Mendocino	75	133	-58
Merced	53	59	-6
Modoc	3	3	0
Mono	6	3	3
Monterey	318	259	59
Napa	162	256	-94
Nevada	66	99	-33
Orange	997	543	454
Placer	110	112	-2
Plumas	12	11	1
Riverside	251	223	28
Sacramento	954	1,146	-192
San Benito	16	12	4
San Bernardino	283	193	90
San Diego	1,485	1,263	222
San Joaquin	348	299	49

Coming & Going
(Driver's License Address Changes)

County	Moved To SF from	Moved Out of SF to	Net
San Luis Obispo	171	111	60
San Mateo	6,854	10,280	-3,426
Santa Barbara	414	201	213
Santa Clara	2,751	2,490	261
Santa Cruz	524	324	200
Shasta	61	65	-4
Sierra	1	3	-2
Siskiyou	11	20	-9
Solano	655	1,073	-418
Sonoma	783	1,359	-576
Stanislaus	207	250	-43
Sutter	10	17	-7
Tehama	5	22	-17
Trinity	3	7	-4
Tulare	55	58	-3
Tuolumne	23	35	-12
Ventura	181	156	25
Yolo	245	212	33
Yuba	22	23	-1
All Counties	32,399	38,529	-6,130
Out of State	12,624	8,201	4,423
Total	45,023	46,730	-1,707

Source: California Department of Finance, 1993. Data covers fiscal year July 1, 1992-June 30, 1993. Out-of-state counts have not been adjusted for non-compliers.

Lacking their own laborers (at the Mexican-American War fewer than 7,000 Spanish-Mexicans resided in California), the Spanish dragooned the Indians. They were brought to the missions where they were trained as field hands and under the tutelage of the padres ushered into Catholicism. The policy, as it worked itself out over the next 75 years, killed almost all of the Indians, mainly by measles, smallpox and other diseases.

The Mexicans overthrew the Spanish in 1821. The missions were secularized in the 1830s, weakening the little protection afforded Indians. Rancheros were carved out of the countryside for the original soldiers and their heirs.

Here Come the Yankees

Meanwhile, the United States had beaten the British and purchased the

Education Level of Population Age 18 & Older

City or County	HS	SC	AA	BA	Grad
Alameda County	24	24	7	17	10
Contra Costa County	24	25	8	19	10
Marin County	17	25	7	26	16
Napa County	25	26	9	14	7
Oakland	21	22	6	15	10
San Francisco	**19**	**20**	**6**	**22**	**17**
San Jose	21	24	8	16	7
Santa Clara County	20	24	8	19	11
San Mateo County	22	24	8	19	10
Solano County	28	29	9	12	5
Sonoma County	25	28	9	15	7

Source: 1990 Census. Figures are percent of population age 18 and older, rounded to the nearest whole number. Not shown are adults with less than a 9th grade education or with some high school education but no diploma or GED. **Key**: HS (adults with high school diploma or GED only, no college); SC (adults with some college education); AA (adults with an associate degree); BA (adults with a bachelor's degree only); Grad (adults with a master's or higher degree).

Midwest. Over the mountains came the Americans, first trappers, then business men and farmers.

When war came in 1846, the Americans didn't so much beat the Mexicans, although there were skirmishes, as overwhelm them by numbers.

Two years later, while building a mill in the Sierra, James Marshall caught sight of shiny flakes in the water. The Gold Rush was on.

Within a year, even though sailors abandoned ships as soon as they arrived, San Francisco's population jumped from 800 to more than 25,000, and the City became the financial and commercial heart for mining towns. Factories were built and thrived.

The Railroad

The continental railroad, built mainly by the Chinese and the Irish, was finished in 1869, a great boost to the West Coast economy. Four years later, cable manufacturer Andrew S. Hallidie built a railroad of a different sort — the city's first cable car. His invention was the safest means of transportation over the city's many hills.

This was the era of fabulous fortunes and fabled men and women. Plagued by thieves and murderers (the section near Pacific Avenue and Kearney Street was known as the Barbary Coast), San Francisco formed a Vigilance Committee and hung or banished the worst of the bad men.

Population Profile by Occupation

City or County	EX	PF	TC	SA	CL	SV	AG	MF
Alameda County	15	17	5	11	18	11	1	22
Contra Costa County	18	16	4	13	17	11	1	19
Marin County	21	22	3	15	14	10	2	13
Napa County	13	15	4	10	14	16	5	23
Oakland	14	18	4	10	18	15	1	20
San Francisco	**16**	**19**	**4**	**12**	**18**	**16**	**1**	**9**
San Jose	14	15	6	11	17	12	1	25
San Mateo County	17	15	4	13	19	12	2	29
Santa Clara County	16	19	6	11	16	10	1	21
Solano County	12	12	4	12	17	14	2	16
Sonoma County	13	15	4	13	15	13	4	24

Source: 1990 Census. **Key**: EX (executive and managerial); PF (professional specialty); TC (technicians); SA (sales); CL (clerical and administrative support); SV (service occupations, including household, protective and other services); AG (agricultural including farming, fishing, forestry); MF (manufacturing including precision production, craft , repair; also machine operators, assemblers, inspectors, equipment cleaners and handlers, helpers and laborers). Figures are percent of population, rounded to the nearest whole number.

Great mansions were erected on Nob Hill. Streets were laid out, parks planted, the arts encouraged, and vice, to a certain extent, ignored. San Francisco has always been sympathetic to the failings of the flesh, the foundation of its modern sexual tolerance.

San Francisco entered the 20th century confident of its future and boasting a population of 342,782.

The Great Quake

Six years later, on April 18, a great earthquake struck the City. Very little damage but the resultant fires destroyed the financial section and most of the downtown. The fire line was Van Ness Avenue. If you want to see Victorians, don't look east of Van Ness; look west.

About 700 people were killed in the earthquake, 300,000 lost their homes and the damage exceeded $500 million, in those days an enormous sum.

But San Francisco came roaring back, part of its legend. The destroyed neighborhoods were rebuilt, the saved expanded.

In 1915, a new San Francisco showed itself off to the world by hosting the Panama-Pacific International Exposition, celebrating the opening of the Panama Canal. By 1930, the city's population had almost doubled to 634,394.

The 1930s also saw San Francisco shine. While other cities stagnated in the

Religion in San Francisco

Denomination	Churches	Members	Total
Advent Christian	1	39	45
African Methodist Episcopal Zion	2	773	900
American Baptist	15	5,865	5,714
Assembly of God	16	2,518	3,491
Catholic	58	NA	195,160
Christian & Missionary Alliance	4	485	629
Church of Christ	1	30	34
Disciples of Christ	2	213	268
Church of Christ, Scientist	8	NR	NR
Church of God (Anderson, Ind.)	2	63	73
Church of God (Cleveland, Tenn.)	3	201	230
Church of God (Prophecy)	1	31	35
Latter-day Saints	5	NA	1,937
Church of the Brethren	1	50	57
Church of the Nazarene	5	354	517
Church of Christ	8	1,809	2,287
Cumberland Presbyterian	2	729	764
Episcopal	19	4,625	6,456
Estonian Evangelical Lutheran	1	80	92
Evangelical Free	1	200	350
Evangelical Lutheran	12	1,949	2,702
Free Methodist	1	90	90
Friends	1	62	128
Apostolic Catholic Assyrian	1	42	193
Foursquare Gospel	1	130	149
Latvian Evangelical Lutheran	1	336	388
Lutheran-Missouri Synod	7	1,586	1,923
Mennonite	1	33	66
Mennonite General Conference	2	72	94
Open Bible Standard	1	NR	NR
Orthodox Church in America	3	NR	NR
Pentecostal Holiness	1	7	8
Christian Brethren	1	60	75
Presbyterian (USA)	18	4,057	4,644
Reformed Church in America	2	150	225
Salvation Army	7	742	822
Seventh-day Adventist	8	1,382	1,582
Southern Baptist	22	3,930	4,499
Unitarian-Universalist	1	586	696
United Church of Christ	8	1,215	1,391

Religion in San Francisco

Denomination	Churches	Members	Total
United Methodist	18	5,556	6,360
Jewish*	22	NA	45,500
Independent, Charismatic*	5	NA	3,225
Independent, Non-Charismatic*	3	NA	1,450
San Francisco totals	302	56,953	315,599

Source: Glenmary Research Center, Atlanta, GA, 1990. **Key**: No. (Number of churches in the county); Members (Communicant, confirmed, full members); Total (All adherents); NA (Not applicable); NR (Not reported). *Estimates.

Depression, San Francisco (and its neighbors) built the region's two great public works: the Bay Bridge, 1936, and the Golden Gate Bridge, 1937.

After the War

World War II brought another population boom. Tens of thousands, many of them Blacks from the South, came to the City to build ships and work in the war industries. Thousands of GIs embarked for the Pacific through the port of San Francisco. In 1945, San Francisco served as host for the formation of the United Nations.

The postwar period is often portrayed as period of stagnation. San Francisco's population, fattened to 827,000 by the war, melted away over 200,000 residents by 1980. The new suburbs attracted the City's middle class, leaving behind a disproportionate number of the poor and the old.

Unfortunate decisions were made. Victorians were demolished to make way for ugly public housing. Neighborhoods were sacrificed to freeways, and the Embarcadero freeway commissioned, cutting off the Bay. The Embarcadero was to have run up to Golden Gate Bridge but citizens revolted and stopped it well short of Fisherman's Wharf.

The port, always the pride of the City, faded in the postwar years. Oakland and the oil wharves of Contra Costa County now handle most of the shipping to Northern California.

Hippies, Drugs and Cults

San Francisco celebrates the Hippie era but it made drug usage popular, not only here but throughout the country. Modern crime in the City owes much to drugs.

Eccentrics have always been welcome in the City but in the 1970s the unusual became the tragic. Jim Jones established his People's Temple on Geary Boulevard, cozied up to politicians and was on his way to fame and fortune before tripping over his own malevolence. The whole business ended sordidly

Voter Registration
(San Francisco & Other Counties & Cities)

City or County	Democrat	Republican	*Declined
Alameda County	427,339	158,312	76,640
Berkeley	51,989	7,938	9,898
Contra Costa County	251,577	175,133	42,575
Marin County	77,524	45,203	19,111
Oakland	144,722	21,103	18,072
San Francisco	**269,968**	**71,774**	**61,264**
San Jose	191,951	122,251	44,901
San Mateo County	180,560	109,620	42,556
Santa Clara County	387,353	273,721	99,197
Solano County	93,224	51,708	18,577
Sonoma County	134,534	73,907	22,641

Source: Secretary of State, October, 1993. *Voters who declined to state any political party affiliation.

in South America with the shooting death of a congressman and the suicide of hundreds, including Jones.

Months later, Dan White, a disgruntled ex-firemen and politician, climbed through a city hall window and gunned down Mayor George Moscone and Harvey Milk, the City's first openly-gay member of the board of supervisors.

White's lawyer said his man was thrown out of whack, in part, by eating many cupcakes, a tactic known in local lore as the "Twinkies Defense." The jury bought this and other arguments and let White off with voluntary manslaughter. That night, gays rioted in the downtown. After serving his term, White committed suicide.

San Francisco, probably because it is small, is an intimate town. The movers and shakers, the activists generally know each other. When Milk and Moscone died, a lot of fun went out of public life.

The '80s — Highs and Lows

In the 1980s, the homeless began appearing in great numbers, particularly in the downtown and around city hall. San Francisco is a humane town and the City tried to do well by its unfortunates.

But crime rose, appearances suffered and confidence eroded in the ability of government to solve problems.

The City closed out the 1980s on what promised to be a high note — a Series showdown in October 1989 between the Giants and the A's — but just as the third game was to start, the Loma Prieta earthquake struck, reminding all that nature was constantly rolling the dice in Northern California. The Bay

Presidential Voting in San Francisco

Year	Democrat	D-Votes	Republican	R-Votes
1948	Truman*	167,726	Dewey	160,135
1952	Stevenson	167,282	Eisenhower*	188,531
1956	Stevenson	161,766	Eisenhower*	173,648
1960	Kennedy*	197,734	Nixon	143,001
1964	Johnson*	230,758	Goldwater	92,994
1968	Humphrey	177,509	Nixon*	100,970
1972	McGovern	170,882	Nixon*	127,461
1976	Carter*	133,733	Ford	103,561
1980	Carter	133,184	Reagan*	80,967
1984	Mondale	193,278	Reagan*	90,219
1988	Dukakis	201,887	Bush*	72,503
1992**	Clinton*	230,007	Bush	56,373

Source: Calif. Secretary of State. *Election winner nationally. **Ross Perot (28,574).

Bridge collapsed in one spot and many structures in the Marina District were badly damaged.

If problems abounded, however, so did triumphs, although perhaps less appreciated. The City joined Contra Costa and Alameda counties in constructing a rail rapid transit system called BART. Service started in 1972. The international airport was expanded several times to keep up with growing air traffic. Davies Symphony Hall was built. The downtown, not without opposition, underwent a building boom. It's a much different, livelier downtown than it was 30 years ago.

After years of decline, the population in the 1980s began coming up, much of increase coming from Asians and Hispanics. When people vote for a city with their feet, when they commit themselves to reside in that city, that's a strong vote of confidence.

The Forty-Niners, with their winning ways, put a lot of sparkle in the town.

The Nineties

New mayor. Much more awareness of diversity. The mayor's race, for the first time, saw a serious Asian candidate.

Also much more awareness of the complexity of diversity. For a long time, people approached minorities as if they were a single block, as in, the minority is now a majority, and as if all minorities were oppressed and just hungering to vote liberal.

Now differences among minorities are getting more attention. Jordan, the new mayor, is a former police chief who drew a lot of support from the Asian community. (He's also a liberal and a consensus builder but in San Francisco, which likes its liberals to be flaming, many consider him a conservative.)

For all the misery of the 1989 earthquake, many San Franciscans were glad it demolished the much despised freeway that had intruded into the beloved waterfront. Already the waterfront, with clear vistas to the Bay, is undergoing a renaissance.

A Word About Government

San Francisco is the only city in California that is also a county. Instead of a city council, San Francisco elects an 11-member board of supervisors as its legislative body. Members serve four years. The mayor also is elected directly to a four-year term and can veto legislation by the board.

Because it is a charter city, San Francisco can amend its powers at the polls without seeking permission from the state Legislature. Almost every election features ballot amendments.

2/San Francisco School Rankings

Reading, Writing, Math, Science & History Tests

ALTHOUGH SAN FRANCISCO has many high-scoring schools, the question — how good are the schools — is difficult to answer because scores are greatly influenced by parents and background. If your mother and father attended college and drummed into you that you should attend college, well, chances are good — many studies strongly indicate — that you're going to score high on tests that try to determine the minimum you should know.

That's what the CAP tests attempted to do: they tested basic knowledge. The tests are now history, shot down in the political wars that regularly sweep the state. The last CAP test was confined to eighth graders and given in 1992. New tests were introduced in 1993 but the first results won't be issued until 1994.

In the meantime the CAP tests results are among the best we have for determining not how individual students or classes did, but for how the school is made up demographically. High scores generally identify well-to-do or educated neighborhoods; middling scores, middle-class neighborhoods; low, poor neighborhoods. For more discussion see the chapters on how public schools work and San Francisco integration.

These rankings, issued by the California Department of Education, are slightly weighted to allow for enrollment differences but are very close to unalloyed percentiles.

What Percentiles Mean

If a school scores in the 91st percentile, it has done better than 91 percent of the other public schools in the state. If it scores in the 51st percentile, it has done better than 51 percent of the others; the 40th rank, better than 40 percent of the others. If a school scores in the first percentile, 99 percent of the other schools have scored higher.

Rankings

These rankings are drawn from state tests given over three years, 1988, 1989, 1990, and from the 1992 eighth grade test.

For the most part, the rankings will follow a pattern. High one year will be high the next, low will be low.

When the numbers fluctuate wildly, the number of children who took the tests will often be low. In a small class, one or two kids having a bad or good day will cause wide swings. Sometimes the children fail to understand instructions and this lowers their grade. Sometimes they just have an off day.

A Cautionary Note

Ranking systems don't recognize overall gains or losses. If every school in California raised raw scores 20 percent, some schools would still be ranked at the bottom, a few at the top. The same if every raw score dropped. A ranking system shows how one school did against all other schools. There is no one perfect method of testing.

SAN FRANCISCO UNIFIED SCHOOL DISTRICT
Districtwide

3rd Grade	1988	1989	1990	1992
Reading	40	48	41	—
Writing	37	43	37	—
Math	50	54	50	—
No. Tested	4,422	4,340	4,219	—
6th Grade	1988	1989	1990	1992
Reading	29	26	24	—
Writing	32	31	30	—
Math	37	37	32	—
No. Tested	3,794	3,782	3,792	—
8th Grade	1988	1989	1990	1992
Reading	29	30	28	29
Writing	37	—	—	34
Math	46	48	45	49
History	35	39	33	31
Science	25	27	27	27
No. Tested	3,970	3,844	3,705	3,725
12th Grade	1988	1989	1990	1992
Reading	25	34	29	—
Writing	—	22	26	—
Math	48	59	57	—
No. Tested	3,703	3,548	3,453	—

A.P. Giannini Middle

6th Grade	1988	1989	1990	1992
Reading	23	19	26	—
Writing	40	31	31	—
Math	45	44	50	—
No. Tested	278	283	295	—

8th Grade	1988	1989	1990	1992
Reading	44	46	16	36
Writing	54	—	—	43
Math	64	67	50	77
History	54	34	28	42
Science	44	31	27	31
No. Tested	321	320	326	337

Abraham Lincoln High

12th Grade	1988	1989	1990	1992
Reading	12	17	11	—
Writing	—	23	17	—
Math	32	49	49	—
No. Tested	397	355	399	—

Alamo Elementary

3rd Grade	1988	1989	1990	1992
Reading	95	83	94	—
Writing	90	92	89	—
Math	97	90	94	—
No. Tested	118	115	108	—

Alvarado Elementary

3rd Grade	1988	1989	1990	1992
Reading	7	14	5	—
Writing	5	6	4	—
Math	9	14	9	—
No. Tested	58	46	56	—

Aptos Middle

6th Grade	1988	1989	1990	1992
Reading	32	32	26	—
Writing	44	32	38	—
Math	33	32	29	—
No. Tested	257	271	334	—

SAN FRANCISCO UNIFIED (Continued)

Aptos Middle

8th Grade	1988	1989	1990	1992
Reading	50	27	18	25
Writing	55	—	—	25
Math	67	29	29	43
History	56	23	23	35
Science	34	14	18	28
No. Tested	341	257	239	332

Argonne Elementary

3rd Grade	1988	1989	1990	1992
Reading	75	83	65	—
Writing	77	84	63	—
Math	77	86	79	—
No. Tested	65	54	59	—

Balboa High

12th Grade	1988	1989	1990	1992
Reading	5	19	6	—
Writing	—	13	3	—
Math	4	7	6	—
No. Tested	324	237	187	—

Benjamin Franklin Middle

6th Grade	1988	1989	1990	1992
Reading	5	4	5	—
Writing	6	12	10	—
Math	19	11	20	—
No. Tested	224	145	165	—

8th Grade	1988	1989	1990	1992
Reading	2	6	4	3
Writing	2	—	—	13
Math	15	21	41	25
History	3	10	10	3
Science	1	4	15	6
No. Tested	251	210	208	207

Bessie Carmichael Elementary

3rd Grade	1988	1989	1990	1992
Reading	17	24	28	—
Writing	18	20	45	—
Math	13	30	42	—
No. Tested	51	59	52	—

Bret Harte Elementary

3rd Grade	1988	1989	1990	1992
Reading	5	9	2	—
Writing	4	11	8	—
Math	4	18	4	—
No. Tested	63	61	58	—

Bryant Elementary

3rd Grade	1988	1989	1990	1992
Reading	16	24	12	—
Writing	20	29	20	—
Math	13	49	34	—
No. Tested	39	48	43	—

Buena Vista Annex

3rd Grade	1988	1989	1990	1992
Reading	19	43	36	—
Writing	5	24	16	—

3rd Grade	1988	1989	1990	1992
Math	23	57	33	—
No. Tested	36	47	64	—

Burton High

12th Grade	1988	1989	1990	1992
Reading	40	54	31	—
Writing	—	70	36	—
Math	62	72	62	—
No. Tested	123	145	171	—

Cabrillo Elementary

3rd Grade	1988	1989	1990	1992
Reading	78	72	89	—
Writing	62	55	80	—
Math	84	66	95	—
No. Tested	71	58	55	—

Claire Lilienthal Elementary

3rd Grade	1988	1989	1990	1992
Reading	94	93	95	—
Writing	94	95	97	—
Math	87	92	99	—
No. Tested	27	27	30	—

Clarendon/Second Community

3rd Grade	1988	1989	1990	1992
Reading	79	87	90	—
Writing	69	80	85	—
Math	91	90	90	—
No. Tested	82	82	74	—

Cleveland Elementary

3rd Grade	1988	1989	1990	1992
Reading	10	10	13	—
Writing	13	10	16	—
Math	12	5	12	—
No. Tested	59	64	59	—

Commodore Sloat Elementary

3rd Grade	1988	1989	1990	1992
Reading	53	90	69	—
Writing	60	83	66	—
Math	54	84	87	—
No. Tested	65	71	64	—

Commodore Stockton Elementary

3rd Grade	1988	1989	1990	1992
Reading	24	50	17	—
Writing	15	37	19	—
Math	43	66	36	—
No. Tested	150	135	111	—

Daniel Webster Elementary

3rd Grade	1988	1989	1990	1992
Reading	9	14	13	—
Writing	6	9	8	—
Math	7	10	17	—
No. Tested	48	44	51	—

Douglas Traditional

3rd Grade	1988	1989	1990	1992
Reading	70	24	49	—
Writing	44	21	31	—

3rd Grade	1988	1989	1990	1992
Math	61	11	35	—
No. Tested	56	61	46	—

Edison Elementary

3rd Grade	1988	1989	1990	1992
Reading	11	2	4	—
Writing	10	4	2	—
Math	5	3	7	—
No. Tested	79	78	84	—

Edward Taylor Elementary

3rd Grade	1988	1989	1990	1992
Reading	17	20	26	—
Writing	21	29	31	—
Math	11	24	32	—
No. Tested	189	102	107	—

El Dorado Elementary

3rd Grade	1988	1989	1990	1992
Reading	32	47	50	—
Writing	43	51	42	—
Math	21	51	59	—
No. Tested	43	52	47	—

Everett Middle

6th Grade	1988	1989	1990	1992
Reading	22	28	22	—
Writing	23	23	28	—
Math	26	29	18	—
No. Tested	221	227	192	—
8th Grade	1988	1989	1990	1992
Reading	11	25	17	19
Writing	11	—	—	17
Math	12	32	24	33
History	13	17	16	22
Science	10	19	17	17
No. Tested	259	217	228	195

Fairmount Elementary

3rd Grade	1988	1989	1990	1992
Reading	6	6	25	
Writing	4	10	19	
Math	3	7	29	
No. Tested	72	85	73	

Filipino Education Center

3rd Grade	1988	1989	1990	1992
Reading	2	4	—	
Writing	8	2	—	
Math	34	20	—	
No. Tested	9	14	—	

Francis Scott Key Elementary

3rd Grade	1988	1989	1990	1992
Reading	46	63	46	
Writing	48	64	53	
Math	82	76	74	
No. Tested	71	76	86	

Francisco Middle

6th Grade	1988	1989	1990	1992
Reading	15	7	2	—
Writing	12	7	5	—

6th Grade	1988	1989	1990	1992
Math	36	34	23	—
No. Tested	250	272	287	—
8th Grade	1988	1989	1990	1992
Reading	10	18	13	6
Writing	16	—	—	8
Math	42	37	42	24
History	15	21	14	7
Science	9	12	15	7
No. Tested	291	280	244	274

Frank McCoppin Elementary

3rd Grade	1988	1989	1990	1992
Reading	81	79	75	—
Writing	68	78	80	—
Math	89	82	76	—
No. Tested	74	67	57	—

Galileo High

12th Grade	1988	1989	1990	1992
Reading	1	1	1	—
Writing	—	1	1	—
Math	21	14	15	—
No. Tested	333	349	340	—

Garfield Elementary

3rd Grade	1988	1989	1990	1992
Reading	15	50	23	—
Writing	14	34	14	—
Math	29	66	26	—
No. Tested	44	43	40	—

George Peabody Elementary

3rd Grade	1988	1989	1990	1992
Reading	88	77	32	—
Writing	86	80	35	—
Math	97	90	62	—
No. Tested	58	41	58	—

George Moscone Elementary

3rd Grade	1988	1989	1990	1992
Reading	31	36	35	—
Writing	33	31	23	—
Math	41	54	40	—
No. Tested	58	63	58	—

George Wash. Carver Elementary

3rd Grade	1988	1989	1990	1992
Reading	87	90	91	—
Writing	83	88	98	—
Math	91	98	97	—
No. Tested	62	50	52	—

George Washington High

12th Grade	1988	1989	1990	1992
Reading	23	23	37	—
Writing	—	25	31	—
Math	62	60	66	—
No. Tested	587	561	528	—

Glen Park Elementary

3rd Grade	1988	1989	1990	1992
Reading	16	8	27	—
Writing	21	8	17	—

SAN FRANCISCO UNIFIED (Continued)

Glen Park Elementary

3rd Grade	1988	1989	1990	1992
Math	19	17	22	—
No. Tested	57	48	44	—

Golden Gate Elementary

3rd Grade	1988	1989	1990	1992
Reading	3	5	1	—
Writing	7	8	1	—
Math	17	17	1	—
No. Tested	77	77	64	—

Grattan Elementary

3rd Grade	1988	1989	1990	1992
Reading	35	52	39	—
Writing	27	24	17	—
Math	61	53	55	—
No. Tested	40	44	51	—

Guadalupe Elementary

3rd Grade	1988	1989	1990	1992
Reading	35	34	27	—
Writing	32	25	41	—
Math	37	45	45	—
No. Tested	61	66	54	—

Hawthorne Elementary

3rd Grade	1988	1989	1990	1992
Reading	66	70	52	—
Writing	51	54	68	—
Math	75	61	88	—
No. Tested	93	94	99	—

Herbert Hoover Middle

6th Grade	1988	1989	1990	1992
Reading	74	70	61	—
Writing	79	65	59	—
Math	86	86	66	—
No. Tested	459	392	355	—

8th Grade	1988	1989	1990	1992
Reading	78	80	81	71
Writing	82	—	—	73
Math	91	94	89	86
History	89	86	87	79
Science	67	72	70	62
No. Tested	393	463	441	326

Hillcrest Elementary

3rd Grade	1988	1989	1990	1992
Reading	8	17	21	—
Writing	5	15	12	—
Math	4	13	8	—
No. Tested	93	68	82	—

Horace Mann Middle

6th Grade	1988	1989	1990	1992
Reading	23	26	17	—
Writing	26	37	28	—
Math	16	32	17	—
No. Tested	142	214	164	—

8th Grade	1988	1989	1990	1992
Reading	24	36	18	28
Writing	24	—	—	63
Math	29	44	15	31
History	30	52	24	46
Science	23	49	23	32
No. Tested	135	154	166	160

Int'l Studies Academy

12th Grade	1988	1989	1990	1992
Reading	71	74	42	—
Writing	—	75	29	—
Math	72	60	59	—
No. Tested	64	81	85	—

J. Eugene McAteer High

12th Grade	1988	1989	1990	1992
Reading	17	14	29	—
Writing	—	14	12	—
Math	17	31	26	—
No. Tested	281	340	326	—

James Denman Middle

6th Grade	1988	1989	1990	1992
Reading	16	2	8	—
Writing	19	5	10	—
Math	13	10	9	—
No. Tested	232	206	228	—

8th Grade	1988	1989	1990	1992
Reading	14	6	7	15
Writing	14	—	—	14
Math	9	9	8	26
History	11	12	9	10
Science	10	7	6	13
No. Tested	207	196	203	199

James Lick Middle

6th Grade	1988	1989	1990	1992
Reading	6	2	3	—
Writing	21	2	10	—
Math	14	3	7	—
No. Tested	178	123	167	—

8th Grade	1988	1989	1990	1992
Reading	3	1	7	2
Writing	7	—	—	14
Math	3	6	7	12
History	4	2	7	8
Science	5	4	4	5
No. Tested	109	121	114	167

Jean Parker Elementary

3rd Grade	1988	1989	1990	1992
Reading	15	9	11	—
Writing	16	17	9	—
Math	19	17	19	—
No. Tested	65	59	68	—

Jefferson Elementary

3rd Grade	1988	1989	1990	1992
Reading	93	79	90	—
Writing	82	65	79	—
Math	92	69	87	—
No. Tested	83	85	85	—

John O'Donnell High

12th Grade	1988	1989	1990	1992
Reading	9	9	9	—
Writing	—	3	8	—
Math	15	8	10	—
No. Tested	74	106	113	—

John Muir Elementary

3rd Grade	1988	1989	1990	1992
Reading	2	1	1	—
Writing	1	1	1	—
Math	7	1	1	—
No. Tested	69	55	50	—

John Swett Elementary

3rd Grade	1988	1989	1990	1992
Reading	53	57	53	—
Writing	58	52	43	—
Math	64	41	45	—
No. Tested	56	63	61	—

Jose Ortega Elementary

3rd Grade	1988	1989	1990	1992
Reading	48	42	19	—
Writing	40	33	21	—
Math	30	18	8	—
No. Tested	51	51	47	—

Junipero Serra Elementary

3rd Grade	1988	1989	1990	1992
Reading	22	8	14	—
Writing	14	9	14	—
Math	10	8	30	—
No. Tested	42	41	40	—

Lafayette Elementary

3rd Grade	1988	1989	1990	1992
Reading	28	56	23	—
Writing	19	42	16	—
Math	25	48	41	—
No. Tested	82	93	80	—

Lakeshore Elementary

3rd Grade	1988	1989	1990	1992
Reading	90	76	78	—
Writing	91	81	77	—
Math	93	87	77	—
No. Tested	91	97	82	—

Lawton Elementary

3rd Grade	1988	1989	1990	1992
Reading	87	95	98	—
Writing	85	87	92	—
Math	91	91	95	—
No. Tested	67	67	62	—
6th Grade	1988	1989	1990	1992
Reading	98	94	82	—
Writing	89	92	87	—
Math	97	90	83	—
No. Tested	55	76	58	—

8th Grade	1988	1989	1990	1992
Reading	98	94	98	98
Writing	98	—	—	80
Math	98	95	98	95
History	98	95	97	97
Science	96	80	91	96
No. Tested	58	35	50	52

Leonard Flynn Elementary

3rd Grade	1988	1989	1990	1992
Reading	8	42	58	—
Writing	14	45	43	—
Math	7	47	74	—
No. Tested	81	58	60	—

Longfellow Elementary

3rd Grade	1988	1989	1990	1992
Reading	82	68	76	—
Writing	83	66	69	—
Math	91	70	84	—
No. Tested	71	76	69	—

Lowell High

12th Grade	1988	1989	1990	1992
Reading	99	99	99	—
Writing	—	98	99	—
Math	99	99	99	—
No. Tested	618	634	609	—

Luther Burbank Middle

6th Grade	1988	1989	1990	1992
Reading	13	9	10	—
Writing	15	23	18	—
Math	12	7	11	—
No. Tested	247	244	219	—
8th Grade	1988	1989	1990	1992
Reading	13	15	13	13
Writing	15	—	—	28
Math	9	15	20	17
History	15	18	21	18
Science	10	18	15	12
No. Tested	251	237	222	207

Marina Middle

6th Grade	1988	1989	1990	1992
Reading	39	35	41	—
Writing	45	49	57	—
Math	44	54	50	—
No. Tested	264	268	290	—
8th Grade	1988	1989	1990	1992
Reading	51	54	61	62
Writing	72	—	—	69
Math	61	62	53	71
History	62	70	56	53
Science	42	51	49	48
No. Tested	314	294	266	286

Marshall Elementary

3rd Grade	1988	1989	1990	1992
Reading	35	47	35	—
Writing	26	43	16	—
Math	47	57	23	—
No. Tested	49	60	46	—

SAN FRANCISCO UNIFIED (Continued)
M.L. King Academic

6th Grade	1988	1989	1990	1992
Reading	24	28	19	—
Writing	21	31	39	—
Math	28	31	26	—
No. Tested	149	173	182	—

8th Grade	1988	1989	1990	1992
Reading	31	29	33	36
Writing	39	—	—	33
Math	43	37	37	46
History	45	26	22	28
Science	37	27	23	38
No. Tested	128	183	131	167

McKinley Elementary

3rd Grade	1988	1989	1990	1992
Reading	4	29	58	—
Writing	7	16	25	—
Math	3	18	35	—
No. Tested	34	28	24	—

Miraloma Elementary

3rd Grade	1988	1989	1990	1992
Reading	65	41	39	—
Writing	67	60	23	—
Math	71	76	55	—
No. Tested	63	50	47	—

Mission High

12th Grade	1988	1989	1990	1992
Reading	1	2	2	—
Writing	—	1	1	—
Math	6	12	7	—
No. Tested	349	286	241	—

Monroe Elementary

3rd Grade	1988	1989	1990	1992
Reading	86	68	51	—
Writing	91	58	41	—
Math	91	88	70	—
No. Tested	64	56	69	—

New Traditions Center

3rd Grade	1988	1989	1990	1992
Reading	73	84	38	—
Writing	87	51	55	—
Math	84	71	79	—
No. Tested	19	22	23	—

Paul Revere Elementary

3rd Grade	1988	1989	1990	1992
Reading	3	9	9	—
Writing	5	9	13	—
Math	3	6	12	—
No. Tested	91	79	95	—

Potrero Hill Middle

6th Grade	1988	1989	1990	1992
Reading	8	4	2	—
Writing	14	12	5	—
Math	25	14	5	—
No. Tested	211	205	186	—

8th Grade	1988	1989	1990	1992
Reading	6	8	6	3
Writing	6	—	—	7
Math	14	14	30	16
History	7	11	7	2
Science	3	4	9	2
No. Tested	183	178	166	153

Presidio Middle

6th Grade	1988	1989	1990	1992
Reading	63	69	70	—
Writing	62	84	78	—
Math	84	87	86	—
No. Tested	300	281	289	—

8th Grade	1988	1989	1990	1992
Reading	81	79	76	61
Writing	90	—	—	84
Math	87	88	92	84
History	83	89	79	68
Science	77	77	69	65
No. Tested	324	289	306	282

Raoul Wallenberg Traditional High

12th Grade	1988	1989	1990	1992
Reading	88	76	75	—
Writing	—	80	84	—
Math	93	92	91	—
No. Tested	108	132	105	—

Rafael Weill Elementary

3rd Grade	1988	1989	1990	1992
Reading	4	22	2	—
Writing	5	13	6	—
Math	9	18	17	—
No. Tested	61	54	48	—

Redding Elementary

3rd Grade	1988	1989	1990	1992
Reading	33	29	24	—
Writing	19	23	17	—
Math	64	59	56	—
No. Tested	64	66	69	—

Robert L. Stevenson Elementary

3rd Grade	1988	1989	1990	1992
Reading	40	40	57	—
Writing	44	33	63	—
Math	58	79	68	—
No. Tested	57	69	68	—

Rooftop Elementary

3rd Grade	1988	1989	1990	1992
Reading	73	90	97	—
Writing	77	85	90	—
Math	88	89	96	—
No. Tested	59	57	60	—

Roosevelt Middle

6th Grade	1988	1989	1990	1992
Reading	37	31	40	—
Writing	38	39	39	—
Math	54	61	63	—
No. Tested	221	243	239	—

8th Grade	1988	1989	1990	1992
Reading	56	46	54	71
Writing	68	—	—	69
Math	87	70	68	87
History	53	47	50	52
Science	49	55	48	59
No. Tested	234	263	244	245

San Francisco Community Alternative

3rd Grade	1988	1989	1990	1992
Reading	35	78	32	—
Writing	50	87	29	—
Math	46	81	50	—
No. Tested	15	20	17	—

San Francisco Community Alternative

6th Grade	1988	1989	1990	1992
Reading	58	21	35	—
Writing	37	46	57	—
Math	51	30	50	—
No. Tested	18	20	17	—
8th Grade	1988	1989	1990	1992
Reading	4	65	64	24
Writing	19	—	—	50
Math	19	43	33	17
History	4	28	91	29
Science	10	35	38	42
No. Tested	6	18	13	12

Sanchez Elementary

3rd Grade	1988	1989	1990	1992
Reading	9	8	12	—
Writing	5	5	5	—
Math	7	15	8	—
No. Tested	72	57	57	—

Sheridan Elementary

3rd Grade	1988	1989	1990	1992
Reading	44	67	51	—
Writing	62	61	35	—
Math	41	42	45	—
No. Tested	58	57	52	—

Sherman Elementary

3rd Grade	1988	1989	1990	1992
Reading	92	98	94	—
Writing	83	92	83	—
Math	98	98	98	—
No. Tested	76	82	70	—

Sir Francis Drake Elementary

3rd Grade	1988	1989	1990	1992
Reading	37	27	6	—
Writing	20	29	14	—
Math	23	17	6	—
No. Tested	56	57	43	—

Spring Valley Elementary

3rd Grade	1988	1989	1990	1992
Reading	34	43	30	—
Writing	30	25	17	—
Math	46	65	63	—
No. Tested	104	74	71	—

Starr King Elementary

3rd Grade	1988	1989	1990	1992
Reading	9	9	12	—
Writing	10	8	10	—
Math	26	17	16	—
No. Tested	64	57	61	—

Sunnyside Elementary

3rd Grade	1988	1989	1990	1992
Reading	43	57	54	—
Writing	27	63	41	—
Math	30	75	47	—
No. Tested	42	50	35	—

Sutro Elementary

3rd Grade	1988	1989	1990	1992
Reading	62	69	50	—
Writing	46	48	52	—
Math	74	75	84	—
No. Tested	39	50	49	—

Treasure Island Elementary

3rd Grade	1988	1989	1990	1992
Reading	52	42	38	—
Writing	53	41	28	—
Math	69	76	39	—
No. Tested	138	159	140	—

Ulloa Elementary

3rd Grade	1988	1989	1990	1992
Reading	54	50	51	—
Writing	44	48	53	—
Math	51	62	70	—
No. Tested	58	67	62	—

Visitacion Valley Elementary

3rd Grade	1988	1989	1990	1992
Reading	31	23	36	—
Writing	43	38	40	—
Math	63	38	69	—
No. Tested	69	72	74	—

Visitacion Valley Middle

6th Grade	1988	1989	1990	1992
Reading	3	3	2	—
Writing	9	7	7	—
Math	2	5	3	—
No. Tested	188	139	125	—
8th Grade	1988	1989	1990	1992
Reading	1	7	4	5
Writing	1	—	—	8
Math	3	19	7	4
History	2	3	4	4
Science	2	5	2	5
No. Tested	165	129	138	124

West Portal Elementary

3rd Grade	1988	1989	1990	1992
Reading	63	70	50	—
Writing	45	51	45	—
Math	65	65	58	—
No. Tested	98	77	102	—

SAN FRANCISCO UNIFIED (Continued)

William De Avila Elementary

3rd Grade	1988	1989	1990	1992
Reading	42	55	19	—
Writing	35	54	16	—
Math	72	57	37	—
No. Tested	61	62	73	—

William Cobb Elementary

3rd Grade	1988	1989	1990	1992
Reading	49	59	43	—
Writing	33	67	46	—
Math	46	60	68	—
No. Tested	55	42	47	—

Woodrow Wilson High

12th Grade	1988	1989	1990	1992
Reading	1	1	1	—
Writing	—	1	1	—
Math	4	5	7	—
No. Tested	197	207	186	—

Yick Wo Elementary

3rd Grade	1988	1989	1990	1992
Reading	54	30	29	—
Writing	58	39	25	—
Math	63	49	28	—
No. Tested	30	31	27	—

3/San Francisco Neighborhoods

Diverse Communities in a Diverse City

OTHER COUNTIES HAVE TOWNS and cities; San Francisco has neighborhoods. Within the borders of the City, residents identify location by Noe Valley, Sunset, Pacific Heights and over a dozen other neighborhoods.

Books and boosters sing the praises of neighborhood diversity and are fond of noting the different housing styles, but sometimes the business is overdone.

Some neighborhoods are a hodgepodge of buildings. Old homes have been demolished, new ones erected. Many buildings have been divided into condos. San Francisco is famous for opposing change but change does come.

San Francisco has a distinct Chinatown but Chinese and Chinese-Americans are found in many other neighborhoods.

The Richmond and Sunset districts are considered separate neighborhoods but in housing styles they are quite similar.

Neighborhoods share important characteristics: the sections west of Twin Peaks are in the summer fog belt. If you don't like fog, you might confine your search to the east side of the City. See chapter on weather.

In politics, the Sunset, Parkside, West of Twin Peaks, the Pacific Heights, Sea Cliff, Chinatown and North Beach are considered conservative, which in the parlance of the outside world means moderate to liberal.

Western Addition, Bernal Heights, Haight Ashbury, Potrero Hill, Eureka Valley and the downtown are considered liberal, which means very liberal. Other neighborhoods fall between.

On some maps, "neighborhoods" disappear — folded into other neighborhoods. Hayes Valley is often counted as part of the Western Addition, the Inner Sunset as part of the Sunset, Chinatown as part of North Beach.

All this granted, however, in many ways the neighborhoods are individu-

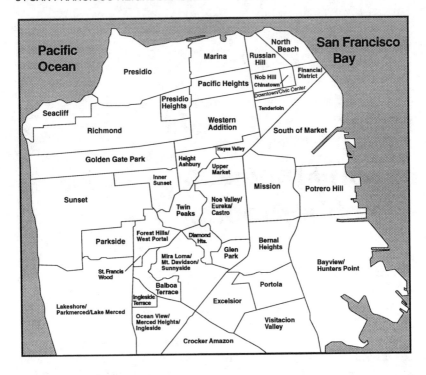

alistic. San Francisco was built out from the downtown, from east to west and from north to south. The great majority of the housing was erected from 1850 to 1950. When it became timely to develop the outlying sections, developers built according to the styles and market values of their eras.

Pacific Heights and Haight-Ashbury have Victorian homes; these neighborhoods were developed in the latter half of the 1800s. The Sunset was built during the early 20th century, a time when Americans were switching from horses to cars. Many homes in the Sunset and Richmond districts have one-car garages, the garage typically placed under the living room.

The land near San Francisco State University was developed after World War II. Homes and apartments there tend to have a 1950s look.

San Francisco is ethnically diverse: People of all races are scattered around the City. But it also has its neighborhoods or pockets of ethnic groups: Blacks, Chinese, Hispanics, Japanese, Italians, Irish and various other nationalities, including Koreans, Samoans, Vietnamese and Russians.

The City also divides by age and sexual persuasion. Many students live next to San Francisco State University and the University of San Francisco. Many homosexuals favor Castro Street and environs.

The state in its 1993 count tallied 332,538 residential units: 55,446 single homes, 49,784 single attached, 227,195 apartments, 113 mobile homes.

Number & Value of Owner-Occupied Dwellings

County	<$100K -199K	$200K -299K	$300K -399K	$400K -499K	$500K -plus
San Francisco	11,694	24,950	19,365	7,454	9,180
Alameda	84,603	78,954	31,943	11,925	10,300
Contra Costa	77,620	45,841	26,233	12,644	12,038
Marin	4,651	12,958	13,324	7,285	11,422
Napa	11,897	5,001	1,846	686	905
San Mateo	11,896	35,570	32,257	17,631	25,925
Santa Clara	42,597	97,300	55,842	26,942	35,779
Solano	48,566	10,459	2,058	447	287
Sonoma	36,506	24,181	7,883	2,912	2,318

Source: 1990 Census. The chart shows the number of owner-occupied dwellings within a designated price range.

A word about crime. It varies from neighborhood to neighborhood, and often from block to block. The poorer neighborhoods generally are higher in crime than the rich and middle-class sections. See chapter on crime.

Like all cities, San Francisco demands wariness. Homicides totaled 117 in 1992. The counts for the preceding five years are, 94, 101, 73, 92, and 103, reports the FBI. The unofficial count for 1993 is 132, the police report.

Not everyone can afford their first pick in housing. Sometimes the choice comes down to a bigger, cheaper unit in a marginal or transition neighborhood or part of that neighborhood against a smaller, more expensive unit in a stable neighborhood. For a single person, the first might be quite acceptable. For a parent, the second might be preferable.

Take your time. Ask questions. Drive the neighborhoods. Think about what you value, in safety, schools, commuting, closeness to parks and other amenities. Here is a capsule overview of many neighborhoods. Local Realtors and rental agents will usually have more detailed information.

Bayview, Hunters Point

Working-class neighborhood on southeast side of the City, near navy yard and Candlestick Park. A mix of single-family houses, apartments, four-plexes, factories. During World War II, many southern African-Americans settled in these neighborhoods. The area is now attracting Asians, many Hispanics, a few Caucasians.

Third Street, running north and south, is the main commercial strip. After several years of doing without a supermarket, Bayshore landed one in 1991.

Hunters Point, the shipyard that used to employ thousands, is in limbo. The site has potential but cleanup and infrastructure problems are many and the city government has shown little interest in addressing them. Artists and small

Median & Average Prices of Owner-Occupied Homes

County	Units	Median	Average
San Francisco	72,643	$298,900	$322,684
Alameda	217,725	227,200	248,918
Contra Costa	174,376	219,400	254,100
Marin	49,630	354,200	378,356
Napa	20,335	183,000	217,930
San Mateo	123,279	343,900	369,486
Santa Clara	258,460	289,400	324,548
Solano	61,817	147,300	163,275
Sonoma	73,800	201,400	228,273

Source: 1990 Census. Median means halfway. In 100 homes, the 50th is the median.

businesses have leased space at the shipyard.

The neighborhood is a mixed bag. On one block, residents sitting amiably in front of their homes and barbecuing with neighbors. Many homes, yards well cared for. Around the corner, burned-out cars abandoned in the middle of the street. Security grates and bars installed over many doors and windows.

City hall wants to make improvements in Bayshore, a touchy point because in past redevelopment efforts, a lot of housing for poor and low-income people has been wiped out. Plans call for adding commercial space and about 3,800 apartments and homes.

Commute good. Right off the freeway. Neighborhood associations. People always trying to make improvements. Rents, housing, cheap.

Bernal Heights

One of the older neighborhoods that declined for decades but made a comeback in the 1980s. Many residents own homes, which helps neighborhood stability. Spread over several hills. Good views of Bay and hills to the west. Trees and small lawns and shrubs adorn the fronts of mostly single-family homes, many of which have been remodeled.

Protected by the hills, Bernal Heights escapes the fog and enjoys some of the nicest weather of the City. Close to downtown. Excellent commute. Businesses along Cortland Avenue.

Neighborhood activists came to life in early 1980s and pressured city hall to make long overdue street improvements and pay more attention to planning. When property values rose, some were concerned about gentrification — a great influx of newcomers with lots of money who would drive up values and force the poor and working class out. Didn't happen but reputation of neighborhood as nice place to live improved. One resident called Bernal Heights a "village in the middle of San Francisco."

Number of Units Available at Selected Rents

County	<$100 -249	$250 -499	$500 -749	$750 -999	$1,000 -plus
San Francisco	17,319	49,287	65,672	38,086	24,070
Alameda	17,718	63,179	89,053	36,171	11,832
Contra Costa	6,977	18,083	43,319	18,295	7,417
Marin	1,322	3,386	11,642	9,293	8,005
Napa	856	3,877	6,191	1,817	584
San Mateo	2,625	9,310	41,360	24,449	15,827
Santa Clara	7,785	18,199	86,385	59,775	30,576
Solano	3,264	14,445	16,488	4,491	569
Sonoma	3,010	13,767	23,250	8,361	2,284

Source: 1990 Census. The chart shows the number of rental units counted within a designated range of rates.

In 1993, when only bank decided to pull out of Bernal Heights, residents organized, secured more accounts and persuaded it to stay.

Several parks, including Bernal Heights and Holly.

Crocker-Amazon

Blue collar, middle-class neighborhood on southern border of City, near Highway 101 and Interstate 280. Stucco and wood homes.

Many lawns and landscaping well kept, an indication of social stability. Window bars and door grills on some streets.

Close to Cow Palace and McLaren Park, one of biggest in San Fran.

A silent neighborhood. Rarely makes the news. No tourist attractions that call attention. Nothing chi-chi or artsy. Bedroom.

Eureka Valley — The Castro

About a mile southeast of downtown. Noted for its large gay population and interest in rights of gays. Many shops, restaurants, bars along Castro Street. Movie house. Bookstores. Hilly. Pretty. Many Victorians. Much care lavished on neighborhood and homes. Free and easy style.

No apologies here for sexual orientation. A neighborhood that will charm and shock granny. For some gays, almost a holy place, and according to polls, the most popular spot for gay tourists in the country.

Here's where a lot of actions were started that led to more freedom, less persecution of gays.

On the somber side, the Castro intentionally calls attention to AIDS and the deaths it has caused.

Buses to downtown. Close to the cultural offerings of the City. East of Twin Peaks, which means some protection from the fog.

Median & Average Rents of Renter-Occupied Dwellings

County	Units	Median	Average
San Francisco	198,974	$613	$650
Alameda	222,014	570	592
Contra Costa	95,962	613	642
Marin	33,386	763	806
Napa	13,775	561	583
San Mateo	95,164	711	764
Santa Clara	210,111	715	752
Solano	41,148	521	537
Sonoma	52,479	576	600

Source: 1990 Census. Units are total number of renter-occupied dwellings. Rents are stated as monthly payments. Median means halfway. In 100 homes, the 50th is the median.

Excelsior

Working class neighborhood, south of Bernal Heights. Favored in past by Italians, now home to many Hispanics. Described as a transition between Hunters Point, low income, and Outer Mission, more middle class.

Homes, about 50 years old, are usually single-family, stucco and wood frame construction built over one- and two-car garages. Some apartments along with duplexes and four-plexes. Public housing.

Appearances range from dilapidated and in need of paint and remodeling to near-mint condition. Many in-law units, portions of homes that have been remodeled as rental units, sources of additional income.

Bedroom neighborhood. A short bus ride to downtown. Near Highways 101 and 280. Includes McLaren Park.

Balboa High School, which serves the neighborhood and other southern sections, was threatened with closure in 1991 but parents, alumni and students rallied to its survival and persuaded the school board to keep it open.

Forest Hills-West Portal, St. Francis Wood

Although Forest Hills-West Portal border Twin Peaks, its prices and architectural style are so different as to make it a separate neighborhood.

Mix of two-story houses with gables and Tudor styling and single-story homes built over the garages. Trees line the streets. Well-kept lawns. Older homes have been remodeled inside and converted into apartments or condos. Most homes owner-occupied.

St. Francis Wood, built in the 1910s, routinely carries the tag "ritzy." Fountains and gateways. Shaded streets. Impressive homes. Active homeowner associations. Kind of neighborhoods that pay attention to quality, planning and conditions that might breed crime. Low in crime (but take precautions).

Open to ocean fog. Some views. A short drive to the Pacific. You can smell the salt air. Buses and streetcars to the downtown. Nice places but bring bucks.

Haight-Ashbury

During the 1960s, the Haight was the home of the flower children — hippies and would-be hippies who came to San Francisco searching for excitement and freedom from less liberal surroundings. Many old Victorians and lofts became communes for writers, musicians, dancers and other artists.

Today, the flower children are gone and the old Victorians have been gentrified into boutiques and offices, or duplexes and triplexes. Expensive. Yet many young people and artists share the rent in the older homes.

On-street parking is in short supply.

Drugs, crime troublesome. The Haight, because of fame, attracts wandering young who see it as a shrine to yesteryear. Residents and businesses are pressing for more cops and trying to discourage drug dealing.

Next to Golden Gate Park, a cornucopia of museums, flora, activities. Book, art, record stores. Bike rentals. Clothing stores. Groceries.

All San Fran neighborhoods have their restaurant rows. The Haight's have won a reputation for being pleasant. The Pacific is within a half-hour walk.

Buses and streetcars. About five miles from the downtown, which is long in San Fran, but a hop-and-a-skip for the rest of the world.

Hayes Valley

A neighborhood that died and now is emerging from its grave.

Located in the downtown between Larkin Street on the west, Webster on the west, Fulton on the north and Fell on the south.

Years ago, a well-known neighborhood, mentioned frequently in local histories, Hayes Valley declined when Highway 101 spur was run through it. Many of the stores went empty, crime became a problem. People started to include the fragments in the Western Addition.

Then that great urban renewer, the 1989 earthquake, weakened and forced the dismantling of the freeway spur, and a new Hayes emerged: artsy, small shops, diverse. Some concern that gentrification will force out the many African-American residents. City hopes to tear down a housing project with crime problems and build townhouses.

Lakeshore

The last neighborhood in the City to be developed. Located on the Pacific on the southern border. Includes San Francisco State University, Lake Merced, two golf courses, a shore park and the only "suburban" shopping plaza in the City, Stonestown. Also Parkmerced complex, short and tall (12-story) apartments. Built for elderly, it now houses all ages.

Just below Sloat Boulevard, the northern boundary, middle-class homes built just after World War II. Small tracts, condos and single homes, very nice, tucked here and there. Dominant type of housing in the district is the apartment. Middle-class neighborhood. Fog country. Bundle up.

By San Fran standards, a long way to the downtown. But freeways and Junipero Serra Boulevard are close by. BART station nearby in Daly City.

For amusements, the zoo, the golf courses, the lake, the Pacific (gorgeous sunsets), Golden Gate Park close by.

Marina, Pacific Heights, Presidio Heights

Most prestigious neighborhoods in the City, especially Pacific Heights.

Marina took a bad hit in the 1989 quake: homes and apartments destroyed. But since then repairs have been made.

Home to corporate executives, civic officials, lawyers and, if there is such a group, plain old people with money. Great views of Golden Gate. Close to pleasures and restaurants of the downtown. Marinas. Jogging, strolling, sunbathing along the shore. Palace of Fine Arts west of the Marina.

Close to the Presidio, army base that is being turned into park land. Fort Mason, on the shore, has exhibits, plays.

Mansions in Pacific Heights, condos and apartments as you descend into Marina District. Also many single homes in Marina. Luxury high-rises on east side of Heights. Custom homes by famous architects of West. Diverse styles.

Located just west of Pacific Heights, Presidio Heights is a small enclave of elegant homes. No apartments.

Residents of these areas shop Union Street or Chestnut, both fashionable. Victorians on Union have been converted into stores.

Close to downtown. A nothing commute. Controlled parking; residents get parking stickers. No bars on windows but many alarm systems. Compared to other neighborhoods, low in crime.

Cow Hollow, located just north of Pacific Heights, is sometimes included in the heights. Also a preferred neighborhood. Housing prices vary in these neighborhoods but many top $1 million.

The San Andreas Fault runs right up San Francisco. This is earthquake country and if you can't accept the risks, you shouldn't live in the City.

If buying a home, ask many questions, get the foundation examined by an expert. Realtors, by state law, are required to give you information about structural flaws and earthquake faults.

Other drawbacks: tourist country. People walk and drive through the neighborhoods. Some concern that Presidio as a park will attract too many people. Fog shoots through Golden Gate, adds great beauty, allure to the views.

Mission District

Large, vibrant neighborhood that for the first half of this century was home to many Irish and now is favored by Hispanics and, lately, Chinese storekeep-

Home Price Sampler — Classified Ads

Balboa Terrace
3-bedroom, 1.5-bath, exquisite, $489,000.
5-bedroom, 4-bath, remodeled, $525,000.

Bayview-Hunters Point
2-bedroom owner unit + 1-bedroom unit, $159,000.
3-bedroom, 2-bath, secure parking, private court, $187,000.

Bernal Heights
2-bedroom, 1-bath, formal dining room, parking, room & bath down, $199,000.
3-bedroom, 2.5-bath, remodeled, gourmet kitchen, 2-car parking, $349,000.

Crocker-Amazon
3-bedroom, 1-bath, full basement, move-in condition, $236,500.
3-bedroom, 1-bath, $279,000.

Diamond Heights
1-bedroom, view, parking, pool, $149,950.
2-bedroom, 2-bath, view, $227,000.

Eureka Valley-The Castro
3-bedroom, 2.5-bath, condo, private garden, fireplace, views, $369,000.
2-story remodeled Edwardian, 3-bedroom, 2-bath, patio, garden, $389,950.

Excelsior
3-bedroom home, family room, remodeled kitchen & bath, $219,000.
2-bedroom, dining, fireplace, remodeled kitchen, breakfast area, studio with entry, garage, yard, $244,500.

Financial District
1-bedroom, 1-bath, patio, $365,000.
2-bedroom, 2-bath, fireplace, bay view, 1-floor, parking, security, $649,000.

Forest Hill-West Portal
4-bedroom, 2-bath, corner, 2-story, views, $399,000.
5-bedroom, 3.5-bath, gourmet kitchen, decks, view, family room, $699,000.

Glen Park
4-bedroom, 3-bath, 1920s decor with updated systems, $279,500.
2-bedroom fixer-upper, Victorian cottage, views, $188,500.

Golden Gate Heights
1+ bedrooms & 1 bath up + rooms & bath down, view, garden, hardwood floors, fireplace, yard, $299,000.
12-room home, remodeled, views, $589,000.

Haight-Ashbury
2-bedroom, sunny corner unit, fireplace, parking, $219,000.
4-bedroom, 3-bath, Victorian, renovated, $589,000.

Ingleside Terrace
3-bedroom, 2-bath, formal dining, fireplace in living room, family room, $228,888.
Home, 4-bedroom, 3.5-bath, family room, 2-car garage, $599,000.

Lakeshore
2-bedroom, 1-bath up, 1-bedroom, 1-bath down, split level, living room, formal dining, remodeled kitchen, 2-car garage, $349,000.
3-bedroom, 2-bath, condo, $369,000.

Marina
1-bedroom, 1-bath, garage, $210,000.
3+ bedrooms, 3.5-bath, fireplace, formal dining, big kitchen, room & bath down, sunny large yard, deck, $699,000.

Mission
3-bedroom, 2-bath, big 2-story home, $179,000.
Vacant flats & garage, large rooms, yard, $259,000.

Mount Davidson
2-bedroom + den, 2-bath, formal living & dining rooms, garage, corner lot, $385,000.
3-bedroom, 4.5-bath, fireplaces, spa & exercise room, garage, view, decks, $629,000.

Nob Hill
3-bedroom, 3-bath, remodeled, fireplace, deck,

ers, but the mix here can be described as United Nations. Having escaped the 1906 fires, the Mission has a fair number of Victorians. Also many apartments. Some public housing. Low rents.

Starts near the downtown and can end, depending on who does the defining, at the south county border. Site of the first Spanish settlements in San Francisco. Mission Dolores, built in 1791, still stands and is popular with tourists. About 5,000 Indians are buried in the churchyard.

The Mission District, however, is not touristy. Too many working people for that. But it has a reputation for being colorful, exuberant and cosmopolitan, and at the same time friendly.

Home Price Sampler — Classified Ads

$399,950.

2-bedroom, 2.5-bath, 2 decks, 1-car garage, remodeled, $409,950.

Noe Valley

3-bedroom, 2-bath, views, garden, $379,000.

3-bedroom, 2-bath, views, $399,000.

North Beach

3-room, 2-story 1906 penthouse condo, nice location, $169,000.

One 5-room & two 4-room flats, nice location, $529,000.

Ocean View

Legal 2 units on huge lot, live in one, rent one, each are 2-bedroom, 1-bath, $209,950.

4-bedroom, 2-bath, beautiful tri-level, remodeled, panoramic views, $298,000.

Outer Mission

2-bedroom, 1-bath, big basement, $189,500.

3-bedroom, 1-bath, 2-car garage, $239,000.

Pacific Heights

1-bedroom, 1-bath, parking, $177,000.

6+ bedrooms, 7-bath, garden, 4-car garage, $1,995,000.

Parkside

3-bedroom, 2-bath, garden, parking, $349,000.

2 bedrooms up, 1 bedroom down, view, $218,500.

Potrero Hill

2-bedroom, 2-bath, fireplace, bay bridge view, $239,000.

1906 warehouse loft, 1,800 sq. ft., 20-ft. ceilings, patio, hardwood floors, fireplace, carpet, covered parking, bay view, $350,000.

Presidio Heights

3-bedroom, 2-bath, upgraded, top floor, parking, $399,000.

5-bedroom, 3-bath, renovated, garden, parking, $749,000.

Richmond-Seacliff

2-bedroom + sunroom, 25 x 120 lot, view of ocean, $278,000.

3-bedroom, 1.5-bath owner unit + two 2-bedroom, 1-bath rental units, $699,000.

Russian Hill

2-bedroom, 1-bath, view, gourmet kitchen, parking, $399,000.

3+ bedrooms, 2-story, renovated, fireplace, deck, 2-car garage, $699,000.

St. Francis Wood

3-bedroom, 2-bath, marble, fireplace, views, $529,000.

5-bedroom, 4-bath, Tudor, yard, $1,195,000.

South of Market-China Basin

Top floor loft, $265,000.

1-bedroom lofts, 16-foot ceilings, decks, huge windows, $119,000 to $172,000.

Sunset

2-bedroom, 2.5-bath + commercial, $309,000.

2-bedroom home up, preschool down, owner operation, $388,000.

Twin Peaks

View studio, 1-bath, deck, parking, $101,000.

Upper Market

Large Victorian home on quiet street, 4-car parking, $265,000.

2-bedroom condo, views, deck, parking, $379,000.

Visitacion Valley

2-bedroom, 1-bath, full basement, hardwood floors, yard, $165,000.

4-bedroom, 3-bath, newer home, super clean, $215,000.

Western Addition-Hayes Valley

Victorian, 2-level, 2-bedroom, 2 fireplaces, garden, parking, $265,000.

3 units, 2 Victorian flats + 3-bedroom cottage, 2-car parking, $398,000.

Source: Survey of San Francisco classified advertising listings in fall, 1993.

Small shops, groceries, lively restaurants, cheap food. Lots of talk.

People crowd the shops along Mission and Dolores streets. Murals decorate walls.

Hispanic includes Mexican but also people from many parts of South and Central America. Cinco de Mayo parade. Carnaval.

Crime a recurring and serious problem in some sections despite several efforts down through the years to improve matters. Many blocks enjoy relative peace and many residents go about their business without getting into trouble. Cops have beefed up presence.

Commute great. Buses and BART. Protected from fog by Twin Peaks.

Nob Hill, Russian Hill

A neighborhood whose name has entered the language as metaphor for great riches. If you live on "Nob Hill" you have arrived.

The hill once was home to the Bonanza kings (mining) and the Big Four — Leland Stanford, Charles Crocker, Mark Hopkins (for whom the hotel was named) and Collis Huntington — builders of the transcontinental railroad. Great views of Bay and Golden Gate.

Many of the great homes were destroyed in the fire that followed the 1906 earthquake. Or they were dynamited to stop the fire's spread.

Modern Nob Hill: Several hotels surrounding a small park. Grace Cathedral. Just off the hill — apartment buildings. Many tourists. Restricted parking. Great commute. Walk down the hill and you're in financial district. Cable cars.

Russian Hill, located just north of Nob Hill, also has great views. More of a residential neighborhood, it lacks — and doesn't want — the glitz and popularity of Nob Hill. Couple of restaurants. Little else in the way of businesses. High-rise apartments and three-story flats. Many nice homes, some oddly shaped to fit contours of hills. Steepest streets in the City. One of most desirable locations in City.

Noe (no-ee) Valley, Glen Park

Another choice neighborhood, Noe Valley nestles on east slope of Twin Peaks and is bordered on the south by Diamond Heights and on the north by hills. You can reach it by driving west on 24th street.

About 25 years ago, it was a working-class neighborhood with fading Victorians, many of them subdivided into apartments.

Since then the homes have been generally and nicely refurbished, greatly adding to the beauty of the neighborhood, and many of the apartments folded up — the pluses and minuses of gentrification.

Small stores — meat, fish, produce — some saloons and highly rated neighborhood restaurants. Window boxes filled with brightly colored flowers adorn many of the homes and the yards are landscaped with mature trees and shrubs.

The smell of eucalyptus trees tints the air in some sections. Residents are supposedly hard line about protecting the charms of Noe Valley.

In the streets near the Mission District, door grills suggest crime may be a problem.

Easy commute. BART station at 24th Street. Buses to downtown. Some Noe streets narrow traffic to one way.

Glen Park is a small, hilly neighborhood south of Noe Valley, just east of Diamond Heights. Homes old but well tended. Lawns and shrubs also show much care.

Small shopping section on Bosworth, near a BART station. On-street parking is controlled by the issuance of parking stickers to residents.

North Beach, Chinatown

Not too long ago, it was almost impossible to say North Beach without adding Italian. Many Italians settled in the neighborhood and the restaurants, bakeries and delicatessens and shops strongly reflected Italia.

The Italian presence is still strong but — an old San Francisco story — it's being replaced by other immigrant groups, Chinese from Taiwan and Hong Kong, and Laotians and Vietnamese. Many Italians have moved to the suburbs.

It might be more accurate to say that the Chinese section of North Beach is expanding. Chinatown, centered on Grant Avenue, has always been considered part of North Beach.

Even this is misleading. Many Chinese and Chinese-Americans, having saved enough money, have also moved to the suburbs or to outlying districts, like the Sunset. The new North Beach residents tend to be immigrants.

North Beach's glittery strip of Broadway, for years the exclusive domain of topless clubs, is taking on a new look, reflecting the Asian influx. A quick tour of the area, however, reveals that the night life is still very active but almost all of the strip joints are gone, replaced by cafes.

Kids play in the streets. Women walk to morning Mass at Saints Peter and Paul. Old men chat at Washington Square. Fisherman's Wharf and Pier 39, the little restaurant-amusement plaza, are part of North Beach.

With Embarcadero Freeway torn down, businesses are coming to life along the waterfront.

In many ways, a great neighborhood, full of restaurants, mainly seafood and Italian and Chinese, interesting people, bookstores and things to do, places to visit. In 1993, residents successfully fought the opening of "chain" coffee houses (Starbuck's, etc.). People want to keep the local flavor.

Parking's a problem but you can walk to work. Housing a mix: apartments with bay windows overlook busy streets. At Telegraph Hill, the streets and the prices ascend rapidly. Great views.

Ocean View, Ingleside

Middle-class neighborhoods in southwest section, ethnically diverse. Homes generally single-family, many built between 1900 and 1940. Wood and stucco, zero lot lines. Gentle hills.

Close to Pacific. Good views of the San Bruno Mountain and Mt. Davidson. Also nearby, San Francisco State University, Lake Merced, Stonestown Shopping Center, and to east, City College.

Safety grates cover some doors and windows. News stories in 1993 about residents complaining of drug dealing and crime.

Citizen groups are working to divert the young people into safer pursuits. Fog belt.

One of the longer hauls to the downtown, but buses and BART available, Interstate 280 close by.

Outer Mission

A neighborhood in transition. Older residents who have owned their single homes for 40 years or more are being replaced by younger families who are remodeling and occupying homes.

Lawns small, houses generally stucco over a wood frame. A few Victorians. Graffiti mar signs and public structures but, in safety, the Outer Mission is rated higher than other sections of the City. City College, many activities and classes, sits on western border, a plus for the neighborhood.

Interstate 280 runs through Outer Mission. Short drive to downtown. Buses. BART station at Geneva Avenue. On some maps, shown as Sunnyside with some sliding into the Excelsior.

Potrero Hill

Considered by some to be part of South of Market, Potrero Hill lies between the Bayshore Freeway and the Bay and 15th Street on the north and Army Street on the south. Despite an industrial setting, nearly half the area's residents own and occupy their own single-family homes, a mixture of Victorians and wood-frame houses that cling to Potrero Hill's slopes. Great views of the Bay.

Some upscaling, artists and professionals, in the 1980s on the north side of the hill. The neighborhood includes wholesale furniture centers.

Sheltered by the hills from the fog. Warmer than other neighborhoods.

Mixed group, Whites, Blacks and Hispanics.

Susan Shepard, in her book, *In the Neighborhoods*, mentions that the eastern portion of Portrero Hill was settled by Irish ironworkers who facetiously named it Dogpatch, after the many packs of dogs that used to race through the neighborhood.

Presidio

Possibly the oldest neighborhood in San Francisco. Located east and west of the Golden Gate Bridge. One of the choicest spots in the City.

Settled first by the Spanish who built the fort (Presidio). Later taken over by the U.S. Army and for the last 140 years or so used as a military base. Thousands of soldiers have been stationed at the Presidio and treated at its hospitals.

When the Soviet Union went belly up and the Cold War collapsed, the Pentagon decided to give up the Presidio. Some of the land and buildings are to go to the Golden Gate Recreational Area. The Army wants to keep the golf course. Mikhail Gorbachev, the man who helped made the closing possible, has set up his institute in one of the buildings. Sweet irony.

The Army's out in 1994. Letterman Hospital, except for a clinic, closed in 1991. Some neighbors fear the hospital may be reopened as a research facility for the University of California.

Richmond District-Seacliff

The neighborhood north of Golden Gate Park, south of the Presidio. Middle class. Many Chinese-Americans and a mixture of hyphenated Americans. First residents included Russians, refugees from the Revolution. Russian church with onion domes on Geary Boulevard.

Homes, for the most part, built between 1900 and 1940, a mix of styles, the most popular probably the single home, zero lot line with the living room over the (small) garage. Some quite striking stuff, Mediterranean style, on bluffs overlooking the Pacific in section called Seacliff where homes command seven-digit price tags. Streets clean. Homes generally well kept. Much remodeling. Graffiti scarce. Gates on many doorways, indicating some concern about crime. But reputation is low in crime.

The park is a big plus, all sorts of activities, and on occasion, probably a minus: traffic, visitors taking up parking, bums sleeping in the bushes and filtering into the neighborhood.

The Presidio is being turned into a park. Lincoln Park, with the Palace of the Legion of Honor and a golf course, is located down on the ocean. Short walk to the Pacific. Richmond also encompasses the University of San Francisco (Jesuit). Books and basketball.

Fog belt. In summer, it can get cold and windy. Some people love the fog, some hate it, find it depressing. In winter, often clear. See chapter on weather.

Seacliff is an upper-class neighborhood perched on hills. Single homes. Great views of Pacific and Golden Gate.

Geary Boulevard is a straight shot to downtown. Buses. BART doesn't run in this direction. Still, an easy commute. Many restaurants and shops along Geary and Clement. The two streets add much to the pleasures of the district.

Sears used to run big store on Geary but it closed in 1990, to be replaced later by a Mervyns.

South of Market-China Basin

Also known as SOMA. Located above and below the entrance to the Bay Bridge, and south of Market Street.

An industrial-commercial-residential section that's been changing for years and is coming to symbolize, especially with the Yerba Buena project, the new San Francisco.

Yerba Buena, 87 acres between Third and Fourth Streets, includes the

---

SOME CHURCHES TO CLOSE

With fewer parishioners and repair costs high, the archdiocese of San Francisco will close 11 churches in 1994. They are, All Hallows, St. Benedict's, St. Brigid's, St. Edward the Confessor, St. Francis of Assisi, Holy Cross, St. Joseph's, Church of the Nativity, St. Thomas More.

Moscone Convention Center and, recently opened, the Center for Arts and the Gardens.

Neighborhood also includes factory outlets, ballroom, bars, apartment housing for poor and elderly, warehouse lofts used by artists, galleries, piers and a variety of small industries. Warehouse-discount store opened in 1992. The neighborhood is relatively cheap, it's close to the downtown, it's making a transition upscale.

Several office-residential buildings have already been constructed. The neighborhood, especially down near the water, is taking on a new exciting look. The City for years has been working through plans to overhaul China Basin and build apartments, condos and housing for 17,200 residents in 8,600 housing units, plus offices, stores and commerce for 23,000 jobs. Job has the green light. Also being discussed for area, a ball park to house Giants.

Sunset District

One of the largest neighborhoods of San Francisco. Borders but stands aloof from the zoo, Golden Gate Park and the Pacific. They attract visitors and tourists; the Sunset doesn't.

Middle class. Not free of crime but low compared to other neighborhoods.

Population about 67,000, reports 1990 census, but some people place Forest Hills, St. Francis Woods and Parkside in the Sunset and put the population close to 100,000. The Sunset is defined alternately as a district including neighborhoods and as a neighborhood.

Glorious sunsets, balmy winters, mild summers — when the fog lifts. In the summer, it often doesn't. Great if you love the cold, the damp and the dim. Not so good if you don't.

Commute, very good. By MUNI bus, about a half hour to downtown San Francisco. Shorter if you drive.

Streets clean. Homes painted. Graffiti rare, confined mainly to bus stops.

Used to be almost 100 percent Caucasian, mostly Irish and German descent, now about 50 percent Asian or Asian-American, mainly Chinese descent, census reports. Some Hispanics, few Blacks, Russians.

Sand dunes in the last century, the district started to develop in the early 1900s, when trolley lines were extended and the downtown ran out of building space. In the 1930s and early 1940s, contractor Henry Doelger built thousands of homes and set the architectural look of the district.

At that time, builders were wrestling with a new problem: what to do with the car. The horse, noble but stinky, had been shunted into the stable, separate from the house. The horseless carriage, now being mass produced, could be brought into the house, but where.

Doelger stuck it under the living room. The typical Sunset home is a two-story affair: garage on the ground floor, stairs to the second floor, living room with picture window looking out to street, kitchen to rear of living room, and off the hallway, two bedrooms and one bathroom. In many homes, a third bedroom and a second bathroom were added.

Lots 25 feet wide. No front yard or just a patch of grass. Small rear yard. Pinched views, if any, of the Pacific. Stucco relieved by decorative balconies, tile and other knickknacks.

Doelger priced his homes at $5,000 each, which in the Depression was a lot of money but not an overwhelming amount, and as much as anything this defined the social character of the Sunset.

It was built for people ascending into the middle class. The Sunset is sometimes criticized for being bland — the White Cliffs of Doelger — but had it added views, rooms and more yard space, it would have priced itself beyond its intended market.

First came the Irish and the Germans, immigrants or their children. As the initial wave grew old and the kids moved to the suburbs, many of the homes came on the market, to be purchased by Chinese immigrants or their children moving out of Chinatown. One publication said that the Asian boom started when home prices soared in the Richmond District (heavily Asian), driving buyers to the other side of Golden Gate Park.

Ten or twenty or thirty years from now ... who knows ... perhaps the Sunset will catch the Hispanic middle class moving out of the Mission District.

Fearing their children would lose their religion in public schools, the Irish in San Francisco and elsewhere built their own schools.

Four Catholic elementary schools and two high schools have been built in or near the Sunset, and one school, St. Anne's, runs an afternoon program for Chinese children.

Before moving in, check with the local public school and also ask about the transition to middle school and high school. See chapter on San Francisco schools.

On pleasant evenings, people jog or stroll to the ocean. Besides playgrounds and Golden Gate park, there's a community center, a senior's center, social clubs, and Stern Grove, which offers popular Sunday concerts.

Restaurants and shops many and diverse: Irish pubs, Chinese diners, kosher markets. Most are concentrated on a few streets, among them Judah, Noriega and Taraval. Stonestown Mall is located just south of the Sunset.

See the shore for apartments and drive around Judah Street for homes built around the turn of the century.

Inner Sunset, which includes the giant University of California Medical, is sometimes broken out as a separate neighborhood. Hilly. Older homes, more in tune with the nearby Haight.

Tenderloin

Depressed neighborhood undergoing interesting changes. Meets housing needs of poor and elderly. Bordered by shopping district and major hotels.

Crime hot spot. Attracts many tourists.

By day, full of business people, conventioneers, and government workers. At night, along the western edge, frequented by people going to opera or symphony. Also has Museum of Modern Art. Exhibit hall. Big new library under construction.

Boundaries described as Market on the south, Post on the north, Van Ness on the west, Powell on the east.

Porno theaters and bookstores. Pimps, prostitutes, druggies, winos, decent people down on their luck, derelicts passed out on street. Many homeless, some quite aggressive in panhandling.

Many efforts to deal with problems; many failures.

Many Vietnamese families, refugees from the wars. Kids play among riff-raff of the streets. The Vietnamese also run many the shops.

Within walking distance of downtown. Good place to save commuting costs. But take care.

Treasure Island

San Francisco's newest neighborhood — maybe. Located mid Bay, Treasure Island was built from fill and is connected to Yerba Buena Island, the middle anchor for the Bay Bridge.

San Francisco owned Treasure Island until the Navy took it over in 1942.

With the end of the Cold War, Treasure Island is to be decommissioned and chances are good that the land will revert to San Francisco. Much red tape needs to be waded through, many arguments resolved over use.

Twin Peaks, Mt. Davidson, Diamond Heights

Right about the middle of San Francisco several hills rise to about 900 feet and run north-south for about two miles. Views great. You can see the Pacific and, if faced east, the Bay. Golden Gate Park is within a mile. Market Street, which leads directly to the downtown, a short distance off, is at the base of the eastern slopes.

Tie the package together and you come up with some of the most desirable neighborhoods in the City. How desirable is a matter of argument because someone will always argue that many homes are plain middle-class suburban.

In describing San Francisco, Realtors and writers frequently use the term "West of Twin Peaks." This is the fog line. The hills block the fog from the downtown neighborhoods or impede its progress. If you live on the west side, if you can see the Pacific, you will often be socked in by the summer fog. Some love it, some hate it. Your choice.

Many of these tracts were developed just before and after World War II, and the general housing looks modern compared to, say, the Victorian neighborhoods. Tudors, Spanish styles with terra-cotta roofs, mostly single homes but some townhouses, American substantial, American flimsy, the posh and the plain can be found in these neighborhoods, which include St. Francis Wood, Sherwood Forest, Forest Hill, Balboa Terrace (Some of these neighborhoods are profiled in this chapter.)

Crime low but residents wary. Homes have alarms, not barred windows.

Lot of tender loving into homes and lawns and appearances. Mature trees on some streets. Hedges and flower gardens.

Mt. Davidson, 925 feet, is topped by a cross, popular with Easter worshippers. A park, heavily wooded, protects the top from further development but blocks some views. Many townhouses on Diamond Heights.

On top of Mt. Sutro, to the north, is planted a tall (977 feet) electronics tower, hated by many but a fascinating sight when fog rolls in. Looks like a sailing ship emerging from a cottony sea.

Off the track for tourists but, for its views, placed on the 49-mile scenic drive, which means extra outside traffic. Streets wide. Parking restricted on some streets. Located within or near this district is the Laguna Honda Home.

The twin peaks, which the Spanish explorers called Los Pechos de la Choca, or the Breasts of the Indian Maiden, rise to 904 feet and 913 feet.

If shopping for a home or apartment in these neighborhoods, a map is a must. The streets curl all over the place.

Visitacion Valley

Bedroom neighborhood on southern border. Historically, a transition neighborhood for people on their way up from some of the poorer sections and it still seems to be following that path. Good ethnic mix.

Younger working-class people are buying older rental homes, remodeling and occupying them.

Single homes, row on row. Stucco. Living room over the garage, a common pattern in San Francisco. Zero side yards. Near the county line, off Geneva Street, you'll find townhouses and apartments.

Neighborhood that requires map. Many streets deadend at McLaren Park or Highway 101. Bars on some windows. Concern about crime in Sunnydale, the largest public-housing project in the City. Shopping done at small stores, many family owned. Views from some locations.

Buses to downtown. You can pick up BART a few miles east, on Geneva. A short drive on Highway 101. Also a short drive to the airport, one of the biggest employers on the Peninsula. Candlestick Park (Giants and Forty-Niners) just over the freeway. Cow Palace, which hosts sporting and recreational events, is just across the border in Daly City.

McLaren Park, which has a golf course, is one of the biggest in the City.

Western Addition-Hayes Valley

Located just west of city hall in the downtown. Sometimes called the "Fillmore." A mixed neighborhood where the poor blend with the middle class and well-to-do. Gates on doorways indicator of concern over crime.

Home to the 5-acre Japanese Cultural and Trade Center which includes a consulate, hotel, restaurant, two Japanese-language theaters and three Buddhist temples.

Includes Cathedral Hill and St. Mary's, the last hurrah for grand churches in San Fran. An interesting, striking cathedral. Organ employed for concerts.

Before World War II, about 5,300 Japanese lived in the neighborhood. When they were interned, thousands of Blacks from the South, hired to work in the shipyards and local industries, moved in, and the housing units multiplied. After the war, many Japanese returned and an effort was made to provide the neighborhood with decent housing.

The Addition bordered the fire line of the 1906 earthquake. East of the line the homes were destroyed, west they were saved. The district salvaged a great store of Victorians. In a misguided effort that supposedly lost more housing than it produced, many Victorians were demolished and replaced by projects. In recent years, the remaining Victorians, which had faded with neglect, made a comeback. Many have been restored. Remodelings are common.

Recently opened, the Fillmore Center, 1,113 apartments over five blocks (Steiner and Turk streets). Subsidies available for low income. Homes and apartments on the northern border of the district glide into Pacific Heights, the most prestigious neighborhood in the City.

Some concern that the poor are being driven out of neighborhood but it is also argued that the Western Addition was overdue for a change, and that any change would have caused dislocations.

Commute a nothing. You can walk to the downtown and to the opera, Davies Symphony Hall and San Fran's largest library. On Laguna Street, one of the hidden treasures of the district, the University of California Extension. Many classes. Summer fog often makes its way down to Western Addition.

Mixed races, incomes, housing styles — truly diverse, still defining itself. Fewer Blacks and Japanese now. More immigrants from other Asian countries. In a way, an old San Francisco story, one group, yielding to another, and that to another, with some friction and much blending, and efforts to get along.

4/San Mateo County at a Glance

Population, Income, Voter Registration, Trends

ONE OF THE MOST SCENIC COUNTIES IN CALIFORNIA, San Mateo is an urban-suburban county quietly undergoing fundamental but familiar changes.

Its cities, with one exception, are low in crime. Many of its schools score among the highest in the state but some are struggling.

The county, since its inception, has served as home to some of the richest in California and home to many of the newest to California. This tradition continues, the latest arrivals including Hispanics, Asians and Filipinos.

In the big picture, the county is considered one of the most desirable addresses in the state. San Mateo owes much of its prestige to its history, its amenities, its topography and its location.

Geography, Weather, Location

To the immediate north is San Francisco. Just over the southern border is Palo Alto and Silicon Valley. The Bay laps the eastern shore. The sun sets over the Pacific on the western shore. Both shores ascend to the hills and ridges of the Santa Cruz Mountains, which afford delightful vistas (home sites) of Bay and Ocean.

For most towns, the average rainfall is less than 20 inches. But it can reach 50 inches in the mountains. Temperatures rarely fall below freezing, rarely rise above 90. Humidity rarely bothers anyone. Rarely does thunder or lightning strike. Except for the fog, the weather might as well have been invented by the visitors' bureau. And some people love the fog.

Commuting-Travel

Two freeways traverse the county north and south. Two bridges connect

San Mateo County Population

City or Area	Male	Female	Total	*Total
Atherton	3,536	3,627	7,163	7,272
Belmont	11,780	12,347	24,127	25,056
Brisbane	1,514	1,438	2,952	3,105
Broadmoor	1,830	1,909	3,739	NA
Burlingame	12,513	14,288	26,801	27,831
Colma	544	559	1,103	1,160
Daly City	44,914	47,397	92,311	98,316
East Palo Alto	11,961	11,490	23,451	24,472
El Granada	2,246	2,180	4,426	NA
Emerald Lake Hills	1,665	1,663	3,328	NA
Foster City	14,072	14,104	28,176	29,249
Half Moon Bay	4,536	4,350	8,886	10,141
Highlands	1,383	1,261	2,644	NA
Hillsborough	5,138	5,529	10,667	11,060
Menlo Park	13,324	14,716	28,040	29,407
Millbrae	9,696	10,716	20,412	21,125
Montara	1,270	1,282	2,552	NA
Moss Beach	1,506	1,496	3,002	NA
North Fair Oaks	7,454	6,458	13,912	NA
Pacifica	18,630	19,040	37,670	39,080
Portola Valley	2,056	2,138	4,194	4,293
Redwood City	33,294	32,778	66,072	69,917
San Bruno	19,776	19,185	38,961	40,275
San Carlos	12,565	13,602	26,167	27,147
San Mateo	41,467	44,019	85,486	89,355
South San Francisco	26,674	27,638	54,312	56,613
West Menlo Park	1,850	2,109	3,959	NA
Woodside	2,484	2,551	5,035	5,247
Remainder	10,510	9,565	20,075	NA
Countywide	320,188	329,435	649,623	680,885

Source: 1990 Census and Demographic Research Unit of the California Dept. of Finance. **Key**: NA (not available). *Population estimates by Dept. of Finance., Jan. 1, 1993.

San Mateo with the East Bay. BART runs trains to Daly City, up on the northern border. CalTrain runs commuter trains from Gilroy in Santa Clara County through San Mateo up to San Francisco. SamTrans buses travel the arterials for passengers. No urban county in California enjoys an easy commute. In the Bay Area, San Mateo does it better than almost all.

Average Household Income

City	1990	*1995	*2000
Atherton	$199,950	$210,300	$227,000
Belmont	65,962	69,700	75,600
Brisbane	46,903	49,600	55,100
Burlingame	58,283	62,600	68,000
Colma	41,530	42,000	43,800
Daly City	50,068	52,700	56,500
East Palo Alto	38,152	41,000	43,200
Foster City	76,156	79,600	85,500
Half Moon Bay	66,536	69,300	77,700
Half Moon Bay, Uninc.	72,447	76,200	85,700
Hillsborough	197,607	208,800	224,900
Menlo Park	74,694	79,700	87,200
Millbrae	59,725	62,500	64,300
Pacifica	55,640	59,000	63,200
Portola Valley	143,807	152,000	164,000
Redwood City	54,879	59,600	66,200
San Bruno	51,589	54,800	58,900
San Carlos	71,368	76,000	81,900
San Mateo	59,084	62,600	67,800
So. San Francisco	49,063	51,600	56,000
Woodside	180,450	190,400	205,000
Remainder	83,763	91,600	97,000
Countywide	63,672	67,500	73,200

Source: Association of Bay Area Governments, *"Projections 92."* Average income per household includes wages and salaries, dividends, interest, rent and transfer payments such as Social Security or public assistance. Based on 1990 Census data, income is stated in 1990 dollars. *Projections.

Last but not least, in the middle of the county, on the east side, sits San Francisco International Airport — a fast ticket to any place in the world.

Nonetheless, the county is part of the real world, with real challenges. Minority enrollments in schools have risen to the point where minority children form the majority. Many minority students are succeeding in school but many others are not. How to get them to succeed, how to fund education, have become crucial questions.

Fingertip Facts

The 1990 census counted 649,628 residents, an increase of 11 percent over the 1980 tally. For some unexplained reason, boys and young men outnum-

Population Profile by Occupation

City or Town	EX	PF	TC	SA	CL	SV	AG	MF
Atherton	30	29	2	19	9	6	1	4
Belmont	21	16	5	14	19	8	1	18
Brisbane	16	12	3	11	24	10	0	25
Broadmoor	15	14	4	14	19	12	1	21
Burlingame	21	14	3	17	19	10	1	15
Colma	16	6	3	8	23	15	3	26
Daly City	11	10	4	11	26	15	1	21
East Palo Alto	8	12	5	7	17	22	4	25
El Granada	20	18	3	12	16	12	1	18
Emerald Lake Hills	21	26	7	14	13	7	1	13
Foster City	25	18	5	19	17	6	*0	11
Half Moon Bay	19	13	3	14	11	12	8	19
Highlands	27	23	4	14	13	9	*0	9
Hillsborough	29	26	2	18	12	6	1	5
Menlo Park	21	29	7	13	12	8	1	9
Millbrae	18	13	3	16	20	13	1	18
Montara	16	20	5	15	11	8	2	23
Moss Beach	16	18	3	15	14	11	4	20
North Fair Oaks	8	9	3	5	11	32	6	26
Pacifica	14	14	4	12	21	12	1	23
Portola	25	41	5	11	9	4	0	5
Redwood City	16	13	4	12	17	14	2	21
San Bruno	15	11	3	12	22	12	1	23
San Carlos	22	17	4	16	16	8	1	15
San Mateo	18	14	4	14	18	12	2	18
South San Francisco	12	9	3	11	23	14	1	26
West Menlo Park	21	33	7	16	11	3	1	8
Woodside	28	26	4	16	10	5	3	8
San Mateo County	17	15	4	13	19	12	2	29

Source: 1990 Census. Figures are percent of population, rounded to the nearest whole number. **Key**: EX (executive and managerial); PF (professional specialty); TC (technicians); SA (sales); CL (clerical and administrative support); SV (service occupations, including household, protective and other services); AG (agricultural including farming, fishing, forestry); MF (manufacturing including precision production, craft, repair; also machine operators, assemblers, inspectors, equipment cleaners and handlers, helpers and laborers). *Less than 0.5 percent.

bered women. Two examples: Under 5 years: boys 23,151; girls, 21,642. Ages 5 through 17: boys 50,171; girls, 47,522.

Not until the sexes reach their 30's do they approach parity, and on the nether side of life, the guys flame out much earlier than the gals. Men over age

55 numbered 60,351 in the census. Women over 55 came in at 77,439. If you're a woman shopping for a mate, you'll be pleased to know that never-married males in the county outnumber never-married females 85,178 to 66,096.

The state in 1993 estimated the population at 680,885, the majority, about 65 percent, living in single or single-attached homes.

San Mateo County boasts 40 miles of coast and beaches and encompasses 440 square miles, about one-third the size of its southern neighbor, Santa Clara County, and about ten times the size of its northern neighbor, San Francisco.

From north to south, the county is about 40 miles, and from east to west, at the widest point, about 15 miles.

Running up the center of the county is the San Andreas Fault. Yes, this is earthquake country. The whole Bay Area is earthquake country.

The 1989 earthquake gave the county a rousing jolt. Windows broke, chimneys toppled, water and gas lines ruptured and thousands, possibly millions of glasses and jars toppled and broke. No one was killed in the county.

Should you worry about the Next One? Some do. Some don't. But you should read the literature on earthquakes and get prepared. The beginning of your telephone book is a good place to start.

City and County

There are two San Mateos, which sometimes proves confusing. San Mateo, the city, is the second most populous city in San Mateo, the county. The county government legislates generally for all who do not reside within a city. County supervisors represent districts but they are elected countywide.

In some instances, the county government performs services that in other states are provided by cities. The county provides medical care for the poor, even if they live in a city.

About 91 percent of the county's residents reside in 21 cities. Besides the City of San Mateo, they are: Atherton, Belmont, Brisbane, Burlingame, Colma, Daly City, East Palo Alto, Foster City, Half Moon Bay, Hillsborough, Menlo Park, Millbrae, Pacifica, Portola Valley, Redwood City, San Bruno, San Carlos, San Mateo, South San Francisco, and Woodside.

Coming & Going
(Driver's License Address Changes)

County	Moved To SM from	Moved Out of SM to	Net
Alameda	2,554	3,999	-1,445
Alpine	2	2	0
Amador	20	50	-30
Butte	135	212	-77
Calaveras	25	63	-38
Colusa	6	17	-11
Contra Costa	1,140	1,942	-802
Del Norte	6	7	-1
El Dorado	89	179	-90
Fresno	167	205	-38
Glenn	6	17	-11
Humboldt	61	86	-25
Imperial	9	13	-4
Inyo	5	2	3
Kern	64	79	-15
Kings	17	22	-5
Lake	45	120	-75
Lassen	6	21	-15
Los Angeles	2,248	1,619	629
Madera	21	39	-18
Marin	436	539	-103
Mariposa	11	15	-4
Mendocino	52	87	-35
Merced	54	74	-20
Modoc	0	6	-6
Mono	2	2	0
Monterey	181	245	-64
Napa	66	154	-88
Nevada	56	184	-128
Orange	585	500	85
Placer	88	280	-192
Plumas	17	29	-12
Riverside	143	176	-33
Sacramento	490	1,155	-665
San Benito	12	32	-20
San Bernardino	191	176	15
San Diego	633	678	-45
San Francisco	10,280	6,854	3,426

Coming & Going
(Driver's License Address Changes)

County	Moved To SM from	Moved Out of SM to	Net
San Joaquin	177	400	-223
San Luis Obispo	137	135	2
Santa Barbara	170	164	6
Santa Clara	5,968	6,515	-547
Santa Cruz	252	297	-45
Shasta	45	118	-73
Sierra	1	3	-2
Siskiyou	12	24	-12
Solano	379	792	-413
Sonoma	331	781	-450
Stanislaus	147	359	-212
Sutter	18	33	-15
Tehama	10	27	-17
Trinity	2	17	-15
Tulare	41	44	-3
Tuolumne	28	94	-66
Ventura	188	228	-40
Yolo	127	162	-35
Yuba	15	25	-10
All Counties	27,971	30,098	-2,127
Out of State	6,028	6,652	-624
Total	33,999	36,750	-2,751

Source: California Department of Finance, 1993. Data covers fiscal year July 1, 1992-June 30, 1993 Out-of-state counts have not been adjusted for non-compliers.

City councils, directly elected by local residents, run the city governments. All use city managers. The council sets policy; the manager executes it. Often the reality is that the managers and other administrators, being trained in the business, exert a great deal of influence on policy.

With few exceptions, San Mateo cities are oriented toward the Bay, where the weather is milder.

Many cities now are turning inward, trying to "redevelop" (a legal term dealing with tax structuring and building incentives) their old neighborhoods, especially the downtowns.

Of the remaining government entities, school boards are probably the most important. Some are confined to one city, some cover several cities. The boards hire and fire superintendents and help set policy for schools.

The Past — The Indians

The Indians arrived maybe 20,000 years ago. They spoke the Costanoan dialect and gathered in small tribes that went by such names as Iamsin, Salson, Puyson, Shiwam. Stocky and copper-skinned, the Spanish described them, with beards and mustaches.

The Indians lived on a gruel made of local edibles and gathered buckeye nuts, acorns, blackberries and huckleberries. Fish were netted, oysters and clams scooped up. Snares, spears and bows and arrows were used to trap or kill deer, rabbits, squirrels, pheasants, quail and other small game.

The Indians lived by streams, had no written language, kept pretty much to themselves and were utterly unprepared for what followed.

The Spanish

Although they had claimed California since the 1500s, the Spanish rarely ventured north from Mexico. Not until 1769 did Gaspar de Portola lead the first expedition to explore what is now San Mateo County and to discover San Francisco Bay. For more than 200 years Europeans had sailed the coast of California without finding the Golden Gate. In 1776, Colonel Juan Bautista de Anza, on his way to San Francisco with the first settlers, camped about mid-peninsula near a stream he named after Saint Matthew, "San Mateo."

Spanish policy was to take the Indians to the San Francisco mission and indoctrinate them in the tenets of the Church. Unfortunately, the padres could not know that the Indians had no immunity to European diseases.

Many died. Some fled. Some rebelled. A few turned outlaw. Pomponio was the most famous. He raided settlements, killed other Indians and at least one soldier before he was betrayed by a woman. He escaped, was caught again and went to the wall. A creek and later a state beach were named in his memory.

When the Spanish arrived, historians estimate that about 1,500 Indians lived in or near the county.

Within 100 years, after many Indians were taken from interior villages and brought to San Mateo, only eight Indians were reported living on the Peninsula.

Meanwhile, hostile Indians along the Mexican border closed the overland route to the Bay Region. Few settlers followed the pioneers, leaving California sparsely populated — less than 7,000 Hispanics in the whole state on the eve of the Mexican-American War.

The Yankee Invasion

Lacking workers, the settlers fell into the only economy that could support them: cattle ranching. Great herds roamed California.

Napoleonic wars weakened Spain. In 1821, Mexico declared her independence and to secure California awarded large grants of land to the sons and daughters and grandchildren of the original settlers.

But hardly had the ink dried on the grants when the Yankee invasion came.

Education Level of Population Age 18 & Older

City or Town	HS	SC	AA	BA	Grad
Atherton	7	19	5	34	31
Belmont	19	29	9	22	12
Brisbane	24	31	6	17	4
Broadmoor	28	21	9	19	5
Burlingame	22	27	9	21	10
Colma	13	25	7	12	2
Daly City	25	24	8	17	5
East Palo Alto	22	18	5	9	5
El Granada	20	27	9	22	13
Emerald Lake Hills	15	23	12	27	15
Foster City	15	26	10	29	15
Half Moon Bay	19	25	9	17	9
Highlands	15	25	7	28	20
Hillsborough	13	23	7	29	24
Menlo Park	13	18	7	28	24
Millbrae	29	24	9	16	7
Montara	14	28	11	25	16
Moss Beach	19	25	10	23	11
North Fair Oaks	20	13	5	8	5
Pacifica	26	29	10	14	7
Portola Valley	4	15	6	34	37
Redwood City	22	24	9	17	8
San Bruno	30	25	9	14	6
San Carlos	20	27	10	21	12
San Mateo	22	25	9	20	9
South San Francisco	28	24	8	14	5
West Menlo Park	14	21	5	29	25
Woodside	10	20	5	31	28
San Mateo County	22	24	8	19	10

Source: 1990 Census. Figures are percent of population age 18 and older, rounded to the nearest whole number. Not shown are adults with less than a 9th grade education or with some high school education but no diploma or GED. **Key**: HS (adults with high school diploma or GED only, no college); SC (adults with some college education); AA (adults with an associate degree); BA (adults with a bachelor's degree only); Grad (adults with a master's or higher degree).

American courts were obliged to uphold the grants but enforcement was slow, few grants were properly surveyed and lawyers' fees were exorbitant. One took over 5,000 acres, including a good deal of Belmont.

Within a few decades the rancheros had been replaced by Yankees who turned to farming and subdividing.

San Mateo became a county in 1856, a complicated maneuver that owed much to a political deal concerning San Francisco. In 1863, the last spike was driven for a rail line between San Jose and San Francisco, which should have opened San Mateo to rapid development. But local service was sacrificed to express runs. Millionaires, meanwhile, tired of the fog of San Francisco, built estates up and down the peninsula and took land off of the market.

The county finished the century with 12,000 residents. Retrospectively, San Mateo County was going to be settled sooner or later. What was needed was good transportation and enough people to spur housing demand.

The 20th Century

The 20th century provided both, in the form of the streetcar, roads, the automobile and four wars that brought millions to the West Coast. Gradually, towns and industries spread down the Bay shore. Some highlights:

• The great earthquake of 1906. It did little damage to San Mateo County, while it destroyed San Francisco and persuaded many that perhaps San Mateo County was safer. Within four years the county's population doubled.

• Hetch Hetchy. To secure its water supply, San Francisco between 1910 and 1934 dammed the Hetch Hetchy Valley in the Sierra and channeled the flow into Crystal Springs Reservoir in San Mateo.

Good for the City, good for San Mateo County. Almost all San Mateo communities now tap into the delicious Sierra water.

Bad, said John Muir and other conservationists, for lovers of nature. Hetch Hetchy was beautiful, the rival of Yosemite and even today someone is always saying, let's blow up the dam and turn Hetch Hetchy back to nature. Don't hold your breath. To protect Crystal Springs, San Francisco purchased thousands of acres in the hills and mountains surrounding the reservoir. Central San Mateo looks like one big forest — great for hiking.

• The airport. San Francisco had thought about building its big one where Treasure Island stands but rational minds won out and in 1926 the City took an option on a couple of hundred acres of marsh off San Bruno.

As with many new ventures, the airport had its bad days. When Lindbergh, piloting a plane with 32 passengers, got stuck in the mud in 1929, some said let's

------

TWO-FOR-ONE FIRE ALARM

In summer 1993, an alarm was triggered at a Daly City bank. Firefighters rushed to their engines. On their way, the battalion chief noticed smoke rising about a half mile away. He diverted one truck.

False alarm at bank, triggered by a malfunction. The other engine found a house ablaze; pot boiled over. Damage extensive but not as bad as might have been.

San Mateo County Ethnic Makeup

City, Town or Area	White	Af.Am.	Hisp.	Asn./PI	N. Am.
Atherton	6,294	56	295	504	9
Belmont	19,540	379	1,755	2,356	88
Brisbane	2,252	45	415	225	12
Broadmoor	1,942	85	586	1,115	7
Burlingame	21,428	252	2,731	2,292	75
Colma	447	18	375	257	5
Daly City	25,299	6,891	20,634	39,010	282
East Palo Alto	2,832	9,727	8,527	2,168	119
El Granada	3,915	23	327	128	26
Emerald Lake Hills	2,992	22	192	116	5
Foster City	19,475	885	1,627	6,114	51
Half Moon Bay	6,522	44	1,978	319	15
Highlands	1,966	92	174	396	10
Hillsborough	8,165	73	436	1,984	4
Menlo Park	20,216	3,382	2,710	1,622	91
Millbrae	14,486	214	2,279	3,360	38
Montara	2,260	11	203	62	16
Moss Beach	2,535	33	338	67	22
North Fair Oaks	4,352	424	8,466	581	78
Pacifica	25,516	1,900	5,099	4,895	204
Portola Valley	3,916	12	124	132	8
Redwood City	43,504	2,240	15,935	4,004	280
San Bruno	23,169	1,536	7,252	6,698	202
San Carlos	22,612	235	1,691	1,554	65
San Mateo, City of	57,900	2,958	13,235	11,032	266
South San Francisco	24,258	2,054	14,731	12,862	285
West Menlo Park	3,508	29	168	248	4
Woodside	4,616	17	192	197	13
Countywide	392,131	34,000	114,627	105,559	2,349

Source: 1990 Census. **Key**: Af.Am. (African-American); Hisp. (Hispanic); Asn./PI (Asian/Pacific Islander); N. Am. (Native American including American Indian, Eskimo and Aleut). Not included, a small number identified by census as "other race."

give up the site. By 1940, however, the airport was handling 18,000 flights and 130,000 passengers a year. During World War II, the military took over and expanded the facility.

After the war, it just kept growing and serving more people and creating more business along the shore. Today, the airport is the mainstay of the county's economy and in a recent 12-month count (1992) handled 32,608,857

San Mateo County Voter Registration

City	Democrat	Republican	All Voters
Atherton	1,417	3,348	5,412
Belmont	7,600	5,243	15,279
Brisbane	1,204	371	2,041
Burlingame	8,191	6,017	16,523
Colma	241	89	399
Daly City	20,769	7,491	34,088
East Palo Alto	6,648	563	8,612
Foster City	7,227	6472	16,683
Half Moon Bay	2,698	2,095	5,881
Hillsborough	1,944	4,381	7,255
Menlo Park	9,035	6,829	18,701
Millbrae	6,017	4,038	11,396
Pacifica	12,942	4,762	21,476
Portola Valley	1,213	1,721	3,362
Redwood City	16,770	10,802	32,795
San Bruno	11,211	4,843	18,950
San Carlos	8,445	7,085	18,132
San Mateo	24,708	16,442	48,053
So. San Francisco	15,059	5,260	23,687
Woodside	1,310	2,009	3,910
Countywide	180,560	109,620	343,765

Source: Secretary of State, October, 1993.

passengers, up over 1 million from the previous year.

• Bridges. The car and the new roads led naturally to bridges across the Bay. The car Dumbarton, 1.2 miles, was built in 1927, the first Bay crossing and has since been rebuilt. San Mateo Bridge came next, 1929. For a while it was billed as the longest bridge in the world, 8 miles.

• Prohibition. It raised hell with law enforcement but is recalled as one of the most colorful eras in San Mateo history. The county's long coast, often shrouded in fog, made it a favorite for smugglers. The forested interior hid countless stills. The law was full of loopholes, the police departments understaffed, the politicians willing to wink at violations. But some escapades did raise the eyebrows.

Bootleggers one night seized the lighthouse at Pigeon Point and used the light to guide their ships in. In Pescadero, they took over the town. A local group dug up a $20,000 cache of liquor buried on the beach. Incensed, the bootleggers invaded Pescadero, applied some muscle and got their booze back.

Gambling flourished. One gambler founded Daly City's first newspaper

Presidential Voting in San Mateo County

Year	Democrat	D-Votes	Republican	R-Votes
1948	Truman*	34,215	Dewey	48,909
1952	Stevenson	50,802	Eisenhower*	87,780
1956	Stevenson	63,637	Eisenhower*	100,049
1960	Kennedy*	97,154	Nixon	104,570
1964	Johnson*	140,978	Goldwater	77,916
1968	Humphrey	106,519	Nixon*	98,654
1972	McGovern	109,745	Nixon*	135,377
1976	Carter*	102,896	Ford	117,338
1980	Carter	87,335	Reagan*	116,491
1984	Mondale	122,268	Reagan*	135,185
1988	Dukakis	135,002	Bush*	102,709
1992**	Clinton*	138,261	Bush	68,414

Source: Calif. Secretary of State. *Election winner nationally. **Ross Perot (46,652).

and led the fight for incorporation. Reforms came slowly, then accelerated after World War II when the county began its suburban phase.

World War II and the Years After

• World War II. County turned into a military camp. Installations were built at many points, including Half Moon Bay and Coyote Point. Cow Palace, built in Thirties, was turned into a motor pool and barracks.

Cheap housing was built along the shore. Many workers migrated in for the jobs. They stayed after the war. Many soldiers, sailors and marines came back.

• The great boom. The figures just about tell the story. On the eve of World War II, San Mateo County had 111,782 residents. By 1950, it had 235,000; ten years later, 445,000; and by 1970, about 556,000.

This was the era when homes seemed to march over the countryside, so strong was the demand. Daly City and South San Francisco provide the best examples of the immediate postwar boom.

You can trace the prosperity of the nation and the county through the housing. The Forties boxes gave way to expanded homes with two-car garages in the Fifties and Sixties. The Seventies and Eighties saw the rise of the

---

WILD KINGDOM

Among the birds and beasts of San Mateo County are mountain lions and rattlesnakes that will leave you alone if you leave them alone, and blackbirds that dive bomb your hair if you blunder too close to their nests during chicking time.

Religion in San Mateo County

Denomination	Churches	Members	Total
African Methodist Episcopal Zion	5	673	1,158
American Baptist	13	2,795	3,392
Assembly of God	23	2,197	3,525
Baptist General Conference	4	188	228
Catholic	39	NA	165,966
Christian & Missionary Alliance	3	122	210
Church of Christ	2	284	345
Disciples of Christ	1	120	150
Christian Reformed	1	233	298
Church of Christ, Scientist	8	NR	NR
Church of God (Anderson, Ind.)	3	167	167
Church of God (Cleveland, Tenn.)	2	67	81
Church of God (Prophecy)	1	31	38
Latter-day Saints	22	NA	9,642
Church of the Nazarene	6	379	457
Church of Christ	9	887	1,090
Conservative Baptist	3	NR	NR
Episcopal	15	4,095	6,683
Evangelical Free	1	17	20
Evangelical Lutheran	10	2,757	3,676
Free Methodist	3	109	147
Greek Orthodox	3	NR	NR
Foursquare Gospel	3	168	204
Lutheran-Missouri Synod	8	2,361	2,907
Missionary	1	32	65
Open Bible Standard	1	NR	NR
Orthodox Church in America	1	NR	NR
Christian Brethren	1	45	60
Presbyterian (USA)	11	8,409	10,205
Reformed Church in America	1	84	161
Salvation Army	1	88	94
Seventh-day Adventist	8	1,064	1,291
Southern Baptist	15	2,291	2,780
Unitarian-Universalist	2	321	423
United Church of Christ	12	2,869	3,482
United Methodist	14	3,183	3,863
Wisconsin Evangelical Lutheran	1	99	142
Jewish*	5	NA	41,500
Independent, Charismatic*	1	NA	3,600
San Mateo County totals	264	43,680	277,206

Source: Glenmary Research Center, Atlanta, Ga. **Key**: No. (Number of churches in the county); Members (Communicant, confirmed, full members); Total (All adherents); NA (Not applicable); NR (Not reported). *Estimates.

townhouse and condo and the estate home on small lots.

Also, the ascendancy of the hotel room. Tourism, thanks to the airport, is probably the county's major industry.

In the 1970's land became scarce and cities more selective in their housing. The 1980 census counted 587,329 residents, the 1990 census 649,628.

The Association of Bay Area Governments predicts that by the year 2010, San Mateo County will have 739,000 residents — a distinct possibility but anti- or slow-growth movements are popular in many cities. School enrollments are rising.

• The new immigration. Changes in immigration law opened the door in the late 1970s and 1980s to many immigrants from Mexico and Central America, and from the Philippines and Asian and Southeast Asian countries.

In the last decade, almost all these groups doubled their numbers in the county. How is everyone getting along? No doubt there is friction and instances where cultures clash. There is the problem of educating children who speak one language and teachers who, for the most part, speak another.

But San Mateo and California in general have learned some lessons in ethnic harmony. The county has a tradition of absorbing immigrants — Irish, Italians, Japanese, Portuguese.

San Mateo County is part of the real world and has real-world problems. But compared to many other counties, it does remarkably well in pursuing peace, tranquillity and happiness.

5/San Mateo County School Rankings

Reading, Writing, Math, Science & History Tests

THESE RANKINGS ARE drawn from state tests given over four years, 1988, 1989, 1990, 1992. For the most part, they will follow a pattern. High one year will be high the next, low will be low.

When the numbers fluctuate wildly, the number of children who took the tests will often be low. In a small class, one or two kids having a bad or good day will cause wide swings. Sometimes the children fail to understand instructions and this lowers their grade. Sometimes they just have an off day.

Ranking systems don't recognize overall gains or losses. If every school in California raised raw scores 20 percent, some schools would still be ranked at the bottom, a few at the top. The same if every raw score dropped. A ranking system shows how one school did against all other schools. There is no one perfect method of testing.

Family background, particularly education of parents, greatly influences how children will score in schools. See introduction to San Francisco scores (Chapter 2) and Chapter 7 on how public schools work.

Also note: Some school districts reorgranized and some grades were added and some dropped.

**BAYSHORE ELEMENTARY
SCHOOL DISTRICT**

(Daly City)

Districtwide

3rd Grade	1988	1989	1990	1992
Reading	64	17	44	—
Writing	50	3	41	—
Math	47	26	11	—
No. Tested	33	38	41	—

6th Grade	1988	1989	1990	1992
Reading	32	20	7	—
Writing	34	25	42	—
Math	1	1	5	—
No. Tested	41	37	31	—

8th Grade	1988	1989	1990	1992
Reading	43	20	39	53
Writing	58	—	—	48
Math	2	1	17	28
History	45	18	4	29

BAYSHORE ELEMENTARY (Continued)
Districtwide

8th Grade	1988	1989	1990	1992
Science	31	21	22	46
No. Tested	30	29	34	31

Bayshore Elementary

3rd Grade	1988	1989	1990	1992
Reading	62	20	45	—
Writing	50	15	38	—
Math	46	29	14	—
No. Tested	33	38	41	—

Robertson Intermediate

6th Grade	1988	1989	1990	1992
Reading	32	22	19	—
Writing	33	27	42	—
Math	7	10	16	—
No. Tested	41	37	31	—
8th Grade	**1988**	**1989**	**1990**	**1992**
Reading	46	20	39	53
Writing	55	—	—	47
Math	8	4	19	29
History	43	19	16	31
Science	30	22	23	42
No. Tested	30	29	34	31

BELMONT ELEM. DISTRICT
(Belmont)
Districtwide

3rd Grade	1988	1989	1990	1992
Reading	74	89	78	—
Writing	81	91	85	—
Math	76	90	87	—
No. Tested	168	208	209	—
6th Grade	**1988**	**1989**	**1990**	**1992**
Reading	98	92	92	—
Writing	93	89	89	—
Math	97	93	95	—
No. Tested	177	174	192	—
8th Grade	**1988**	**1989**	**1990**	**1992**
Reading	92	79	91	95
Writing	92	—	—	93
Math	92	94	95	96
History	90	90	93	88
Science	90	89	95	96
No. Tested	211	180	200	209

Central Elementary

3rd Grade	1988	1989	1990	1992
Reading	61	83	85	—
Writing	80	86	85	—
Math	77	90	75	—
No. Tested	44	74	64	—

Fox Elementary

3rd Grade	1988	1989	1990	1992
Reading	83	90	88	—
Writing	83	93	87	—
Math	64	65	79	—
No. Tested	57	61	63	—

Nesbit Elementary

3rd Grade	1988	1989	1990	1992
Reading	55	73	44	—
Writing	65	73	58	—
Math	67	86	82	—
No. Tested	67	73	82	—

Ralston Intermediate

6th Grade	1988	1989	1990	1992
Reading	94	87	87	—
Writing	87	84	84	—
Math	92	89	89	—
No. Tested	177	174	192	—
8th Grade	**1988**	**1989**	**1990**	**1992**
Reading	89	77	89	93
Writing	89	—	—	92
Math	90	92	93	95
History	88	87	92	87
Science	88	87	94	95
No. Tested	211	180	200	209

BRISBANE ELEMENTARY
SCHOOL DISTRICT
(Brisbane, Daly City)
Districtwide

3rd Grade	1988	1989	1990	1992
Reading	68	76	50	—
Writing	49	63	45	—
Math	49	60	49	—
No. Tested	60	64	62	—
6th Grade	**1988**	**1989**	**1990**	**1992**
Reading	41	68	70	—
Writing	29	73	54	—
Math	30	82	57	—
No. Tested	38	47	40	—
8th Grade	**1988**	**1989**	**1990**	**1992**
Reading	77	86	66	39
Writing	71	—	—	83
Math	56	50	54	83
History	78	89	86	49
Science	69	74	78	58
No. Tested	35	38	38	41

Brisbane Elementary

3rd Grade	1988	1989	1990	1992
Reading	71	79	53	—
Writing	68	60	39	—
Math	76	79	35	—
No. Tested	25	27	37	—

Lipman Intermediate

6th Grade	1988	1989	1990	1992
Reading	74	77	68	—
Writing	41	64	60	—
Math	20	86	49	—
No. Tested	16	24	26	—
8th Grade	**1988**	**1989**	**1990**	**1992**
Reading	74	85	66	41
Writing	66	—	—	80
Math	56	50	56	80

8th Grade	1988	1989	1990	1992
History	77	84	82	49
Science	67	75	77	57
No. Tested	35	38	38	41

Panorama Elementary

3rd Grade	1988	1989	1990	1992
Reading	56	64	49	—
Writing	32	63	52	—
Math	28	42	70	—
No. Tested	35	37	25	—
6th Grade	1988	1989	1990	1992
Reading	21	49	52	—
Writing	22	70	48	—
Math	43	62	68	—
No. Tested	22	23	14	—

BURLINGAME ELEMENTARY SCHOOL DISTRICT
(Burlingame)
Districtwide

3rd Grade	1988	1989	1990	1992
Reading	77	75	95	—
Writing	83	74	90	—
Math	90	66	91	—
No. Tested	174	161	164	—
6th Grade	1988	1989	1990	1992
Reading	87	91	88	—
Writing	98	93	92	—
Math	95	72	83	—
No. Tested	136	196	169	—
8th Grade	1988	1989	1990	1992
Reading	89	94	92	96
Writing	94	—	—	87
Math	94	91	93	90
History	93	95	92	94
Science	88	86	76	92
No. Tested	173	172	161	221

Burlingame Intermediate

6th Grade	1988	1989	1990	1992
Reading	81	86	88	—
Writing	96	87	87	—
Math	91	67	78	—
No. Tested	136	196	169	—
8th Grade	1988	1989	1990	1992
Reading	84	92	90	94
Writing	92	—	—	84
Math	93	88	92	88
History	91	93	90	93
Science	84	84	76	89
No. Tested	173	172	161	221

Franklin Elementary

3rd Grade	1988	1989	1990	1992
Reading	71	95	97	—
Writing	64	89	97	—
Math	63	92	93	—
No. Tested	50	33	39	—

Lincoln Elementary

3rd Grade	1988	1989	1990	1992
Reading	96	83	88	—
Writing	96	89	79	—
Math	97	80	89	—
No. Tested	36	53	50	—

McKinley Elementary

3rd Grade	1988	1989	1990	1992
Reading	73	50	91	—
Writing	84	49	84	—
Math	93	24	70	—
No. Tested	51	52	43	—

Washington Elementary

3rd Grade	1988	1989	1990	1992
Reading	22	27	77	—
Writing	49	24	61	—
Math	36	31	76	—
No. Tested	37	23	32	—

CABRILLO UNIFIED SCHOOL DISTRICT
(El Granada, Half Moon Bay, Montara)
Districtwide

3rd Grade	1988	1989	1990	1992
Reading	74	83	64	—
Writing	67	82	46	—
Math	67	66	43	—
No. Tested	204	222	239	—
6th Grade	1988	1989	1990	1992
Reading	52	48	49	—
Writing	50	54	48	—
Math	79	58	63	—
No. Tested	206	232	164	—
8th Grade	1988	1989	1990	1992
Reading	75	65	84	74
Writing	76	—	—	63
Math	85	85	87	75
History	88	71	76	77
Science	90	87	92	88
No. Tested	205	174	191	196
12th Grade	1988	1989	1990	1992
Reading	83	89	66	—
Writing	—	57	60	—
Math	78	76	72	—
No. Tested	195	164	132	—

Cunha Intermediate

6th Grade	1988	1989	1990	1992
Reading	51	48	50	—
Writing	50	53	46	—
Math	72	58	61	—
No. Tested	206	232	164	—
8th Grade	1988	1989	1990	1992
Reading	72	62	81	73
Writing	72	—	—	63
Math	80	80	84	73
History	83	68	75	75

CABRILLO UNIFIED (Continued)

Cunha Intermediate

8th Grade	1988	1989	1990	1992
Science	88	85	90	85
No. Tested	205	174	191	196

El Granada Elementary

3rd Grade	1988	1989	1990	1992
Reading	71	83	67	—
Writing	82	84	54	—
Math	74	76	52	—
No. Tested	45	54	63	—

Farallone View Elementary

3rd Grade	1988	1989	1990	1992
Reading	78	90	85	—
Writing	75	89	71	—
Math	54	68	58	—
No. Tested	73	80	76	—

Half Moon Bay High

12th Grade	1988	1989	1990	1992
Reading	79	84	65	—
Writing	—	59	56	—
Math	77	75	70	—
No. Tested	194	164	132	—

Hatch Elementary

3rd Grade	1988	1989	1990	1992
Reading	45	47	33	—
Writing	43	53	19	—
Math	59	42	30	—
No. Tested	75	80	84	—

Kings Mt. Primary

3rd Grade	1988	1989	1990	1992
Reading	96	98	71	—
Writing	64	81	63	—
Math	93	59	29	—
No. Tested	11	8	16	—

HILLSBOROUGH ELEM. DISTRICT
(Hillsborough)
Districtwide

3rd Grade	1988	1989	1990	1992
Reading	98	98	92	—
Writing	99	95	93	—
Math	98	99	96	—
No. Tested	1103	85	129	—
6th Grade	1988	1989	1990	1992
Reading	96	95	98	—
Writing	99	95	99	—
Math	97	98	98	—
No. Tested	120	125	118	—
8th Grade	1988	1989	1990	1992
Reading	94	97	98	99
Writing	96	—	—	99
Math	97	96	95	97
History	94	92	97	97
Science	90	92	94	98
No. Tested	123	127	130	120

Crocker Middle

6th Grade	1988	1989	1990	1992
Reading	93	90	97	—
Writing	98	91	98	—
Math	94	96	98	—
No. Tested	120	125	118	—
8th Grade	1988	1989	1990	1992
Reading	93	96	98	99
Writing	95	—	—	99
Math	96	95	94	97
History	94	91	96	97
Science	88	90	93	97
No. Tested	123	127	130	120

South Elementary

3rd Grade	1988	1989	1990	1992
Reading	97	80	80	—
Writing	98	81	83	—
Math	97	94	87	—
No. Tested	47	35	56	—

West Elementary

3rd Grade	1988	1989	1990	1992
Reading	97	99	92	—
Writing	97	95	91	—
Math	96	98	95	—
No. Tested	56	50	73	—

JEFFERSON ELEM. DISTRICT
(Colma, Daly City)
Districtwide

3rd Grade	1988	1989	1990	1992
Reading	68	60	63	—
Writing	67	63	75	—
Math	69	58	65	—
No. Tested	687	681	749	—
6th Grade	1988	1989	1990	1992
Reading	60	52	63	—
Writing	49	56	65	—
Math	66	55	67	—
No. Tested	635	634	719	—
8th Grade	1988	1989	1990	1992
Reading	37	34	56	57
Writing	46	—	—	71
Math	27	32	40	50
History	36	33	40	41
Science	44	30	41	52
No. Tested	560	573	629	709

Brown Elementary

3rd Grade	1988	1989	1990	1992
Reading	62	35	75	—
Writing	62	37	68	—
Math	75	21	61	—
No. Tested	46	51	44	—
6th Grade	1988	1989	1990	1992
Reading	52	32	63	—
Writing	41	31	49	—
Math	68	59	64	—
No. Tested	60	46	52	—

Colma Elementary

3rd Grade	1988	1989	1990	1992
Reading	69	46	57	—
Writing	53	38	47	—
Math	54	64	53	—
No. Tested	64	57	67	—

Columbus Elementary

3rd Grade	1988	1989	1990	1992
Reading	71	67	39	—
Writing	58	69	39	—
Math	68	50	35	—
No. Tested	64	55	77	—
6th Grade	1988	1989	1990	1992
Reading	53	57	49	—
Writing	40	57	64	—
Math	47	49	57	—
No. Tested	55	53	53	—

Edison Elementary

3rd Grade	1988	1989	1990	1992
Reading	65	57	66	—
Writing	79	42	68	—
Math	67	37	52	—
No. Tested	48	59	58	—
6th Grade	1988	1989	1990	1992
Reading	54	77	77	—
Writing	74	85	71	—
Math	44	61	82	—
No. Tested	49	50	59	—

Franklin Intermediate

8th Grade	1988	1989	1990	1992
Reading	38	23	50	67
Writing	33	—	—	80
Math	30	24	50	50
History	36	23	43	46
Science	50	31	55	68
No. Tested	173	179	198	215

Garden Village Elementary

3rd Grade	1988	1989	1990	1992
Reading	59	73	85	—
Writing	62	88	94	—
Math	65	82	86	—
No. Tested	44	45	42	—
6th Grade	1988	1989	1990	1992
Reading	42	87	74	—
Writing	25	71	76	—
Math	48	46	62	—
No. Tested	36	41	47	—

J. F. Kennedy Elementary

3rd Grade	1988	1989	1990	1992
Reading	50	44	50	—
Writing	64	51	65	—
Math	54	38	69	—
No. Tested	84	75	84	—

Pollicita Middle

6th Grade	1988	1989	1990	1992
Reading	34	19	44	—
Writing	30	25	48	—
Math	33	26	42	—
No. Tested	199	227	239	—
8th Grade	1988	1989	1990	1992
Reading	21	40	45	38
Writing	28	—	—	73
Math	11	30	34	38
History	16	23	22	25
Science	21	24	23	34
No. Tested	194	191	208	259

Rivera Intermediate

8th Grade	1988	1989	1990	1992
Reading	54	44	65	72
Writing	72	—	—	54
Math	52	46	44	62
History	65	50	63	60
Science	56	43	51	59
No. Tested	193	203	223	235

Roosevelt Elementary

3rd Grade	1988	1989	1990	1992
Reading	73	70	81	—
Writing	81	59	88	—
Math	52	52	78	—
No. Tested	42	49	57	—
6th Grade	1988	1989	1990	1992
Reading	85	37	64	—
Writing	74	37	74	—
Math	76	39	76	—
No. Tested	54	31	41	—

Tobias Elementary

3rd Grade	1988	1989	1990	1992
Reading	75	78	83	—
Writing	79	89	88	—
Math	60	88	85	—
No. Tested	50	55	41	—
6th Grade	1988	1989	1990	1992
Reading	89	88	84	—
Writing	81	57	76	—
Math	96	85	84	—
No. Tested	38	38	34	—

Washington Elementary

3rd Grade	1988	1989	1990	1992
Reading	52	56	52	—
Writing	68	49	53	—
Math	66	29	35	—
No. Tested	77	91	90	—

Webster Elementary

3rd Grade	1988	1989	1990	1992
Reading	76	50	82	—
Writing	70	54	95	—
Math	72	76	91	—
No. Tested	48	39	54	—
6th Grade	1988	1989	1990	1992
Reading	58	90	80	—
Writing	35	89	72	—
Math	66	88	86	—
No. Tested	60	46	60	—

JEFFERSON ELEM. (Continued)
Westlake Elementary

3rd Grade	1988	1989	1990	1992
Reading	50	86	58	—
Writing	56	93	69	—
Math	85	96	68	—
No. Tested	55	46	57	—
6th Grade	1988	1989	1990	1992
Reading	95	95	47	—
Writing	98	99	78	—
Math	98	97	78	—
No. Tested	35	55	73	—

Woodrow Wilson Elementary

3rd Grade	1988	1989	1990	1992
Reading	62	64	44	—
Writing	52	67	52	—
Math	62	57	50	—
No. Tested	65	59	78	—
6th Grade	1988	1989	1990	1992
Reading	64	32	60	—
Writing	33	34	68	—
Math	75	43	68	—
No. Tested	49	47	61	—

JEFFERSON UNION HIGH DISTRICT
(Daly City, Pacifica)
Districtwide

12th Grade	1988	1989	1990	1992
Reading	35	40	44	—
Writing	—	48	45	—
Math	24	33	34	—
No. Tested	946	917	855	—

Jefferson High

12th Grade	1988	1989	1990	1992
Reading	12	12	18	—
Writing	—	17	22	—
Math	8	9	13	—
No. Tested	198	250	240	—

Oceana High

12th Grade	1988	1989	1990	1992
Reading	56	42	63	—
Writing	—	65	77	—
Math	24	28	41	—
No. Tested	168	158	124	—

Terra Nova High

12th Grade	1988	1989	1990	1992
Reading	53	83	72	—
Writing	—	84	77	—
Math	55	76	63	—
No. Tested	236	200	179	—

Westmoor High

12th Grade	1988	1989	1990	1992
Reading	32	42	47	—
Writing	—	42	35	—
Math	35	35	39	—
No. Tested	322	309	312	—

LA HONDA-PESCADERO UNIFIED
(La Honda, Pescadero)
Districtwide

3rd Grade	1988	1989	1990	1992
Reading	19	83	39	—
Writing	2	56	21	—
Math	31	78	37	—
No. Tested	27	28	40	—
6th Grade	1988	1989	1990	1992
Reading	62	38	25	—
Writing	89	36	45	—
Math	98	90	87	—
No. Tested	20	23	19	—
8th Grade	1988	1989	1990	1992
Reading	2	23	62	32
Writing	25	—	—	65
Math	29	30	36	83
History	1	44	34	66
Science	22	19	23	71
No. Tested	16	26	19	19
12th Grade	1988	1989	1990	1992
Reading	44	22	20	—
Writing	—	69	1	—
Math	41	3	22	—
No. Tested	22	26	26	—

La Honda Elementary

3rd Grade	1988	1989	1990	1992
Reading	64	68	63	—
Writing	22	53	41	—
Math	56	45	25	—
No. Tested	10	14	18	—

Pescadero Elementary

3rd Grade	1988	1989	1990	1992
Reading	7	83	23	—
Writing	11	60	12	—
Math	20	89	49	—
No. Tested	17	14	22	—
6th Grade	1988	1989	1990	1992
Reading	58	41	27	—
Writing	83	37	44	—
Math	96	86	82	—
No. Tested	20	23	19	—

Pescadero High

8th Grade	1988	1989	1990	1992
Reading	10	26	60	35
Writing	27	—	—	65
Math	31	31	39	80
History	3	44	36	67
Science	23	20	25	71
No. Tested	16	26	19	19
12th Grade	1988	1989	1990	1992
Reading	42	26	28	—
Writing	—	69	3	—
Math	44	12	26	—
No. Tested	22	26	26	—

LAGUNA SALADA UNION ELEM. SCHOOL DISTRICT
(Pacifica, San Bruno)
Districtwide

3rd Grade	1988	1989	1990	1992
Reading	76	77	72	—
Writing	67	78	72	—
Math	52	75	65	—
No. Tested	388	430	454	—
6th Grade	1988	1989	1990	1992
Reading	78	83	88	—
Writing	87	73	78	—
Math	70	69	67	—
No. Tested	328	398	439	—
8th Grade	1988	1989	1990	1992
Reading	63	73	66	65
Writing	65	—	—	78
Math	49	61	50	60
History	64	75	67	72
Science	56	64	70	65
No. Tested	347	356	342	381

Cabrillo Elementary

3rd Grade	1988	1989	1990	1992
Reading	79	80	75	—
Writing	61	84	72	—
Math	47	69	65	—
No. Tested	51	67	76	—
6th Grade	1988	1989	1990	1992
Reading	67	75	84	—
Writing	60	54	75	—
Math	59	56	67	—
No. Tested	29	54	51	—
8th Grade	1988	1989	1990	1992
Reading	95	97	98	—
Writing	98	—	—	—
Math	69	87	80	—
History	79	95	99	—
Science	96	97	96	—
No. Tested	9	18	12	—

Fairmont Elementary

3rd Grade	1988	1989	1990	1992
Reading	57	45	42	—
Writing	41	57	30	—
Math	45	29	20	—
No. Tested	51	41	48	—
6th Grade	1988	1989	1990	1992
Reading	51	71	61	—
Writing	58	44	42	—
Math	49	34	66	—
No. Tested	43	35	51	—

Linda Mar Elementary

3rd Grade	1988	1989	1990	1992
Reading	87	76	65	—
Writing	85	78	72	—
Math	56	79	85	—
No. Tested	37	34	33	—

6th Grade	1988	1989	1990	1992
Reading	75	77	89	—
Writing	94	69	61	—
Math	43	69	70	—
No. Tested	31	39	33	—
8th Grade	1988	1989	1990	1992
Reading	31	61	55	—
Writing	25	—	—	—
Math	42	49	47	—
History	37	53	60	—
Science	41	69	74	—
No. Tested	51	54	61	—

Oddstad Elementary

3rd Grade	1988	1989	1990	1992
Reading	95	82	78	—
Writing	76	67	73	—
Math	58	51	52	—
No. Tested	27	41	41	—
6th Grade	1988	1989	1990	1992
Reading	96	66	74	—
Writing	87	59	92	—
Math	62	41	56	—
No. Tested	27	36	38	—

Ortega Elementary

3rd Grade	1988	1989	1990	1992
Reading	83	76	71	—
Writing	60	78	78	—
Math	74	96	70	—
No. Tested	32	42	67	—
6th Grade	1988	1989	1990	1992
Reading	93	84	66	—
Writing	96	78	86	—
Math	85	88	91	—
No. Tested	39	59	53	—
8th Grade	1988	1989	1990	1992
Reading	89	85	84	74
Writing	93	—	—	89
Math	76	74	70	70
History	94	91	85	76
Science	82	72	82	73
No. Tested	88	102	87	177

Pacific Heights Elementary

3rd Grade	1988	1989	1990	1992
Reading	21	13	62	—
Writing	34	21	50	—
Math	7	28	43	—
No. Tested	22	18	23	—
6th Grade	1988	1989	1990	1992
Reading	63	75	84	—
Writing	64	81	68	—
Math	46	53	42	—
No. Tested	23	24	31	—
8th Grade	1988	1989	1990	1992
Reading	40	57	72	51
Writing	40	—	—	41
Math	34	60	49	43

LAGUNA SALADA UNION (Continued)

Pacific Heights Elementary

8th Grade	1988	1989	1990	1992
History	32	70	73	60
Science	30	55	52	48
No. Tested	79	67	70	159

Pacific Manor Elementary

3rd Grade	1988	1989	1990	1992
Reading	79	71	71	—
Writing	64	77	78	—
Math	74	80	75	—
No. Tested	37	34	28	—
6th Grade	1988	1989	1990	1992
Reading	45	70	96	—
Writing	60	72	69	—
Math	84	60	57	—
No. Tested	27	35	40	—

Portola Elementary

3rd Grade	1988	1989	1990	1992
Reading	20	63	38	—
Writing	34	62	48	—
Math	36	66	49	—
No. Tested	24	26	21	—
6th Grade	1988	1989	1990	1992
Reading	78	95	87	—
Writing	90	53	89	—
Math	81	91	88	—
No. Tested	15	9	20	—

Sharp Park Elementary

3rd Grade	1988	1989	1990	1992
Reading	27	68	34	—
Writing	63	60	38	—
Math	38	62	53	—
No. Tested	20	29	30	—
6th Grade	1988	1989	1990	1992
Reading	52	77	59	—
Writing	83	52	59	—
Math	50	52	36	—
No. Tested	26	36	30	—
8th Grade	1988	1989	1990	1992
Reading	35	55	27	89
Writing	37	—	—	98
Math	30	38	37	80
History	47	49	30	88
Science	36	36	54	85
No. Tested	90	85	83	14

Vallemar Elementary

3rd Grade	1988	1989	1990	1992
Reading	91	85	95	—
Writing	91	84	95	—
Math	88	86	94	—
No. Tested	52	57	59	—
6th Grade	1988	1989	1990	1992
Reading	88	88	89	—
Writing	86	82	57	—
Math	71	76	59	—
No. Tested	41	44	57	—

8th Grade	1988	1989	1990	1992
Reading	86	55	82	71
Writing	80	—	—	95
Math	79	71	50	78
History	88	78	64	89
Science	88	85	97	91
No. Tested	30	30	29	31

Westview Elementary

3rd Grade	1988	1989	1990	1992
Reading	29	76	32	—
Writing	68	71	45	—
Math	20	44	15	—
No. Tested	35	41	28	—
6th Grade	1988	1989	1990	1992
Reading	45	80	70	—
Writing	60	81	79	—
Math	50	77	35	—
No. Tested	27	27	35	—

LAS LOMITAS ELEM. SCHOOL DISTRICT
(Atherton, Menlo Park)
Districtwide

3rd Grade	1988	1989	1990	1992
Reading	99	99	99	—
Writing	99	98	97	—
Math	99	98	98	—
No. Tested	76	60	83	—
6th Grade	1988	1989	1990	1992
Reading	99	98	98	—
Writing	98	98	98	—
Math	98	97	98	—
No. Tested	54	69	56	—
8th Grade	1988	1989	1990	1992
Reading	99	99	99	98
Writing	99	—	—	99
Math	99	98	98	99
History	99	99	99	98
Science	99	98	99	99
No. Tested	57	65	55	55

La Entrada Middle

6th Grade	1988	1989	1990	1992
Reading	98	96	96	—
Writing	97	96	96	—
Math	97	94	94	—
No. Tested	54	69	69	—
8th Grade	1988	1989	1990	1992
Reading	98	99	99	98
Writing	99	—	—	99
Math	99	97	97	99
History	99	98	99	98
Science	99	97	99	98
No. Tested	57	65	55	55

Las Lomitas Elementary

3rd Grade	1988	1989	1990	1992
Reading	99	99	98	—
Writing	98	96	93	—

3rd Grade	1988	1989	1990	1992
Math	99	96	96	—
No. Tested	76	60	83	—
6th Grade	1988	1989	1990	1992
Reading	—	—	96	—
Writing	—	—	96	—
Math	—	—	97	—
No. Tested	—	—	56	—

MENLO PARK CITY ELEM. SCHOOL DISTRICT
(Atherton, Menlo Park)
Districtwide

3rd Grade	1988	1989	1990	1992
Reading	98	95	97	—
Writing	98	93	94	—
Math	97	95	95	—
No. Tested	136	144	166	—
6th Grade	1988	1989	1990	1992
Reading	98	98	98	—
Writing	98	98	98	—
Math	97	98	98	—
No. Tested	134	143	136	—
8th Grade	1988	1989	1990	1992
Reading	97	99	99	98
Writing	99	—	—	98
Math	94	98	98	98
History	98	97	99	99
Science	96	95	96	99
No. Tested	130	139	132	130

Encinal Elementary

3rd Grade	1988	1989	1990	1992
Reading	—	—	96	—
Writing	—	—	85	—
Math	—	—	89	—
No. Tested	—	—	102	—
6th Grade	1988	1989	1990	1992
Reading	97	98	98	—
Writing	98	98	98	—
Math	94	97	97	—
No. Tested	70	67	67	—
8th Grade	1988	1989	1990	1992
Reading	91	96	96	—
Writing	94	—	—	—
Math	76	98	98	—
History	93	97	97	—
Science	89	93	93	—
No. Tested	57	72	72	—

Hillview Elementary

6th Grade	1988	1989	1990	1992
Reading	97	92	95	—
Writing	88	92	97	—
Math	94	96	97	—
No. Tested	64	76	136	—
8th Grade	1988	1989	1990	1992
Reading	98	99	99	97
Writing	99	—	—	97

8th Grade	1988	1989	1990	1992
Math	97	97	97	97
History	99	95	99	99
Science	98	96	96	98
No. Tested	73	67	132	130

Laurel Elementary

3rd Grade	1988	1989	1990	1992
Reading	94	92	92	—
Writing	94	90	90	—
Math	93	93	93	—
No. Tested	63	63	63	—

Oak Knoll Elementary

3rd Grade	1988	1989	1990	1992
Reading	96	89	95	—
Writing	95	85	93	—
Math	96	89	94	—
No. Tested	73	81	64	—

MILLBRAE ELEMENTARY SCHOOL DISTRICT
(Millbrae)
Districtwide

3rd Grade	1988	1989	1990	1992
Reading	77	87	86	—
Writing	82	81	82	—
Math	80	72	75	—
No. Tested	196	198	192	—
6th Grade	1988	1989	1990	1992
Reading	78	68	75	—
Writing	94	78	73	—
Math	89	85	87	—
No. Tested	170	191	186	—
8th Grade	1988	1989	1990	1992
Reading	81	70	76	73
Writing	84	—	—	94
Math	92	81	83	93
History	75	47	80	85
Science	87	49	93	78
No. Tested	184	208	196	206

Green Hills Elementary

3rd Grade	1988	1989	1990	1992
Reading	85	75	91	—
Writing	92	70	83	—
Math	94	62	77	—
No. Tested	53	52	46	—

Lomita Park Elementary

3rd Grade	1988	1989	1990	1992
Reading	61	42	62	—
Writing	52	36	55	—
Math	39	41	37	—
No. Tested	28	35	48	—

Meadows Elementary

3rd Grade	1988	1989	1990	1992
Reading	83	98	96	—
Writing	84	98	91	—
Math	80	95	95	—
No. Tested	52	56	52	—

MILLBRAE ELEMENTARY (Continued)

Spring Valley Elementary

3rd Grade	1988	1989	1990	1992
Reading	49	55	49	—
Writing	58	44	55	—
Math	46	39	53	—
No. Tested	63	55	46	—

Taylor Intermediate

6th Grade	1988	1989	1990	1992
Reading	73	64	66	—
Writing	88	72	69	—
Math	81	79	82	—
No. Tested	170	191	186	—
8th Grade	1988	1989	1990	1992
Reading	78	69	75	72
Writing	81	—	—	93
Math	90	78	80	91
History	74	47	78	82
Science	83	48	91	77
No. Tested	184	208	196	206

PORTOLA VALLEY ELEM. SCHOOL DISTRICT
(Portola Valley)
Districtwide

3rd Grade	1988	1989	1990	1992
Reading	99	99	99	—
Writing	99	98	99	—
Math	98	99	98	—
No. Tested	56	61	55	—
6th Grade	1988	1989	1990	1992
Reading	99	98	99	—
Writing	99	99	98	—
Math	99	97	99	—
No. Tested	68	54	60	—
8th Grade	1988	1989	1990	1992
Reading	99	99	95	99
Writing	99	—	—	99
Math	99	97	98	98
History	99	99	98	99
Science	99	97	95	98
No. Tested	65	51	59	64

Corte Madera Elementary

6th Grade	1988	1989	1990	1992
Reading	97	97	98	—
Writing	97	99	97	—
Math	99	96	98	—
No. Tested	68	54	60	—
8th Grade	1988	1989	1990	1992
Reading	99	98	95	99
Writing	99	—	—	99
Math	98	96	97	98
History	98	98	98	99
Science	98	96	94	97
No. Tested	65	51	59	64

Ormondale Elementary

3rd Grade	1988	1989	1990	1992
Reading	98	98	99	—
Writing	97	97	98	—
Math	97	98	96	—
No. Tested	56	61	55	—

RAVENSWOOD CITY ELEM. SCHOOL DISTRICT
(Menlo Park, East Palo Alto)
Districtwide

3rd Grade	1988	1989	1990	1992
Reading	1	3	16	—
Writing	1	18	21	—
Math	1	15	1	—
No. Tested	391	342	367	—
6th Grade	1988	1989	1990	1992
Reading	2	2	3	—
Writing	3	19	3	—
Math	1	2	3	—
No. Tested	276	281	337	—
8th Grade	1988	1989	1990	1992
Reading	2	2	2	1
Writing	1	—	—	17
Math	1	1	1	1
History	1	1	1	1
Science	1	2	1	1
No. Tested	181	179	237	301

Belle Haven Elementary

3rd Grade	1988	1989	1990	1992
Reading	17	16	20	—
Writing	32	42	37	—
Math	22	26	18	—
No. Tested	51	44	57	—
6th Grade	1988	1989	1990	1992
Reading	4	1	8	—
Writing	8	7	15	—
Math	6	8	6	—
No. Tested	60	48	48	—
8th Grade	1988	1989	1990	1992
Reading	—	—	—	10
Writing	—	—	—	10
Math	—	—	—	4
History	—	—	—	3
Science	—	—	—	1
No. Tested	—	—	—	41

Brentwood Oaks

3rd Grade	1988	1989	1990	1992
Reading	10	7	11	—
Writing	11	9	16	—
Math	14	7	8	—
No. Tested	152	144	145	—

Costano Elementary

6th Grade	1988	1989	1990	1992
Reading	36	5	16	—
Writing	35	13	22	—

6th Grade	1988	1989	1990	1992
Math	25	12	43	—
No. Tested	40	46	34	—
8th Grade	1988	1989	1990	1992
Reading	—	—	—	1
Writing	—	—	—	47
Math	—	—	—	2
History	—	—	—	1
Science	—	—	—	3
No. Tested	—	—	—	39

James B. Flood Elementary

3rd Grade	1988	1989	1990	1992
Reading	—	74	98	—
Writing	—	84	95	—
Math	—	90	97	—
No. Tested	—	32	26	—
6th Grade	1988	1989	1990	1992
Reading	—	69	78	—
Writing	—	64	70	—
Math	—	37	63	—
No. Tested	—	24	34	—
8th Grade	1988	1989	1990	1992
Reading	—	—	—	95
Writing	—	—	—	80
Math	—	—	—	71
History	—	—	—	80
Science	—	—	—	85
No. Tested	—	—	—	23

Menlo Oaks Intermediate

6th Grade	1988	1989	1990	1992
Reading	12	13	10	—
Writing	23	18	7	—
Math	9	12	9	—
No. Tested	76	73	113	—
8th Grade	1988	1989	1990	1992
Reading	—	12	8	1
Writing	—	—	—	35
Math	—	3	3	4
History	—	7	4	2
Science	—	10	9	2
No. Tested	—	65	81	50

Ravenswood Middle

8th Grade	1988	1989	1990	1992
Reading	9	9	9	14
Writing	8	—	—	7
Math	3	4	4	11
History	3	7	7	21
Science	4	11	7	11
No. Tested	181	114	130	54

Ronald McNair

6th Grade	1988	1989	1990	1992
Reading	3	12	2	—
Writing	9	25	10	—
Math	4	9	8	—
No. Tested	100	90	93	—

8th Grade	1988	1989	1990	1992
Reading	—	—	—	1
Writing	—	—	—	5
Math	—	—	—	3
History	—	—	—	3
Science	—	—	—	2
No. Tested	—	—	—	94

Willow Oaks

3rd Grade	1988	1989	1990	1992
Reading	1	12	18	—
Writing	2	18	23	—
Math	4	15	8	—
No. Tested	138	122	101	—

REDWOOD CITY ELEM. SCHOOL DISTRICT
(Atherton, Redwood City)
Districtwide

3rd Grade	1988	1989	1990	1992
Reading	50	50	37	—
Writing	46	50	39	—
Math	39	41	33	—
No. Tested	635	642	611	—
6th Grade	1988	1989	1990	1992
Reading	38	36	39	—
Writing	27	52	48	—
Math	41	65	45	—
No. Tested	623	636	653	—
8th Grade	1988	1989	1990	1992
Reading	30	25	5	32
Writing	33	—	—	41
Math	35	21	26	34
History	36	24	19	25
Science	33	23	23	32
No. Tested	621	595	635	594

Clifford Elementary

3rd Grade	1988	1989	1990	1992
Reading	61	77	74	—
Writing	72	67	78	—
Math	59	57	80	—
No. Tested	65	62	61	—
6th Grade	1988	1989	1990	1992
Reading	81	63	70	—
Writing	59	77	84	—
Math	79	90	65	—
No. Tested	55	51	60	—

Cloud Elementary

3rd Grade	1988	1989	1990	1992
Reading	85	71	65	—
Writing	80	82	56	—
Math	90	60	76	—
No. Tested	43	62	44	—
6th Grade	1988	1989	1990	1992
Reading	91	90	92	—
Writing	66	97	96	—
Math	92	97	97	—
No. Tested	43	54	57	—

REDWOOD CITY (Continued)

Fair Oaks Elementary

3rd Grade	1988	1989	1990	1992
Reading	9	1	5	—
Writing	10	2	3	—
Math	23	1	7	—
No. Tested	35	23	33	—
6th Grade	1988	1989	1990	1992
Reading	1	2	—	—
Writing	2	4	—	—
Math	6	14	—	—
No. Tested	61	41	—	—

Ford Elementary

3rd Grade	1988	1989	1990	1992
Reading	64	71	62	—
Writing	42	65	60	—
Math	45	62	38	—
No. Tested	76	68	64	—
6th Grade	1988	1989	1990	1992
Reading	48	30	—	—
Writing	51	69	—	—
Math	40	48	—	—
No. Tested	47	47	—	—

Garfield Elementary

3rd Grade	1988	1989	1990	1992
Reading	18	12	32	—
Writing	13	16	37	—
Math	40	25	33	—
No. Tested	18	25	21	—
6th Grade	1988	1989	1990	1992
Reading	3	8	8	—
Writing	11	19	32	—
Math	8	25	16	—
No. Tested	31	48	49	—

Gill Elementary

3rd Grade	1988	1989	1990	1992
Reading	52	66	39	—
Writing	50	52	32	—
Math	52	45	48	—
No. Tested	52	86	61	—
6th Grade	1988	1989	1990	1992
Reading	76	73	47	—
Writing	54	76	57	—
Math	71	65	69	—
No. Tested	56	61	72	—

Hawes Elementary

3rd Grade	1988	1989	1990	1992
Reading	64	50	15	—
Writing	53	57	18	—
Math	45	36	17	—
No. Tested	58	70	78	—
6th Grade	1988	1989	1990	1992
Reading	59	38	—	—
Writing	48	57	—	—
Math	56	62	—	—
No. Tested	51	52	—	—

Hoover Elementary

3rd Grade	1988	1989	1990	1992
Reading	14	4	5	—
Writing	9	4	7	—
Math	4	4	7	—
No. Tested	36	36	45	—
6th Grade	1988	1989	1990	1992
Reading	8	4	13	—
Writing	2	14	24	—
Math	10	27	22	—
No. Tested	73	79	53	—

Kennedy Intermediate

8th Grade	1988	1989	1990	1992
Reading	36	26	23	33
Writing	32	—	—	39
Math	34	17	23	39
History	37	24	20	20
Science	39	26	29	31
No. Tested	288	321	328	329

McKinley Intermediate

8th Grade	1988	1989	1990	1992
Reading	26	34	13	36
Writing	36	—	—	46
Math	39	36	35	36
History	36	25	23	38
Science	30	28	23	32
No. Tested	333	274	307	265

Orion Elementary

3rd Grade	1988	1989	1990	1992
Reading	62	39	55	—
Writing	65	18	28	—
Math	58	19	45	—
No. Tested	25	18	17	—
6th Grade	1988	1989	1990	1992
Reading	89	83	50	—
Writing	68	61	72	—
Math	82	76	50	—
No. Tested	27	11	8	—

Roosevelt Elementary

3rd Grade	1988	1989	1990	1992
Reading	59	68	52	—
Writing	60	80	50	—
Math	36	60	43	—
No. Tested	65	56	63	—
6th Grade	1988	1989	1990	1992
Reading	76	67	72	—
Writing	56	81	66	—
Math	83	88	56	—
No. Tested	49	58	53	—

Selby Lane Elementary

3rd Grade	1988	1989	1990	1992
Reading	32	56	67	—
Writing	28	51	58	—
Math	29	74	59	—
No. Tested	75	64	53	—
6th Grade	1988	1989	1990	1992
Reading	45	83	61	—

6th Grade	1988	1989	1990	1992
Writing	20	86	49	—
Math	37	84	55	—
No. Tested	64	69	53	—

Taft Elementary

3rd Grade	1988	1989	1990	1992
Reading	51	26	24	—
Writing	45	28	23	—
Math	25	22	11	—
No. Tested	87	72	71	—
6th Grade	1988	1989	1990	1992
Reading	11	7	22	—
Writing	13	9	19	—
Math	26	16	23	—
No. Tested	66	65	63	—

SAN BRUNO PARK ELEM. SCHOOL DISTRICT (San Bruno)
Districtwide

3rd Grade	1988	1989	1990	1992
Reading	90	65	83	—
Writing	93	82	76	—
Math	82	66	72	—
No. Tested	250	250	258	—
6th Grade	1988	1989	1990	1992
Reading	87	71	82	—
Writing	84	65	78	—
Math	83	72	69	—
No. Tested	239	217	218	—
8th Grade	1988	1989	1990	1992
Reading	78	57	69	68
Writing	77	—	—	82
Math	61	51	54	50
History	60	40	50	64
Science	68	54	57	65
No. Tested	245	317	232	215

Allen Elementary

3rd Grade	1988	1989	1990	1992
Reading	80	43	79	—
Writing	80	64	64	—
Math	69	42	55	—
No. Tested	54	58	68	—
6th Grade	1988	1989	1990	1992
Reading	73	43	85	—
Writing	68	66	66	—
Math	86	68	71	—
No. Tested	58	49	50	—

Belle Air Elementary

3rd Grade	1988	1989	1990	1992
Reading	49	62	50	—
Writing	51	73	43	—
Math	35	62	36	—
No. Tested	38	42	41	—
6th Grade	1988	1989	1990	1992
Reading	43	50	52	—

6th Grade	1988	1989	1990	1992
Writing	59	31	34	—
Math	64	39	40	—
No. Tested	34	44	33	—

Crestmoor Elementary

3rd Grade	1988	1989	1990	1992
Reading	96	74	79	—
Writing	98	91	87	—
Math	99	63	71	—
No. Tested	26	28	30	—
6th Grade	1988	1989	1990	1992
Reading	85	77	89	—
Writing	75	50	92	—
Math	67	75	96	—
No. Tested	27	25	26	—

El Crystal Elementary

3rd Grade	1988	1989	1990	1992
Reading	79	78	90	—
Writing	88	90	83	—
Math	32	76	86	—
No. Tested	35	24	22	—
6th Grade	1988	1989	1990	1992
Reading	58	69	50	—
Writing	76	43	61	—
Math	71	77	25	—
No. Tested	27	20	25	—

John Muir Elementary

3rd Grade	1988	1989	1990	1992
Reading	93	66	71	—
Writing	98	73	75	—
Math	92	70	69	—
No. Tested	52	53	44	—
6th Grade	1988	1989	1990	1992
Reading	73	77	59	—
Writing	65	88	91	—
Math	64	79	46	—
No. Tested	38	39	46	—

Parkside Intermediate

8th Grade	1988	1989	1990	1992
Reading	74	54	69	68
Writing	73	—	—	79
Math	62	51	56	50
History	59	39	50	65
Science	65	53	57	65
No. Tested	245	317	232	215

Rollingwood Elementary

3rd Grade	1988	1989	1990	1992
Reading	83	66	85	—
Writing	81	75	72	—
Math	69	62	82	—
No. Tested	45	45	53	—
6th Grade	1988	1989	1990	1992
Reading	98	88	92	—
Writing	95	84	64	—
Math	79	75	84	—
No. Tested	55	40	38	—

SAN CARLOS ELEM. DISTRICT
(San Carlos)
Districtwide

3rd Grade	1988	1989	1990	1992
Reading	94	95	94	—
Writing	95	98	98	—
Math	96	98	97	—
No. Tested	214	193	218	—
6th Grade	1988	1989	1990	1992
Reading	92	90	81	—
Writing	91	94	90	—
Math	91	89	95	—
No. Tested	179	196	183	—
8th Grade	1988	1989	1990	1992
Reading	94	94	89	96
Writing	95	—	—	95
Math	91	92	89	87
History	94	97	86	96
Science	92	94	94	94
No. Tested	189	165	163	188

Arundel Elementary

3rd Grade	1988	1989	1990	1992
Reading	87	66	86	—
Writing	88	96	95	—
Math	93	95	96	—
No. Tested	42	50	65	—

Brittan Acres Elementary

3rd Grade	1988	1989	1990	1992
Reading	86	98	96	—
Writing	90	97	94	—
Math	87	97	95	—
No. Tested	73	46	52	—

Central Intermediate

6th Grade	1988	1989	1990	1992
Reading	86	84	75	—
Writing	85	90	85	—
Math	85	82	91	—
No. Tested	179	196	183	—
8th Grade	1988	1989	1990	1992
Reading	93	93	86	95
Writing	94	—	—	93
Math	87	89	86	84
History	94	95	84	95
Science	90	93	93	93
No. Tested	189	165	163	188

Heather Elementary

3rd Grade	1988	1989	1990	1992
Reading	90	91	84	—
Writing	91	96	88	—
Math	95	95	86	—
No. Tested	50	48	50	—

White Oaks Elementary

3rd Grade	1988	1989	1990	1992
Reading	90	95	92	—
Writing	91	94	99	—
Math	96	97	95	—
No. Tested	49	49	51	—

SAN MATEO-FOSTER CITY
SCHOOL DISTRICT
(Foster City, San Mateo)
Districtwide

3rd Grade	1988	1989	1990	1992
Reading	83	88	87	—
Writing	83	90	83	—
Math	85	89	81	—
No. Tested	847	927	907	—
6th Grade	1988	1989	1990	1992
Reading	69	75	80	—
Writing	75	81	59	—
Math	81	80	69	—
No. Tested	820	907	820	—
8th Grade	1988	1989	1990	1992
Reading	84	83	77	88
Writing	91	—	—	85
Math	75	83	75	73
History	91	93	90	89
Science	80	82	76	84
No. Tested	836	821	850	886

Abbott Middle

6th Grade	1988	1989	1990	1992
Reading	61	65	72	—
Writing	76	81	61	—
Math	87	86	78	—
No. Tested	151	158	164	—
8th Grade	1988	1989	1990	1992
Reading	76	79	61	78
Writing	74	—	—	84
Math	80	90	70	73
History	79	86	50	62
Science	76	78	75	49
No. Tested	183	179	165	170

Audubon Elementary

3rd Grade	1988	1989	1990	1992
Reading	77	96	86	—
Writing	62	97	87	—
Math	68	93	75	—
No. Tested	102	102	99	—

Bayside Middle

6th Grade	1988	1989	1990	1992
Reading	40	49	44	—
Writing	38	41	37	—
Math	27	46	27	—
No. Tested	180	190	153	—
8th Grade	1988	1989	1990	1992
Reading	28	39	44	49
Writing	36	—	—	53
Math	19	35	25	23
History	34	56	50	64
Science	46	36	37	51
No. Tested	150	176	205	162

Baywood Elementary

3rd Grade	1988	1989	1990	1992
Reading	93	82	81	—
Writing	96	87	73	—

3rd Grade	1988	1989	1990	1992
Math	78	69	69	—
No. Tested	58	74	84	—

Borel Middle

6th Grade	1988	1989	1990	1992
Reading	74	75	78	—
Writing	77	83	59	—
Math	85	74	63	—
No. Tested	234	271	256	—
8th Grade	1988	1989	1990	1992
Reading	73	80	80	87
Writing	73	—	—	63
Math	62	80	78	63
History	81	87	90	76
Science	72	85	82	92
No. Tested	246	230	218	275

Bowditch Middle

6th Grade	1988	1989	1990	1992
Reading	72	80	84	—
Writing	75	84	71	—
Math	79	82	80	—
No. Tested	255	288	247	—
8th Grade	1988	1989	1990	1992
Reading	96	94	92	95
Writing	98	—	—	95
Math	93	89	92	92
History	99	99	98	98
Science	93	96	90	94
No. Tested	257	236	262	279

Foster City Elementary

3rd Grade	1988	1989	1990	1992
Reading	90	87	86	—
Writing	95	92	84	—
Math	93	86	84	—
No. Tested	134	130	167	—

George Hall Elementary

3rd Grade	1988	1989	1990	1992
Reading	69	69	66	—
Writing	56	76	47	—
Math	80	64	56	—
No. Tested	72	74	65	—

Highlands Elementary

3rd Grade	1988	1989	1990	1992
Reading	69	96	97	—
Writing	83	93	98	—
Math	89	91	96	—
No. Tested	54	54	48	—

Horall Elementary

3rd Grade	1988	1989	1990	1992
Reading	69	75	80	—
Writing	56	57	68	—
Math	74	62	60	—
No. Tested	44	84	76	—

Laurel Elementary

3rd Grade	1988	1989	1990	1992
Reading	86	93	82	—

3rd Grade	1988	1989	1990	1992
Writing	54	90	82	—
Math	82	93	72	—
No. Tested	51	57	59	—

Meadow Heights Elementary

3rd Grade	1988	1989	1990	1992
Reading	71	77	88	—
Writing	65	67	75	—
Math	71	80	95	—
No. Tested	83	68	64	—

North Shoreview Elementary

3rd Grade	1988	1989	1990	1992
Reading	77	29	57	—
Writing	77	43	61	—
Math	50	24	58	—
No. Tested	42	55	43	—

San Mateo Park Elementary

3rd Grade	1988	1989	1990	1992
Reading	78	78	83	—
Writing	67	64	86	—
Math	54	68	66	—
No. Tested	71	79	52	—

Parkside Elementary

3rd Grade	1988	1989	1990	1992
Reading	51	75	57	—
Writing	78	89	47	—
Math	86	94	40	—
No. Tested	67	79	71	—

Sunnybrae Elementary

3rd Grade	1988	1989	1990	1992
Reading	45	79	79	—
Writing	78	89	67	—
Math	49	85	85	—
No. Tested	69	71	79	—

SAN MATEO UNION HIGH SCHOOL DISTRICT
(Burlingame, Millbrae, San Bruno, San Mateo)
Districtwide

12th Grade	1988	1989	1990	1992
Reading	66	69	71	—
Writing	—	87	90	—
Math	77	84	85	—
No. Tested	1802	1788	1578	—

Aragon High

12th Grade	1988	1989	1990	1992
Reading	81	84	84	
Writing	—	95	89	
Math	84	88	90	
No. Tested	315	357	309	

Burlingame High

12th Grade	1988	1989	1990	1992
Reading	59	83	69	—
Writing	—	87	86	—

SAN MATEO UNION HIGH (Continued)

Burlingame High

12th Grade	1988	1989	1990	1992
Math	80	87	74	—
No. Tested	282	285	226	—

Capuchino High

12th Grade	1988	1989	1990	1992
Reading	34	17	42	—
Writing	—	43	38	—
Math	63	33	41	—
No. Tested	240	214	204	—

Hillsdale High

12th Grade	1988	1989	1990	1992
Reading	64	68	70	—
Writing	—	70	82	—
Math	61	79	79	—
No. Tested	390	327	264	—

Mills High

12th Grade	1988	1989	1990	1992
Reading	81	68	67	—
Writing	—	90	94	—
Math	87	82	90	—
No. Tested	262	293	262	—

San Mateo High

12th Grade	1988	1989	1990	1992
Reading	73	80	81	—
Writing	—	95	92	—
Math	74	89	88	—
No. Tested	293	286	300	—

SEQUOIA UNION HIGH DISTRICT
(Atherton, Belmont, Redwood City, Woodside)
Districtwide

12th Grade	1988	1989	1990	1992
Reading	85	77	82	—
Writing	—	83	85	—
Math	90	88	90	—
No. Tested	1,026	977	914	—

Carlmont High

12th Grade	1988	1989	1990	1992
Reading	90	88	80	—
Writing	—	91	90	—
Math	88	90	90	—
No. Tested	227	249	196	—

Menlo-Atherton High

12th Grade	1988	1989	1990	1992
Reading	94	91	93	—
Writing	—	90	92	—
Math	96	94	97	—
No. Tested	280	263	268	—

Sequoia High

12th Grade	1988	1989	1990	1992
Reading	70	50	50	—
Writing	—	67	63	—

12th Grade	1988	1989	1990	1992
Math	69	58	59	—
No. Tested	293	237	221	—

Woodside High

12th Grade	1988	1989	1990	1992
Reading	71	55	73	—
Writing	—	76	75	—
Math	91	57	70	—
No. Tested	210	211	208	—

SOUTH SAN FRANCISCO UNIFIED SCHOOL DISTRICT
(Daly City, San Bruno, South San Francisco)
Districtwide

3rd Grade	1988	1989	1990	1992
Reading	75	82	83	—
Writing	81	78	79	—
Math	61	68	67	—
No. Tested	646	641	662	—
6th Grade	1988	1989	1990	1992
Reading	67	71	73	—
Writing	68	56	54	—
Math	61	55	60	—
No. Tested	620	630	668	—
8th Grade	1988	1989	1990	1992
Reading	81	67	66	59
Writing	81	—	—	59
Math	71	64	50	62
History	71	58	60	67
Science	61	57	46	54
No. Tested	624	619	655	712
12th Grade	1988	1989	1990	1992
Reading	46	55	56	—
Writing	—	60	57	—
Math	37	41	34	—
No. Tested	648	572	515	—

Alta Loma Jr. High

8th Grade	1988	1989	1990	1992
Reading	82	64	65	60
Writing	84	—	—	44
Math	50	60	40	54
History	77	66	68	69
Science	60	52	57	50
No. Tested	193	180	225	244

Buri Buri Elementary

3rd Grade	1988	1989	1990	1992
Reading	80	81	80	—
Writing	64	77	79	—
Math	78	69	82	—
No. Tested	70	65	75	—
6th Grade	1988	1989	1990	1992
Reading	74	70	66	—
Writing	68	46	55	—
Math	66	49	78	—
No. Tested	51	78	68	—

El Camino Sr. High

12th Grade	1988	1989	1990	1992
Reading	34	68	54	—
Writing	—	70	60	—
Math	34	49	30	—
No. Tested	345	272	256	—

Foxridge Elementary

3rd Grade	1988	1989	1990	1992
Reading	77	90	89	—
Writing	94	89	87	—
Math	84	75	77	—
No. Tested	58	56	61	—
6th Grade	1988	1989	1990	1992
Reading	75	77	70	—
Writing	83	49	73	—
Math	70	61	56	—
No. Tested	68	55	56	—

Hillside Elementary

3rd Grade	1988	1989	1990	1992
Reading	66	43	82	—
Writing	68	53	88	—
Math	41	30	68	—
No. Tested	43	36	41	—
6th Grade	1988	1989	1990	1992
Reading	73	68	87	—
Writing	69	65	95	—
Math	49	54	75	—
No. Tested	38	31	31	—

Junipero Serra Elementary

3rd Grade	1988	1989	1990	1992
Reading	87	82	88	—
Writing	79	78	92	—
Math	75	71	86	—
No. Tested	53	58	56	—
6th Grade	1988	1989	1990	1992
Reading	64	74	76	—
Writing	67	39	61	—
Math	61	68	56	—
No. Tested	56	60	59	—

Los Cerritos Elementary

3rd Grade	1988	1989	1990	1992
Reading	72	61	30	—
Writing	82	72	42	—
Math	50	68	36	—
No. Tested	56	57	49	—
6th Grade	1988	1989	1990	1992
Reading	63	72	72	—
Writing	76	81	54	—
Math	52	61	38	—
No. Tested	49	40	49	—

Martin Elementary

3rd Grade	1988	1989	1990	1992
Reading	38	64	75	—
Writing	59	68	68	—
Math	32	50	89	—
No. Tested	45	51	35	—

6th Grade	1988	1989	1990	1992
Reading	10	34	39	—
Writing	26	53	28	—
Math	21	44	46	—
No. Tested	41	43	43	—

Monte Verde Elementary

3rd Grade	1988	1989	1990	1992
Reading	73	72	72	—
Writing	75	72	57	—
Math	75	76	44	—
No. Tested	52	50	56	—
6th Grade	1988	1989	1990	1992
Reading	76	72	45	—
Writing	54	59	40	—
Math	79	57	39	—
No. Tested	31	60	64	—

Parkway Jr. Hi.

8th Grade	1988	1989	1990	1992
Reading	49	47	26	33
Writing	55	—	—	41
Math	44	33	23	44
History	45	31	25	55
Science	44	43	19	46
No. Tested	233	217	221	209

Ponderosa Elementary

3rd Grade	1988	1989	1990	1992
Reading	90	75	88	—
Writing	88	77	82	—
Math	71	55	57	—
No. Tested	54	51	50	—
6th Grade	1988	1989	1990	1992
Reading	61	83	88	—
Writing	65	56	68	—
Math	53	34	67	—
No. Tested	46	29	46	—

Serra Vista Elementary

3rd Grade	1988	1989	1990	1992
Reading	59	87	82	—
Writing	76	88	75	—
Math	66	55	52	—
No. Tested	48	50	56	—
6th Grade	1988	1989	1990	1992
Reading	85	71	70	—
Writing	86	64	51	—
Math	76	64	70	—
No. Tested	45	59	57	—

Skyline Elementary

3rd Grade	1988	1989	1990	1992
Reading	61	89	78	—
Writing	81	79	76	—
Math	66	66	65	—
No. Tested	57	79	86	—
6th Grade	1988	1989	1990	1992
Reading	68	70	69	—
Writing	70	74	62	—
Math	86	76	72	—
No. Tested	89	73	89	—

S. SAN FRANCISCO UNIFIED (Continued)

South San Francisco High

12th Grade	1988	1989	1990	1992
Reading	55	45	55	—
Writing	—	53	49	—
Math	47	36	42	—
No. Tested	293	293	250	—

Spruce Elementary

3rd Grade	1988	1989	1990	1992
Reading	38	25	27	—
Writing	32	20	11	—
Math	31	37	26	—
No. Tested	50	45	55	—
6th Grade	1988	1989	1990	1992
Reading	25	37	39	—
Writing	29	29	34	—
Math	17	42	35	—
No. Tested	57	48	52	—

Sunshine Gardens Elementary

3rd Grade	1988	1989	1990	1992
Reading	59	70	89	—
Writing	70	60	91	—
Math	24	62	45	—
No. Tested	60	43	42	—
6th Grade	1988	1989	1990	1992
Reading	57	70	60	—
Writing	66	44	42	—
Math	50	31	61	—
No. Tested	49	54	54	—

Westborough Jr. High

8th Grade	1988	1989	1990	1992
Reading	91	79	93	78
Writing	89	—	—	86
Math	95	89	89	80
History	87	66	81	75
Science	83	70	64	64
No. Tested	198	222	209	259

WOODSIDE ELEM. DISTRICT
(Woodside)
Districtwide

3rd Grade	1988	1989	1990	1992
Reading	98	98	99	—
Writing	98	89	99	—
Math	99	97	99	—
No. Tested	36	35	41	—
6th Grade	1988	1989	1990	1992
Reading	99	98	99	—
Writing	96	99	98	—
Math	97	99	97	—
No. Tested	28	23	38	—
8th Grade	1988	1989	1990	1992
Reading	99	99	98	99
Writing	99	—	—	99
Math	99	96	94	98
History	99	97	96	97
Science	99	99	98	99
No. Tested	27	36	28	38

Woodside Elementary

3rd Grade	1988	1989	1990	1992
Reading	96	96	99	—
Writing	96	82	99	—
Math	98	94	99	—
No. Tested	36	35	41	—
6th Grade	1988	1989	1990	1992
Reading	97	96	98	—
Writing	93	99	97	—
Math	95	98	94	—
No. Tested	28	23	38	—
8th Grade	1988	1989	1990	1992
Reading	98	98	97	99
Writing	98	—	—	99
Math	98	96	93	98
History	98	96	95	97
Science	99	98	97	99
No. Tested	27	36	28	38

6/San Mateo County City Profiles

Trends, Pace of Development, What's Available

SOME GUIDELINES TO BUYING homes or renting in San Mateo County: Views generally cost more. High academic scores, low crime cost more. Old and small and no views or cramped views cost less. Flatland and next to Highway 101, with some exceptions, cost less.

Short commutes, in many instances, cost less. Daly City, one of the "affordable" cities of the county, has its own BART station and one of the shortest drives to downtown San Fran.

A note on the research: number of housing units were provided by the state in 1993. Two sets of population figures were available: the 1990 census and 1993 state guesses of increases or decreases since the census was taken.

Although home prices and rents were taken from the 1990 census and are therefore dated, they are fairly close to the reality of 1994. In recent years, home prices have either stagnated or decreased. Low inflation has stabilized rents.

The home prices and rents are intended to give a rough idea of what the going rate for housing is in each town. But within the towns the variety is great and, of course, prices change.

Your best bet is to drive the neighborhoods. Happy hunting!

Atherton

One of the most prestigious addresses in the Bay Area. Located in south county. Although it's adding homes here and there, Atherton is essentially built out and, in fact, lost population in the last decade, shrinking from 7,797 residents to 7,163, many of them on the gray side.

Those over age 55 outnumber those under 18 years 31 percent to 20 percent. The 1993 population was estimated at 7,272.

A town where the kiddies will get to know each other. The 1990 census counted 352 under the age of 5 — 183 boys and 169 girls.

Many large homes, a few mansions. Bowered lanes, trees, trees, trees. Foliage hides homes from arterial streets. No stores and none allowed. Atherton raises most of its revenues through property tax.

Named after Faxon Atherton, rich hide and tallow trader from Chile who bought over 600 acres and built first south county mansion. Son George married Gertrude Franklin, who as Gertrude Atherton became famous novelist.

Other estates followed, at least one from a Bonanza king (Flood) and over the years they were broken into large lots for modestly luxurious homes, many ranch design. Influenced by Hillsborough, wishing to protect property values and privacy, Atherton incorporated in 1923, adopted rigid zoning codes. Residents shop in Menlo Park, Redwood City, Palo Alto.

The state in 1993 tallied 2,535 residential units — 2,480 or 98 percent single homes, 27 single-family attached, 28 multiple units. Atherton rises from flatlands to hills but no gradations in housing. Luxury homes in the flats, luxury homes in hills. Lot sizes are one-acre minimum. Many are larger.

Bay view from hills. Good commute to Stanford, Silicon Valley. Long haul to San Francisco. But if one freeway is jammed, there's another to try. CalTrain to City or to Silicon Valley. Station in Atherton. Dumbarton Bridge close by.

One park but probably plenty to do. Homes are little rec centers: tennis courts, pools. Private clubs. Private college: Menlo.

School rankings among tops in state — no surprise. Kids attend Encinal and Laurel Elementary in Menlo Park school district, then Menlo-Atherton High in Sequoia Union High district, where life gets a little complicated. See Redwood City profile. Several private schools in town. About half the kids attend private schools, census revealed.

Crime not tracked by FBI but upper-class towns are generally very low in crime. Newspaper report in early 1993 said Atherton, which has own police department, has not had a homicide since 1946.

Atherton, citing safety and traffic reasons, restricted access on certain streets. This caused an argument with unincorporated Fair Oaks neighborhood, which accused Atherton of being elitist. After talks, the barriers were lifted. County is making special effort to improve Fair Oaks.

To prepare for the next earthquake, city hall gave every home a free radio. About 50 elderly live alone in Atherton. Police, using a computer, call each every day.

Belmont

"Beautiful Mountain," a name chosen by realty interests but not exaggerated. Nice city. Commanding views of the Bay.

Winding streets. City rises from flats to steep hills. Many homes have decks; barbecues in the evening. Many homes built after World War II. Some flat tops. Much remodeling. Small lots. Many trees and shrubs and loving care. Sage and chaparral grow on the steeper hillsides.

Shops and restaurants in a small downtown.

Village during 1800s, with large estates for San Francisco millionaires. Among the most famous: William Ralston, one of the silver kings. In his mansion, he entertained Grant, Sherman and Farragut, Bret Harte and Mark Twain. A speculator, Ralston made too many bad guesses. His body was found in the Pacific, a suspected suicide. Ralston Hall still stands, on the site of the College of Notre Dame. The college, incidentally, offers activities — a choir — that include the town.

Subdivision boom came in the 1920s. Remains of old land grants broken up. Many sold to affluent San Franciscans. Belmont incorporated in 1926 to avoid annexation by San Carlos and to keep local control.

Development slowed during Depression. Belmont and Redwood City in Thirties were famed for chrysanthemum growing. Population tripled during WWII. Some electronic industries came in. 1950 census showed 5,500 people, then came the suburban tide, pushing number of residents to 24,505 by 1980.

The 1990 census counted 24,127 residents, a drop of 378. In age, about 22 percent are over 55, about 18 percent under age 18, which suggests a balanced spread. Kids under 5 years: 711 boys, 719 girls. State estimate of residents in 1993 was put at 25,056.

Good housing mix. Belmont has 10,441 residences, of which 6,128 are single homes, 457 single-family attached, 3,852 multiples (1993 estimate).

Dental hygiene company in 1994 to open West Coast headquarters near Highway 101. Belmont to annex some industrial-commercial land.

Crime rate low. Zero homicides in 1992, 1991 and 1990, one in 1989, one in 1988, none in 1987, one in 1986, none in 1985. Like many peninsula cities, Belmont is cracking down on graffiti.

School rankings up there, among top 20th percentile, 80s and 90s. Elementary schools recently renovated. Day care at public schools. DARE program to discourage kids from drinking and drugs. Middle school program revamped in 1991. Periods shortened by six minutes to create seventh period and time to take electives. School district in 1993 said it would build an elementary school in Redwood Shores neighborhood.

Carlmont High offers students a class in how to stop smoking. For high school info, see Sequoia High School District in Redwood City profile.

Good commute. Ralston Avenue on one end connects to Highway 101 and on other, with a short dogleg, to I-280. Ralston also ties into Highway 92, which runs to Half Moon Bay and San Mateo Bridge. CalTrain station near Highway 101. Commuter trains, about 60 daily, are a not-so-minor irritant to motorists. They block traffic along Ralston. Problem should be solved in mid 1990s when an underpass is constructed.

Number & Value of Owner-Occupied Dwellings

City or Area	<$100K -199K	$200K -299K	$300K -399K	$400K -499K	$500K -plus
Atherton	19	19	42	65	1,959
Belmont	171	666	1,704	1,594	1,208
Brisbane	144	259	162	60	19
Broadmoor	169	673	132	15	5
Burlingame	169	451	1,117	1,191	2,011
Colma	37	97	11	2	1
Daly City	2,046	7,373	4,015	354	54
East Palo Alto	2,035	382	47	14	6
El Granada	54	257	468	196	100
Emerald Lake Hills	35	69	159	170	593
Foster City	155	736	1,690	1,682	1,293
Half Moon Bay	111	425	610	311	255
Highlands	7	35	204	352	96
Hillsborough	26	21	29	45	3,151
Menlo Park	695	487	1,044	841	2,455
Millbrae	175	654	1,342	1,255	1,173
Montara	49	188	267	103	73
Moss Beach	31	102	280	105	81
North Fair Oaks	354	803	332	54	62
Pacifica	995	4,826	1,840	369	78
Portola Valley	11	23	33	40	1,091
Redwood City	769	2,832	3,585	2,078	1,487
San Bruno	757	3,046	2,761	543	66
San Carlos	197	928	2,252	1,886	1,772
San Mateo, City of	1,015	4,220	4,523	2,367	2,848
So. San Francisco	1,368	5,337	2,474	552	68
West Menlo Park	21	81	213	347	474
Woodside	24	32	42	89	1,302
Remainder	262	547	879	951	2,144
Countywide	11,896	35,570	32,257	17,631	25,925

Source: 1990 Census. The chart shows the number of owner-occupied dwellings within a designated price range. Data for some towns or residential areas are grouped with those covering a larger geographic area.

Sixteen parks-playgrounds, including one around lake, another at the Bay. Ice skating rink. Art gallery. Branch of county library. Western border backs up to fish-and-game refuge.

Recreation complex recently opened in Island Park development — five baseball-softball fields, two overlaying soccer fields, rec building with meeting hall. On Sunday summer afternoons, free concerts delight visitors to Twin

Median & Average Prices of Owner-Occupied Homes

City or Area	Units	Median	Average
Atherton	2,102	*$500,001	$583,435
Belmont	5,343	408,200	418,021
Brisbane	644	268,400	280,004
Broadmoor	994	256,400	252,374
Burlingame	4,939	461,500	459,866
Colma	148	227,200	232,027
Daly City	13,843	272,100	271,345
East Palo Alto	2,484	159,700	165,261
El Granada	1,075	348,400	359,128
Emerald Lake Hills	1,026	*500,001	496,987
Foster City	5,556	411,700	420,301
Half Moon Bay	1,712	352,500	369,467
Highlands	694	428,700	428,134
Hillsborough	3,273	*500,001	589,615
Menlo Park	5,522	463,600	441,582
Millbrae	4,599	410,200	419,486
Montara	676	339,300	353,225
Moss Beach	599	359,500	375,659
North Fair Oaks	1,605	261,500	270,339
Pacifica	8,108	266,800	274,487
Portola Valley	1,198	*500,001	577,069
Redwood City	10,751	349,500	364,109
San Bruno	7,173	294,600	298,802
San Carlos	7,035	407,500	421,635
San Mateo, City of	14,973	349,800	373,474
So. San Francisco	9,799	271,900	277,168
West Menlo Park	1,136	472,900	473,669
Woodside	1,489	*500,001	569,001
Remainder	4,783	473,975	459,175
Countywide	123,279	343,900	369,486

Source: 1990 Census. Asterisk (*) prices were the maximum reported by census. Actual prices may have been higher. Median means halfway. In 100 homes, the 50th is the median.

Pines Park. Deer in hills. They like to nibble lawns, and occasionally will leap in front of vehicles.

Brisbane

Small town that got bigger in size in the last decade but smaller in population. In the 1990s, Brisbane should add people when development comes in on San Bruno Mountain, 1,315 feet high.

Built on steep, secluded hills overlooking Bay. Sunny. Generally protected from wind. Town promoter supposedly came from Brisbane, Australia.

After over 25 years of debate and protests and under court order, Brisbane approved a residential development for San Bruno Mountain — 589 homes, townhouses, flats on 93 acres near West Hill and North Hill drives. Grading started in 1992. When finished, will add 1,200 people to Brisbane's population, increase of 40 percent. The developer agreed to donate a parcel for a school, $1.5 million for a public services building and $100,000 for child-care services.

Much of Brisbane's housing was built before World War II. Small lots. Some flat tops. With the hills steep and most homes spread over two or more stories, you do a lot of climbing.

The views are sweeping and the town backs up to a large county park.

Brisbane had 3,000 people in 1942, and in 1993 the state estimated the population as 3,105. An intimate town.

Ages fairly balanced: 18 percent over 55 years, 18 percent under 18. Census (1990) counted 184 kids under age 5 — 98 boys, 86 girls.

The state in 1993 tallied 1,400 residential units — 917 single family, 33 single-attached, 387 multiples, 63 mobile homes. Brisbane grew in a jumbled fashion, sustained by FHA loans and war industries. Fearing annexation, it incorporated in 1961.

Crocker Industrial Park was annexed in the 1980s. Land set aside for industry dwarfs residential land. Residential section is buffered from business-industrial-warehouse. Offices and marina east of Interstate 101. Quarry to west of the city. San Francisco used to dump its garbage down near the water.

School rankings spotty but generally well above 60th percentile, indication of strong parental interest in education. Computers, music, speech, remedial and high-achiever programs.

Crime rate not tracked by FBI but probably quite low. There are only two roads into town; no through traffic. Access and familiarity conspire against intruders.

Good commute. San Francisco is right over the border. Freeway close by. Train station in nearby South San Francisco.

Burlingame

A Bay-to-hills town that has a strong commercial base yet is known primarily as a bedroom community, peaceful and well-to-do.

Slumbered through the 19th century and woke up with a bang, literally, when the 1906 earthquake leveled San Francisco. Eyes turned south and the virtues of Burlingame were discovered. Within a year the population had blossomed from 200 to 1,000. Burlingame incorporated in 1908. Named after Anson Burlingame, ambassador to China, who once owned 1,200 acres nearby.

Two Burlingames: residential and office-hotel-business. Located just south of the airport, having flat land, some recovered from the Bay, Burlingame has attracted many businesses. Airport Boulevard shines with sleek hotels, about 3,500 rooms, and office buildings. In recent years, Hyatt opened near the waterfront a 791-room hotel, largest in county. More hotels are in the works.

Moving west from the water, you encounter modest and small homes and apartments, well kept, a nice shopping section with many restaurants, somewhat upscale, and traffic congestion (price of progress).

Then the town ascends to the hills and home prices rise with elevation. Great views of Bay and of planes taking off. Not on the flight path but home buyers should ask neighbors about noise; better safe than sorry.

Streets lined with magnolias, sycamores. Wood shingle roofs, rock gardens, many shrubs. Good-looking neighborhoods. Designs favor ranch style. Council in 1994 voted to restrict size of new homes — no "monsters."

Burlingame borders Hillsborough, top drawer of county and possibly Bay Area, and basks somewhat in glow of neighbor.

Crime rate low suburban average, more thievery than violence. Two homicides in 1992, three in 1991, none in 1990, 1989, 1988, 1987, four in 1986, none in 1985, FBI reports.

Fifteen parks and playgrounds. Tennis and basketball courts. Baseball fields. Fishing pier. Bird sanctuary. Recreational center. Drive-in movies. Regular movies. Good choice of restaurants, in part because of hotels. Sales tax revenues from hotels and from auto row help fund town's amenities.

School rankings high, 70s, 80s, 90s. Enrollment in schools has increased over 25 percent in recent years. Many of the newcomers are Asian and Hispanic, a pattern common almost throughout the county.

Voters in 1993 passed a bond to renovate elementary schools and a parcel tax to improve instructional programs. State accorded "distinguished school" honors to Lincoln Elementary and Burlingame Intermediate.

Annual state tally (1993) showed 12,909 residential units — 6,126 single homes, 339 single-family attached, 6,441 multiples. The last number includes about 3,500 hotel rooms.

Population increased by 628 in the last decade, to 26,801 residents. Another San Mateo town essentially built out.

Great place if you fly a lot. San Francisco International is five minutes up the road. Good commute in other aspects. Highway 101 runs through flatlands, Interstate 280 runs along the western border. CalTrain carries passengers to San Francisco or Silicon Valley. SamTrans buses serve the street routes.

A few injured in 1989 earthquake but none seriously. About 10 chimneys fell. Hotels evacuated, two closed for repairs, then reopened. One hotel, beyond saving, was demolished. City has given owners of unreinforced masonry buildings until 1996 to improve or demolish.

The California caveat applies in Burlingame and in San Mateo and San Francisco counties. If you absolutely can't stand earthquakes, don't settle here. The San Andreas Fault splits both counties. The smart people read up on quakes and take precautions. Be smart.

Home Price Sampler — Classified Ads

Atherton

4-bedroom, 2.5-bath, on 1/2 acre, family room, private lot, $799,000.

Secluded West Atherton 1.1-acre level lot, has plan for a Mediterranean estate, $900,000.

Belmont

3-bedroom, 2-bath, dining room, fireplace, 2-car garage, $359,950.

3-bedroom mini-estate on 1/4 acre, formal dining room, pool, spa, 3-car garage, secluded, woodsy, $399,000.

Brisbane

2-bedroom, 1-bath, condo, new w/w/ carpet, freshly painted, bay view, $170,000.

2-bedroom, on corner lot, 2 bonus rooms, A/C, BBQ area, nice rear yard, $229,000.

Burlingame

3-bedroom, 1-bath, dining room, fireplace, 1-car garage, west of El Camino, $362,000.

Large Victorian built in 1917 on 2+ acres, bay & city views, remodeled, guest house & pool, $5,800,000.

Colma

3-bedroom, 1-bath remodeled, family room, Broadmoor home, $239,950.

3-bedroom, hardwood floors, move-in condition, $299,950.

Daly City

2-bedroom, 2.5-bath, 2-car garage, 2 master suites, private deck, end unit, former model, panoramic bay view, minutes to SF, $219,500.

4-bedroom, 2.5-bath, fireplace & wet bar in family room, patio, view, on cul-de-sac, $250,000.

East Palo Alto

3-bedroom, 1-bath, 2-car garage, open yard, $153,000.

3-bedroom, 1-bath, $165,000.

El Granada

6-bedroom, 3-bath, family room, 2-car garage, Spanish, ocean view, $329,000.

3-bedroom, 3-bath, on 1/2 acre, secluded, room & facilities for horse, $399,000.

Foster City

Waterfront, ground floor, sunny end unit, fireplace, inside laundry area, washer, dryer, refrigerator, $189,950.

Newer home on quiet cul-de-sac, large enclosed yard, bonus room, with built-ins galore, $474,950.

Half Moon Bay

3-bedroom, 2-bath, formal dining, family room, formal entry, sunken living room, see-through fireplace, master bedroom suite, $389,000.

3-bedroom, 2.5-bath, 3,000+ sq. ft., 2-story, walk to the beach, $439,000.

Hillsborough

3-bedroom, 2.5-bath, park-like setting, bonus room, $789,000.

5-bedroom, 3.5-bath, big family room, recently remodeled, large pool, $1,280,280.

Menlo Park

3-bedroom, 2-bath, 2-car garage, dining room, family room, 2 years old, $257,200.

5-bedroom, 3-bath, custom, 3 fireplaces, family room, wine cellar, shop, dining room, well-equipped kitchen, $699,000.

Millbrae

3-bedroom, 2-bath, close to schools & transportation, on quiet, tree-lined street, $315,000.

4-bedroom, 3-bath, gated courtyard entry, large lot, many fruit trees, $599,000.

Miramar

4-bedroom, 2.5-bath, family room, 2 fireplaces, hardwood floors, new, ocean view, walk to the beach, $389,000.

Miramar

4-bedroom, 2.5-bath, oversized lot, one block

Colma

Although its population grew 179 percent in the 1980s, Colma is the smallest and least populated, with the living, city in San Mateo County. Population 1,160 (state estimate 1993).

In 1992, construction began on a BART station, to be opened about 1995. BART is extending its line to San Francisco Airport, or close by.

The town is famous for its cemeteries. Colma is where San Francisco and other towns bury their dead — so far about 1.5 million in number.

Catholic, Chinese, Jewish, Greek, Serbian, Japanese, Italian and pet

Home Price Sampler — Classified Ads

to Miramar Beach, 2 fireplaces, hardwood floors, $413,000.

Montara

4-bedroom, 2.5-bath, family room, new carpets, in the hills, ocean views, $344,950.

4-bedroom, 3-bath, vaulted ceilings, skylights, airy country kitchen, on tree-line cul-de-sac, big lot, $379,000.

Moss Beach

3-bedroom, new, ocean views, lease option possibility, $419,000.

2-story, ocean views, good neighborhood, private spa & patio, $499,000.

Ocean Colony

3-bedroom, 2.5-bath, large country kitchen, dining room, custom office, den/studio, fireplace in master suite, $379,000.

5-bedroom, 3-bath, large corner lot with fenced backyard, $475,000.

Pacifica

3-bedroom rancher, level yard, patio, fireplace, sunny area, $209,950.

4-bedroom, 2.5-bath, custom, fireplace, ocean view, wine cellar, $369,900.

Pescadero

2-bedroom, 1-bath, across from creek, redwoods, rustic atmosphere, $179,900.

2-bedroom, 2-bath, den/office, log home on 15.6 acres, shop, meadow, outbuildings, creek, waterfalls, woods, $395,000.

Portola Valley

3-bedroom, 2-bath, pool, privacy, $479,000.

4-bedroom, 3-bath, $1,106,000.

Princeton

3-bedroom, 2-bath, Jacuzzi in master suite, family room has 10 skylights, remodeled, overlooks harbor, $357,000.

Redwood City

3-bedroom, 1.5-bath, dining room, fireplace, 2-car garage, on west side, $276,000.

4-bedroom, 3-bath, 5-car garage, on .42 acre, new, Spanish style, $749,000.

San Bruno

3-bedroom, 2-baths upstairs, split level, light & bright, convenient to 280, 101, schools & shopping, $258,800.

4-bedroom, 2.5-bath, formal dining, marble entry, hardwood floors under carpets, landscaped, fenced, view, $349,000.

San Carlos

Extra large one bedroom with potential and deep lot, $163,000.

3-bedroom, 2.5-bath, vaulted ceiling & stone fireplace in living room, master suite with deck, in the hills, bay view, $469,000.

San Mateo

2-bedroom, remodeled, new kitchen, new roof & more, $249,999.

6-bedroom, 4-bath, 2-story, 2,900+ sq. ft., contemporary, large, $469,000.

South San Francisco

2-master suite, 3-bath, fireplaces in living & family rooms, almost new carpets throughout, custom, remodeled, $308,000.

4-bedroom, 2.5-bath, on corner lot, 2 family rooms, large worshop, laundry area, office, 2-car garage, 2 decks & patio, $315,000.

Woodside

3-bedroom house, on private 1 acre, 3-stall barn, paddock arena, close in near town, western view, $799,900.

Hilltop Tudor on 6 acres, panoramic view, rolling hills, horse pasture, $995,000.

Source: Survey of San Mateo County classified advertising listings in fall, 1993.

cemeteries — all are located within hilly Colma. William Randolph Hearst and Wyatt Earp are buried here, the latter, a Protestant, in the Jewish cemetery. His wife was Jewish.

For a while Colma was known as Sand Hill or Schoolhouse Station, then Lawndale. Name has been traced to local creek, to gold country town, to derivation of Indian name. Some local wits give credit to lad who got off the train and exclaimed, "Gee, it's cold, ma!" The Pacific fog in the summer reaches Colma.

When San Francisco went through its periodic reforms, sin moved just over the border to Colma and Daly City. Gambling and dog racing flourished, elections were rigged, prize fights were staged. In 1909 in Colma, Jack Johnson knocked out Stanley Ketchel. Booze flowed in Prohibition days.

Gradually, Colma cleaned up its act. Gambling was outlawed. In 1993, Colma went back to its roots. Residents said OK to a cardroom (40 tables).

Colma turned to cemeteries when San Francisco outlawed burials within its borders. Local businesses tied in with cemeteries: stone cutters, florists. Some flowers grown commercially. Golf course located in hills. Commercial zone has auto dealerships. Metro 280, a shopping plaza, opened in 1987.

Colma incorporated as a city in the Twenties — to avoid being annexed — when almost any neighborhood could declare itself a city. About 444 residential units — 208 single homes, 22 single-family attached, 148 apartments (1993). The 1990 census counted 49 boys under age 5 and 53 girls.

Crime not tracked by FBI but people no longer go to Colma to whoop it up.

Daly City

Located just over the border from San Francisco and tied so closely to the City that it could be considered a San Francisco neighborhood.

About 60 percent of work force hold jobs in San Fran. The BART line, one of the main transporters of commuters to the downtown, begins in Daly City (and is being extended to Colma).

Sprawling, hilly town. Starts at Pacific and extends, through one leg, to Highway 101, just short of the Bay. Another leg runs down the ridge overlooking Pacifica. The Pacific bluffs are popular with parasailers.

Most populous city in San Mateo County, 98,316 residents (1993 estimate). Added more people — 13,792 — in the last decade than any other San Mateo city. According to 1990 census, 20 percent of residents are over age 55 and 24 percent are under age 18. Kids under 5 years number 6,555 — 3,403 boys, 3,152 girls.

In recent years, Daly City has been attracting many Asians, Hispanics and Filipinos. Believed to have the largest Filipino community in Northern California. The city has a long history of being an immigrants' town. It also has many second- and third-generation Europeans, immigrants' children who stayed put.

Town celebrates heritage annually with Fiesta Filipina, and in 1992 held its first Gateway Festival, a celebration of all cultures. Voters in 1993 elected Filipino-American to city council, a first.

Named after John Daly, whose mother died of yellow fever in 1854 while they were crossing Panama. Young Daly did odd jobs, saved pennies, bought 250 acres, ran dairy. When the 1906 earthquake leveled San Francisco, thousands fled south. Daly subdivided land, sold to newcomers. The city incorporated in 1911. Like Colma, Daly City before World War II was a refuge for sinners and gamblers.

At end of World War II, developer Henry Doelger, anticipating the great demand for housing, built row upon row of identical homes (small lawn, one tree) over the countryside. Price about $16,000 each.

Other builders followed in his style. These are the homes you see today. Some need paint and show their age. Lovers of beauty scoff about "boxes on the hillside" but Daly City homes meet genuine needs of middle class and young families. Although the homes look dull from outside, many command nice views of hills and Pacific. Many two-story homes.

Residential units in 1993 numbered 30,764, of which 14,776 were single homes, 4,485 single-family attached, 10,889 multiples, 614 mobile homes.

In 1980s, Daly City expanded its housing stock by over 2,600 units, most of them apartments and single-family attached. A lot of "concealed" housing. City hall acknowledges that many "mother-in-law" units are hidden throughout city.

At Daly City, mountains shrink to hills, too low to hold out fog. Summer time is, often, hooded sweatshirt time. The flip side: mild, sunny winters.

Four elementary school districts serve Daly City youngsters.

School rankings bounce all over, from 20th to 90th percentile, but many rankings above the 50th percentile. Jefferson Elementary District, the largest, is 84 percent minority, with Filipino and Hispanic students making up largest blocks, over 63 percent of total (1992 figures). The district has remedial and bilingual tutor programs schools and computer labs at all schools and a gifted (high achiever) program. Also extended day care. Westlake, Colma and Jefferson have received "distinguished school" awards.

Jefferson High School District serves Daly City and Pacifica. Schools include Jefferson and Westmoor in Daly City, and Oceana and Terra Nova in Pacifica. Serramonte High School in Daly City, closed for about 12 years, was reopened in fall 1993. School district allows transfers between schools, space permitting. In recent years, the district has aggressively pursued innovation, the better to handle the diverse needs of students. Call school district — (415) 756-0300 — for information.

Daly City is low to suburban average in crime. Two homicides in 1992, four in 1991, five in 1990, three in 1989, zero homicides in 1988, six in 1987, four in 1986, two in 1985, reports FBI.

Voters in 1993 turned down measure that would have allowed card clubs. Plans are in works to spruce up Mission Street, the main drag. Ground broken in 1993 for county medical center, near city hall. Council has voted in a utility tax to pay some bills.

Daly City surrounds a large unincorporated pocket called Broadmoor Village, population 3,739. Governed by county supervisors but locals exercise much influence. Rare for an unincorporated neighborhood, Broadmoor has its own police force. Residents raised taxes in 1990 to keep police department going. Broadmoor's future: probably absorption by Daly City, which is nibbling away through annexations.

Great commute town. San Francisco is right down the freeway, but never mind the freeway, there's BART, SamTrans and connections to San Fran's Muni system.

Lots to do: 13 parks, 10 tot lots, four community centers, 22 tennis courts, 2 gyms, two swimming pools, nine movie theaters, ocean beach. For adults, there's Serramonte Shopping Center. Fireworks banned in 1991. Cow Palace, a popular convention-exhibit-music hall, is located in Daly City.

Some noise from planes leaving San Francisco Airport, which is being expanded. Recent report said that over 10 years plane noise has increased in some neighborhoods, decreased in Serramonte section. Overall, the report said, noise was "within margin requisite to protect the public health."

East Palo Alto

In 1993, East Palo Alto went from the city with the highest per capita number of homicides in the nation to a city whose problems may be manageable. Specifically, homicides fell from 39 in 1992 to 6 in 1993. The counts for the previous years are 20, 22, 19, 19, 4 and 7.

School scores are low but improvements may also be coming. Many children transfer to high-scoring schools in other cities.

Affordable housing, good commute. Possibly the next boom town for the county. Waterfront location, on the Bay. Golf course on southern border. Parks, wetlands, trails, community pool, other activities.

Regional mall less than 2 miles away. World-renowned university, Stanford, loaded with cultural activities, also less than 2 miles off. Foreign movies, coffee houses, bookstores, art galleries — all within 5-10 minutes. Protected by hills from coastal fogs. Breezes from the Bay. California sunshine. Balmy.

Despite problems, population increased 29 percent in the last decade. State estimated the 1993 population at 24,472.

About a third of the town is under age 18, the 1990 census reported.

Rural to 1940, East Palo Alto took off after World War II when thousands of Blacks, recruited from the South to work in the war industries, settled in the town. The 1940s saw the construction of 871 residential units, the 1950s, the boom era, 2,685 units, followed in the next decade by 1,610 units, then 863 units, and in the last decade, 482 units.

The housing styles tell the story: the flattop roofs of the forties and fifties give way to the slopes of the sixties and seventies, the single garages blossom into two-car spaces, the two-bedroom homes grow into three.

For most of its modern history, East Palo Alto was unincorporated and governed from Redwood City by the board of supervisors. In 1983, residents voted the town into cityhood.

The 1980s saw an influx of Hispanics, many from Central America, and, in smaller numbers, Asians and Pacific Islanders. They account for, respectively, 36 and 9 percent of the population and the city has always had a small number of Caucasians (12 percent-1990 census).

In the historical perspective, people come to East Palo Alto because whatever its problems, it's better than the place they left.

School quality is a complicated business but, as a rule, the poorer the town the lower the test scores. Schools in the Ravenswood Elementary District, which serves East Palo Alto, score generally in bottom 10th and 20th percentile.

Newcomer classes for non-English speaking. Emphasis on teaching basic skills. Stanford University, civic groups have "adopted" schools, try to help with programs.

To head off legal difficulties over accusations of segregation, Palo Alto and Menlo Park schools — scores in the top 10th percentile — and other school districts agreed years ago to accept minority transfers from East Palo Alto.

The last census placed 9 percent of East Palo Alto's elementary-high school kids in private schools.

All of this raises a big point about East Palo Alto. It's not uniformly depressed. Many of its residents live below the poverty line but many live above. The census revealed that 17 percent of the households earned $35,000 to $50,000, and 23 percent over $50,000. About 14 percent of the residents, or 2,227 people, are college grads, the census reported.

The same picture comes through when you drive the streets. On some blocks, many homes are in need of paint, repairs and a lawnmower. On others, quite the opposite.

The city has a new top cop and the sheriff's office, the California Highway Patrol, and Menlo Park and Palo Alto are lending officers to beef up patrols. Police grants from outside in 1993 totaled $1.6 million, an unusually large amount. Outside civic groups are donating time and money to tone up the city administration.

The tradeoff: when it comes to home prices, the market recognizes the problems, which is why you can buy many three-bedroom homes for under $150,000. In 1993, new four-bedroom homes were selling for $190,000.

Residences total 7,307 — single homes 3,542, single attached 243, multiples 3,260, mobile homes 262. The town is switching from majority homeowners to majority tenants, recent statistics indicate.

New city hall. Some new light industry. Other factors working for East Palo Alto: location, land prices, shortage of land on peninsula. Town is near Dumbarton Bridge and Silicon Valley.

Planning now underway for a retail center near Highway 101.

Foster City

Lagoon-island city. Pretty. Cleverly laid out. The Peninsula city that did the best job of putting the Bay into the service of beauty, housing and recreation.

Increased its population by 21 percent in the last decade. About 16 percent of the town is over 55 years, about 21 under age 18, census reported. Kids under

Number of Units Available at Selected Rents

City or Area	<$100 -249	$250 -499	$500 -749	$750 -999	$1,000 -plus
Atherton	0	6	18	11	80
Belmont	28	230	2,230	1,115	537
Brisbane	14	93	245	115	40
Broadmoor	2	6	34	90	42
Burlingame	39	588	3,441	1,482	773
Colma	8	30	110	35	6
Daly City	378	999	6,333	2,848	1,288
East Palo Alto	328	1,261	1,865	428	100
El Granada	8	48	99	99	148
Emerald Lake Hills	2	10	14	13	58
Foster City	3	34	833	1,685	1,842
Half Moon Bay	109	97	160	223	252
Highlands	0	3	30	39	46
Hillsborough	2	5	6	4	97
Menlo Park	241	444	1,684	1,400	1,566
Millbrae	18	191	1,116	817	637
Montara	1	9	32	36	73
Moss Beach	5	21	27	39	73
North Fair Oaks	59	352	969	376	165
Pacifica	182	239	1,750	1,542	609
Portola Valley	5	16	18	50	187
Redwood City	327	1,383	5,911	2,971	1,674
San Bruno	82	470	2,738	1,447	629
San Carlos	33	204	1,284	802	655
San Mateo, City of	288	1,363	6,809	4,908	2,871
So. San Francisco	377	1,007	3,157	1,607	780
West Menlo Park	9	15	83	55	174
Woodside	5	16	23	20	55
Remainder	72	210	341	192	370
Countywide	2,625	9,310	41,360	24,449	15,827

Source: 1990 Census. The chart shows the number of rental units counted within a designated range of rates.

5 years: 843 boys, 687 girls. State estimated 1993 population at 29,249.

No more than a reclaimed island 30 years ago, used for growing hay, Foster City owes its existence to Jack Foster, a rags-to-riches orphan.

He purchased the island, devised an imaginative — and some thought an illegal — government-financing scheme, laid out the streets, brought in seemingly endless loads of fill, built bridges, carved out lagoons, installed sewers and utility lines, and constructed homes — just your basic job of

Median & Average Rents of Renter-Occupied Dwellings

City or Area	Units	Median	Average
Atherton	155	*$1,001	$1,063
Belmont	4,192	697	763
Brisbane	515	617	669
Broadmoor	184	875	895
Burlingame	6,423	682	741
Colma	195	629	637
Daly City	11,988	674	723
East Palo Alto	4,019	532	550
El Granada	410	866	884
Emerald Lake Hills	104	*1,001	993
Foster City	4,442	947	994
Half Moon Bay	871	811	794
Highlands	120	917	966
Hillsborough	131	*1,001	1,146
Menlo Park	5,412	803	839
Millbrae	2,824	770	830
Montara	158	983	970
Moss Beach	172	939	912
North Fair Oaks	1,952	628	670
Pacifica	4,383	749	783
Portola Valley	294	*1,001	1,070
Redwood City	12,438	670	731
San Bruno	5,439	709	749
San Carlos	3,025	744	814
San Mateo, City of	16,489	738	790
So. San Francisco	7,055	670	698
West Menlo Park	350	*1,001	966
Woodside	140	944	908
Remainder	1,284	722	786
Countywide	95,164	711	764

Source: 1990 Census. Units are total number of renter-occupied dwellings. Rents are stated as monthly payments. Median means halfway. In 100 homes, the 50th is the median. Asterisk (*) rents are highest reported by census. Actual may be higher.

building a city from scratch. Foster City has 223 acres of waterways, 13 miles of shoreline and 12 residential islands.

It is a planned city, which may sound unexceptional but most Bay Area cities were not "planned." They started off with a few homes, a railroad station, and a store, gradually built their populations and commercial strips and one day formed a government and set about providing municipal services: parks and recreation, sewage treatment. The planning came late in the game.

In Foster City and large neighborhoods like Redwood Shores in Redwood City, the planning came before — which makes things easier and often nicer. Commercial zones are established, park land and school sites set aside, residential zones defined.

For about 10 years Foster ran the city as a company town but it was only a matter of time before residents, generally professionals, decided they wanted to do the governing. City incorporated in 1971.

But by this time, Foster had defined the character of the city. Nice job, too.

Trails wander along shore. Windsurfers and skiers skim along the water. Ducks and herons glide out of harm's way. Sailing is popular.

Library, an art gallery, a recreation center, 18 parks, tot and preschool programs, teen activities, summer camps, churches, cable television that broadcasts city council meetings. Soccer, baseball, football, many activities. Youth Council, composed of teens, plans dances, social events.

Foster City is big on square dancing, fitness, softball and tennis, and arts and crafts, in that order, says city hall. Concerts in the parks.

Diverse neighborhoods — apartments, townhouses, modest homes, luxury homes. Office buildings (including 22-story tower), neighborhood shopping centers, many restaurants. About 600 firms in city. Headquarters city for VISA.

Crime low (but always take care). One homicide in 1992, two in 1991, one in 1990, one in 1989, none in 1988, 1987, one in 1986, none in 1985. City has own police and fire department.

School rankings up there, 60s, 70s, 80s, 90s, a reflection in part of the middle-class character of Foster City. All lower schools part of San Mateo-Foster City elementary district, which is opening a school and installing magnet programs to encourage integration. In recent years, voters approved tax increases to renovate and add schools and improve programs.

Some residents would like Foster City to have its own unified school district with its own high school or at least the latter. Ideas are at talk-wish stage.

High school students attend San Mateo Union High District — six high schools in San Mateo, Burlingame, Millbrae and San Bruno. The schools pride themselves on running high-powered prep programs that send many kids to college. The vocational program, Two-Plus-Two, ties kids to San Mateo Community College, encourages electronics.

High schools have open enrollment; you pick the school for your kid. School district publishes several pamphlets explaining programs.

Residences number 11,864, of which 4,770 are single homes, 2,508 single attached, 4,582 multiples (1993 count). More homes, condos are planned. Build-out this decade.

A lot of people thought that in a big earthquake Foster City, because it is built on fill, would gurgle down into the Bay. But it makes a big difference, the newspapers belatedly pointed out, how the fill is compacted, what the consistency of mud below is, and how foundations are designed and anchored. Foster

City took 1989 temblor in stride.

Work began in 1993 to improve levees. More a matter of meeting insurance requirement than safety, said city hall.

When Rover poops, better have a scoop. Also better have dog on leash when walking around town. Laws. One-acre dog run behind city hall.

Paint controls. Can't just slap on any color, as one family discovered when it painted house (outside) salmon. Repaint it, said city council, from list of approved colors.

Fairly good commute. Fast shot over San Mateo Bridge to East Bay. A little overly dependent on Highway 101, which at peak hours can be murder. But with a little detour Foster City residents can pick up I-280 to City. CalTrain connection in nearby San Mateo. SamTrans runs buses from Foster City to San Fran. San Francisco International Airport is 10 minutes up the road.

Silicon Valley takes some slogging but it's a better commute than for many towns in Santa Clara County.

Fog rarely a problem. Sheltered by hills, close to Bay.

San Francisco Airport, under pressure from the city council, has promised to keep planes over Bay, and keep noise down over Foster City. If buying a home or renting, ask neighbors about plane noise.

Half Moon Bay

Small town on the Pacific. Pretty. Increased its population by 22 percent in the last decade but considers growth undesirable. Population in 1993 broke the 10,000 mark and now stands at 10,141 (state estimate).

About 24 percent of the residents are under 18 years, 17 percent over 55, the 1990 census reported. Kids under 5 years: 314 boys, 324 girls.

One of the oldest communities in the county and one of the few that can call itself quaint. For a long time a farm town that owed its livelihood to the cultivation of strawflowers, artichokes, cabbages and sprouts. Farming still counts in Half Moon Bay but not nearly as much as it used to.

Mixed housing. Apartments down near shore. Older homes east of Highway 1. To south of town country club estates with fairway homes. Quite nice, quite expensive, the top going for over $1 million. Some upper-middling housing near Frenchman's Creek Road.

Residences in 1993 numbered 3,702— single homes 2,345, single attached 418, multiples 613, mobile homes 326.

Many locals would like to add more people to give the economy a boost and raise money for activities. But a sizeable number like Half Moon Bay small and cozy. Infrastructure a problem; sewage treatment and water lacking to serve many more residents.

Battles and lawsuits and voter measures over development are part of the Half Moon Bay experience. Most recent elections seem to give edge to pro-growthers. Check with city to see what's pending.

Town is built on flat land; few if any view homes. Ocean is within a few blocks of any home. State beach runs along the shore. Hills look down on the city. Fog country. Often socked in during the summer, clear in the winter.

Commute not as bad as might be thought. San Francisco, along Route 1, is a long drive but nearby Route 92, one of the few east-west arterials in the county, takes you over the ridge and down to 280 and 101, the roads to Silicon Valley, San Fran, the Hayward-San Mateo Bridge. On weekends and summer days, roads are often congested with tourists.

Chamber of commerce estimates the rush-hour commute to San Francisco as 47 minutes, to City of San Mateo 24 minutes, to Palo Alto 35 minutes, to Silicon Valley 53 minutes.

Private airfield north of city. If you have bucks, fly to work.

Few pumpkins are grown but Half Moon Bay has won fame in Bay Region for its annual pumpkin festival, which draws about 300,000. The 1993 winner for big pumpkin came in at 740 lbs.

Other more sedate festivals are also celebrated, including Heritage Festival (ethnic diversity). Tourism drives large portion of local economy (restaurants, bed and breakfast places, shops). Business people are trying to boost coast as place to visit. Homes in old section have been restored. Walking tours.

Crime rate not tracked by FBI, but we're talking low to average.

School rankings, with few exceptions, come in well above the 50th percentile, an indication of strong parental and community interest. Hatch Elementary is educating the kids, from kindergarten, in English and Spanish.

Lots of outdoorsy things to do: salmon and cod fishing, whale watching, surfing (it's cold, wear wet suit), horse riding, golfing. Up the road is the village of Princeton with its restaurants, marina and fishing boats.

A surfing magazine in 1993 revealed that some of the finest waves in the world were breaking off a beach just north of Pillar Point. "So heavy, so radical," murmured a local surfer.

Hillsborough

Most prestigious town in the county and maybe Northern California.

Crime rate among lowest, school scores among highest in state. By reputation the bastion of WASP bluebloods; in reality, open to new money and diversity.

No sidewalks or street lamps. Putting-green lawns. Mansions and custom homes galore but also a surprising number of modest homes. Views of Bay.

A town getting a little ethnic, mainly Chinese and Chinese-American. Asian kids make up over 25 percent of school enrollment.

Added 216 people in the last decade. Total in 1993 was put at 11,060. Essentially built out. Many gray heads; 31 percent of the residents are over 55, census reported. The under-18s make up 22 percent of town. Preschoolers number 480 — 257 boys, 223 girls.

Borders Interstate 280 but removed from the more traveled Highway 101. Helps with privacy. Hedges, trees and shrubs hide many homes from street view. No cars parked on the streets.

Private tennis courts and pools. Playground at Vista Park. School grounds serve as playing fields. Annual Concours d'Elegance (car show) for benefit of schools. No industry, no business (except country club). Ladies are active in supporting this and that charity, the arts.

In 1890s, the heirs of first San Francisco millionaires built first country club in California, parceled out nearby land for estates, and later to protect their investment against encroaching town, incorporated section as a city. Country club still in business.

Hillsborough has the lowest tracked crime rate in the county and among lowest in state. No homicides in 1992, 1991, 1990, 1989, 1988, 1987, 1986, 1985, reports FBI. Teenagers used to keep cops busy with keg parties but a new law gives the law a stronger lever to hold hosts responsible for drinking minors.

Single homes dominate. Of town's 3,824 residences, 97 percent (3,780) are classified as single homes, 18 single attached, 21 multiple units, 5 mobile homes. New homes here and there; about 240 constructed in the last decade.

School rankings among tops in state, 90s. Crocker Middle, North Elementary, South Elementary and West Elementary have won state distinguished-school awards. Crocker, in one judging, was named one of best middle schools in nation, and in 1993 won an award, from Sweden, that locals interpreted as deeming Crocker one of the five best schools on the planet.

Hillsborough voters years ago passed a parcel tax for schools and in 1992 renewed the tax, about $227 a year — nice endorsement of education. Schools are keeping computer labs open extra hour a day, reducing class sizes to 25, expanding physical ed for younger children.

Parents with kids in public schools are asked to make "fair share" donation to a private fund collected by parents. Money is fed into schools and academics. About $450,000 is raised annually through private efforts, an unusually large amount. Many kids (about four of every 10) get outside tutoring, news story said in 1993. Science instruction being improved at schools.

Commute not as good as some cities in county but good enough. Up the hill to Interstate 280, down the hill to Highway 101 and airport. CalTrain close by.

If walking dog, bring pooper scooper. It's the law. Deer nibble lawns and gardens.

La Honda

Village, unincorporated, located in valley southwest of Portola Valley. Used to be logging camp and bootleggers' hideout.

In the Twenties, the well-to-do built summer homes that in the Sixties became all-year homes. In the Seventies, others discovered the charms of La Honda and built mansions, which inevitably sparked row over what kind of housing should be allowed and how much.

Argument has been resolved in favor of larger lots and fewer houses. Development would have been limited in any event as the water supply — a stream feeding into reservoirs — does not bubble to excess. The town council has the ear of the board of supervisors and greatly influences matters.

Surrounded by state parks. Protected by mountains from fog. PTA runs activities for the kiddies, soccer, etc. Annual street fair. La Honda embraces the basics of civilized life: one school, one fire station, one grocery store, one restaurant, a pottery shop and two saloons. Who can ask for anything more?

Long commute. When you buy country, you really get, in this case, country.

Menlo Park

South county town, pleasant, upscale. Borders Palo Alto and Stanford and delights in shopping in Stanford Mall and sampling Palo Alto shops but does not want to go as commercial as Palo Alto.

To the east lies East Palo Alto, high crime, low scores, a reminder that all is not well in the world. The school district serving East Palo Alto also includes a small part of Menlo Park. Another neighbor: Atherton, rich and insular.

Added 1,671 residents in the last decade. Population (1993) tallied 29,407.

About 27 percent of the residents are over age 55, about 19 percent under 18. Preschoolers (under 5) number 1,828 — 980 boys, 848 girls (1990 census).

Name given by first settlers, two Irishmen from Menlough in County Galway. Estate town in beginning. Then served as bedroom town for Stanford faculty. Incorporated in 1927, grew modestly, overshadowed by Palo Alto, but part of university ring.

Home of Stanford Research Institute, Sunset Magazine, U.S. Geological Survey, and Raychem. Sun Systems, near Highway 84, is constructing a seven-building research campus. Supposed to be finished in 1998 and house 2,400 people. New supermarket opened in 1991, one of largest in county.

Residential units in 1993 totaled 12,334 — single homes 6,493, single attached 856, multiples 4,977, mobile homes 8. Most homes and apartments were built in the 15 years right after World War II and styles reflect that era. In the 1980s, the town added about 600 single homes and 300 apartments. Many homes sell for well over $500,000. Some mansions $1 million plus.

City has been arguing for years about building 145 luxury homes on 88 acres in hills. Council said yes in 1992. Court supported decision in mid 1993.

Apartment buildings looked well-cared-for. Magnolias and other trees line the streets. In some neighborhoods, trees grow in middle of streets. Lawns well-tended. Menlo Park imposes a special tax to pay for lights and landscaping throughout the town. Residents in 1993 voted to increase taxes to retain three fire stations and keep the current response time.

Crime picture is a little murky. Menlo Park twists and dodges from the Bay up to the hills. The hills are country club, low crime. Bay neighborhoods butt up against East Palo Alto, high crime. One homicide in 1992, two in 1991, one in 1990, four in 1989, one homicide in each of the four previous years, says FBI. Overall crime rate about low-suburban but the eastern neighborhood, called Belle Haven, has suffered from crime.

City in recent years has pumped money, cops (a satellite police station) and attention into this section, trying to boost morale and drive out drug dealing. In 1993, crime in East Palo Alto dropped sharply, a good omen. Homeless shelter next to Highway 101.

For most kids, school rankings way up there, high 90s, an indication that the community values education. Las Lomitas and La Entrada elementaries were named distinguished schools, a state award for good management.

Ravenswood District serves mainly East Palo Alto and has two schools in Menlo Park. Scores are among the lowest in the state, with one exception. Flood Elementary in Menlo Park is scoring in the top 25th percentile.

Many Menlo kids attend Menlo-Atherton High, honored state and nationally for quality programs. Scores in 90s and often number one in the county in academic rankings. School to be expanded. For more on high school, see Redwood City profile.

Education foundation raises money for schools. Parcel tax passed in 1992 for Menlo elementary schools to reduce class sizes and fund libraries and educational programs.

Silicon Valley close, San Francisco distant. CalTrain helps, up to San Fran or down to San Jose. Train station. Dumbarton Bridge to Fremont-Newark starts at Menlo Park. SamTrans buses. Local traffic a bit congested, many of the motorists driving through Menlo Park to get someplace else.

Many activities: swimming, soccer, dance, bridge, tennis, ballet, baseball. Popular gymnastic program, enrolls about 1,200. Nine parks, 14 playgrounds. Farmers market.

Free Spanish lessons for city employees. Menlo Park is attracting more Hispanics; effort by city to be responsive.

Millbrae

Hills to Bay town. Pretty. Well-cared-for. Middle class. Great views from hills. Located immediately east and above San Fran International Airport. Added 354 residents in 1980s. Built out. Estimated 1993 population: 21,125.

About 31 percent of town is over age 55, about 20 percent under 18. The 1990 census counted 537 boys under the age of 5 and 538 girls.

Darius Mills, rich landowner who built mansion, guided early development. Not much happened during most of its pioneer days. High prices discouraged subdividers. After World War I, homes started to cluster about the roadhouse stations along the main thoroughfare through the Peninsula.

Small subdivision in 1921. Big subdivision in 1927, called Highlands, aimed at upper end of market. After struggling with poor services for years and fighting annexation attempts, Millbrae incorporated as a city in 1948 and built its parks and municipal structure.

A lot of home building came after World War II. By 1954, Millbrae had 10,000 residents, by 1970 about 21,000. Population dipped in the 1970s, rose slightly in the 1980s. Like the rest of the county, Millbrae is becoming more diverse, mainly Asians and Hispanics.

Hills keep fog away, a point of pride in Millbrae.

Ten parks, one PAR course. Green Hills Country Club sits in the middle of town. Many activities for seniors, teenagers and kids. Popular arts and wine festival, draws about 100,000.

Western side borders Crystal Spring Reservoir, pretty. Trails for hiking. Shoreline trail recently opened. Shops and restaurants in the downtown, which is being spruced up with planters and brick crosswalks. Big hotels nearby if you want to try their cuisine.

Of Millbrae's 8,216 residential units, single homes account for 5,408, single-family attached 237, multiples 2,568, mobile homes 3. Higher the elevation, higher the price. Many two-story homes in the hills. Decks for viewing. Much landscaping and care. Arguments about views cut off by second-story additions. Near Highway 101 the homes are smaller, more modest but still well-kept. Apartments also near the freeway.

Crime rate low. Zero homicides in 1992, two in 1991, zero in 1990, one in 1989, zero in 1988, one in 1987, two in 1986, one in 1985.

School rankings ascend from the 40th percentile to the 90th. Mills High has been named a distinguished school, a state honor for schools that are well run. Taylor Middle School recently renovated. Day care at town's four elementary schools. Voters in April 1994 will be asked to approve more school funding.

Sitting next to the airport, served by two freeways, Millbrae has to be considered a good commute. CalTrain to Silicon Valley. SamTrans for local bus transportation. When BART reaches the airport, a station will be built at Millbrae. Arguments surfacing over station location. Separation-of-grade being constructed on Millbrae Avenue. Trains now impede traffic.

After homeowners near downtown complained about parking on their streets, city issued parking permits that allow residential parking, discourages others from leaving cars parked all day.

Noise complaints near airport. Millbrae in 1993 received $1 million in fed taxes to insulate 86 homes against sound. Before buying, listen to planes landing and taking off. Talk to neighbors. Airport is to be expanded, new tactics tried to reduce noise.

Montara-Moss Beach

Coastal villages south of Pacifica. Unincorporated, which means they are governed by board of supervisors, sitting in Redwood City. Although talked of as separate hamlets, the two are close together, have connecting streets and common interests: protecting the shore against development.

Pretty. Rustic. Some streets unpaved in Montara. Artsy look. Many pine trees. State beach in Montara, Fitzgerald Marine Reserve in Moss Beach. Lighthouse at Point Montara. Restaurants, stores. Half Moon Bay Airport, private, extends into Moss Beach. If buying or renting, check with neighbors about noise.

Homes east and west of Highway 1. Many down on the ocean.

Montara population, 2,551, of whom 10 percent are over 55 years and 27 percent under 18 years. Kids under 5 number 224.

Moss Beach has 3,002 residents — 12 percent over 55, about 27 percent under 18. Kids: 268 (Census 1990).

Pacifica

On the Pacific. Great views of the ocean. Warm in the winter. Often cold and foggy in the summer. On the map, Pacifica looks like it has scads of land for housing but a great deal has been locked up in parks and watershed. Remainder is often hilly (expensive for building).

The San Francisco Chronicle made a stab in 1991 at identifying the best towns for families in the Bay Region. Pacifica was the only city in San Mateo County that made the list.

The city added 804 residents in last decade, bringing population to 37,670. About 16 percent over age 55, about 25 percent under age 18. Under five years: 1,503 boys, 1,434 girls (1990 census).

After World War II, the housing boom spread out to and down the coast, engulfing old villages: Rockaway Beach, Vallemar, Sharp Park, Edgemar, Pacifica Manor, Linda Mar. Services and schools lagged behind development, planning was haphazard. Naturally the residents became discontented and — a familiar story in California — incorporated the villages in 1957 into city of Pacifica and took over their own planning and governing.

Much of Pacifica is built on mesas, divided by deep ravines. The neighborhoods are separate and distinct. Step out the door and over the fence and you'll usually find yourself among sage and chaparral. Apartments and small shops near the water, off Highway 1, the main drag.

Fishing pier that sticks out far enough into the Pacific to catch salmon, beach promenade, public golf course, beach park, 14 parks, 12 playgrounds, two public swimming pools, tennis, bowling, riding and hiking trails, archery and shooting range, restaurants, hotels. Community center — arts and crafts, bocce, day care, seniors activities. Great hills for skateboards.

Commute is not bad. San Francisco and Interstate 280 are a few miles up the road. Shark Park Road also leads to I-280 and down to Highway 101.

Highway 1 goes from freeway to four-lane road. Although traffic moves, Pacifica would like Highway 1 improved but many don't want to turn it into a freeway, which would spur coastal development.

Crime rate low. Zero homicides in 1992, one in 1991, zero in 1990, two in 1989, zero in 1988, two in 1987, one in 1986, one in 1985, reports FBI.

Served by Laguna Salada Union Elementary District and Jefferson Union High School District. Elementary rankings range from about the 50s to the 90s.

Jefferson High School District serves Daly City and Pacifica. Schools include Jefferson and Westmoor in Daly City, and Oceana and Terra Nova in Pacifica. Serramonte High School in Daly City, closed for about 12 years, was reopened in fall 1993.

School district allows transfers between schools, space permitting. In recent years, the district has aggressively pursued innovation, the better to handle the diverse needs of students. Call school district — (415) 756-0300 — for information on programs offered. Some admissions determined by lottery.

Laguna Salada district in 1992 and 1993 was afflicted with money shortages. Salaries were cut to make up deficit. Teachers unhappy.

Skyline Community College just over the border. Big plus. Community colleges offer many activities, classes.

Pacifica celebrates itself with Fog Fest. Event draws about 50,000 and includes Fog Dance, Fog Jog. Fog pattern: Generally absent in winter. Sunny and mild. Present in summer, cold and overcast often to late afternoon when sun burns through. Some days fog disappears. People tolerate, hate, love it.

Fairly good housing mix. Residences in 1993 totaled 13,831, of which 9,951 were single homes, 716 single-family attached, 3,056 multiples, 108 mobile homes. New homes and old (some flat tops), some custom-built. Many just typical suburban homes, nice, spacious, well kept. Some funky. Parts of Pacifica come across as a sort of artists' colony.

In last decade, Pacifica added about 700 residential units, 60 percent of them single homes. A bedroom town. Largest employers are the school district and the city government, which doesn't make for a strong tax base.

Residents would like to keep small-town flavor and protect beach and country but they also want enough business to generate taxes for amenities and basic services and repairs, such as filling potholes. Parcel tax was imposed in 1991. Upset many, and the town recalled a majority of the city council. New council is all women, a rarity. Voters in 1993 turned down zoning to build on a quarry near the Pacific and said yes to growth control.

Some noise from planes taking off from San Francisco International, which may put up money for sound insulation.

Portola Valley

As the Santa Cruz mountains move south down the Peninsula, some flatten into small hills and plateaus. The Bay hills rise to the east, the mountains to the west, and in between sits Portola Valley, Woodside and the Crystal Springs Reservoir.

Portola Valley is a pretty town, high income, considered a prestige address. Big lots, tall trees, big homes. Woodsy hills mixed with open space. Majestic oaks. Quail flit across the road. One mansion in 1991 came on the market for $15 million — 30 rooms, 10 bathrooms, 13,000 square feet. Described as a "mini-San Simeon." Most homes, however, fall into the category of large suburban. Many are content to nestle in the trees but some command great views of countryside and Bay. Horse country. Corrals and ranches. Stop signs that say "Whoa." Equestrian center. Town was named after Spanish explorer. Boosted by Andrew Hallidie, inventor of cable car, who bought property in valley and donated land for school and post office.

A long commute to San Fran. One freeway, the pleasant I-280. A short commute to Silicon Valley, Palo Alto and Stanford.

Portola Valley, by reputation, is popular with Silicon Valley and Stanford types. The Stanford Linear Accelerator sits just over the city border, and Stanford owns much of the adjoining land.

Another single-home town — 1,699 residential units, of which 95 percent or 1,439 are single homes, 18 single-family attached, 239 multiples, 3 mobile homes (1993 state estimate).

Town incorporated in 1964 to slow growth and stop encroachment from neighbors. Has done just that. Portola Valley started the last decade with 3,939 people and finished with 4,194, an increase of 255 — peanuts by California standards. The state in 1993 estimated the population at 4,293.

Many residents can probably be found in their rocking chairs: 32 percent are over age 55, about 19 percent under age 18. Kids under 5 number 223 — 115 boys, 108 girls (1990 census). These figures do not include Ladera, an unincorporated subdivision off Alpine Road, near Interstate 280. It's considered part of Portola Valley but is actually outside city limits.

Elementary school rankings among highest in the state, not just in the 90s but the high 90s. Distinguished school awards to Ormondale and Corte Madera. Instruction includes art, music, physical education, science. Middle school offers Spanish and French, and computers.

Portola kids attend Woodside High, scores in the top 30th percentiles. The high school, which draws kids from diverse social and ethnic groups, introduces the reality and some complexities of the larger world. For more on high school, see Redwood City profile.

FBI doesn't track crime stats but Portola Valley rarely makes the news. Thieves would have a hard time finding the place.

Princeton, El Granada

Villages, just above Half Moon Bay. Marina at Princeton, which is sheltered by the curve of the Bay. Jumping-off spot for rock cod and salmon fishing. Whale excursions. Nice restaurants. Bed-and-breakfast places. Small

116 SAN MATEO COUNTY CITY PROFILES

airport to the north. In recent years, many fights over how or if restaurant section should be expanded. In 1993 court gave OK to hotel, 11 apartments, restaurant.

El Granada lies east of Highway 1. Secluded (somewhat) subdivision. Homes rise into hills. Nice views of Pacific.

For all practical purposes, these two places should be considered part of Half Moon Bay. People shop in town, send kids to local schools.

Population of both: 4,426, of whom 12 percent are over 55, and 27 percent are under 18. Kids under 5 years: 185 boys and 182 girls (1990 census).

Redwood City

Started 1993 with a hoo-hah over a sign that proclaimed that Redwood City was: "Palo Alto without the attitude."

Some merchants liked it, others didn't. Down it came but the jangly aggressiveness of the slogan caught some of the spirit of Redwood City, the county seat and one of the fastest growing cities of San Mateo County.

Added 11,121 residents in last decade, an increase of 20 percent. State estimated 1993 population at 69,917. Local schools report that 51 percent of kids are Hispanics — a big change that is influencing how schools are run.

Third most populous city in the county. Only city with a port.

Town was named after Redwood Creek, which descended from redwood country. Old lumber port faded away but in 1930s city built new, larger port.

Although Redwood City ascends to the hills, most of the town is laid out on flat land. Housing generally old, bungalows from Thirties, larger homes after World War II. Good mix in designs. Streets laid on a grid pattern — romantic no, efficient yes. Higher the elevation, generally the higher the price.

Nice-looking city in mature way. Many streets have trees. Some homes need sprucing up but many show care. Courts, jail, county buildings in downtown, about 2,000 county workers, plus lawyers and others, the mainstays of the downtown economy.

City leaders have spent millions in redevelopment funds to revive downtown. Efforts include trees, old-fashioned lampposts on Main Street, new jail and police headquarters, and parking garage. Old police station turned into an art center-gallery.

New mall, Sequoia Station, opened in 1993. Includes largest Safeway in Northern California, a bookstore, restaurants, coffee shop, and more.

Good housing mix. Of Redwood City's 27,292 residential units, 12,696 are single homes, 3,052 single-family attached, 10,937 multiples, 607 mobile homes (1993 figures). One homeless shelter.

About 19 percent of the residents are over 55 years, about 22 percent under 18. Kids under 5 years: 2,701 boys, 2,499 girls (1990 census).

Three unincorporated neighborhoods, Selby, Emerald Lake, Fair Oaks, located just outside city limits, add to housing choices. Emerald Lake has 3,328 residents, 19 percent of whom are over age 55, about 23 percent under 18.

The 1990 census did not break out Selby, generally middle class, or Fair Oaks, low income and popular with immigrants.

Redwood City counts seven parks, eight playgrounds, movie complex, 20 public tennis courts, miniature golf, bowling alley, Boys and Girls Center, video arcades, batting cages, ice skating rink, roller rink, two municipal swimming pools, three libraries (including the most popular in the county), nine-hole golf course, four marinas and a field to fly model planes. Theater, art deco design, stages local productions. Annual Sunflower Festival.

Golfers for years have urged the city to build a public course at Edgewood Park but a 1993 study concluded that the course would destroy a habitat needed by the Checkerspot Butterfly. Summer farmers market, produce from local farms. Antique stores on Main Street. Cañada College, located just outside city limits, adds a lot to the city's cultural life.

Some new housing on the waterfront, near Redwood Shores, condos, first-class hotels (tied to airport trade), office buildings, waterways, many streets tree-lined, homes striking and pleasing. Headquarters city for Oracle, the software firm. San Carlos has small airport near the freeway. Some Redwood Shores folks have complained about plane noise.

In the hills, disputes tend to views and sunlight. City passed an ordinance to control building of additions and second stories.

Crime rate about suburban average. Three homicides in 1992, one in 1991, two in 1990, zero in 1989 and 1988, three in 1987, three in 1986, four in 1985. Newspaper reports drug dealing, social problems in some neighborhoods near Highway 101 and in Fair Oaks. As soon as grafitto appears, city tries to have it painted over. If neighbor's party gets loud, call cops. They have a machine that measures sound. First-time offenders are warned, second-timers may be fined.

Elementary school rankings bounce all over, very low to very high. Intermediate rankings are low, high school rankings generally high.

A detailed explanation is beyond the scope of this book but rankings are greatly influenced by demographics of school population — family income, education of parents, push from home.

Redwood City elementary schools are drawing kids from diverse ethnic groups and backgrounds, the poor and low income residing near Highway 101, the middle and upper in the hills and parts of the shore.

The elementary school district reports a student mix of 39 percent White, 51 percent Hispanic (1992 figures). In 1990 school officials reported that 40 percent of the students spoke little or no English. Bilingual programs have been installed at many of the elementary schools.

The district in fall 1994 will start a magnet program designed to mix the kids by ethnicity. Magnet schools run enriched or special programs. The theory is that middle-class kids will attend schools in the poorer neighborhoods if the schools offer something special: extra math, or science, etc.

The kids in the low-income sections will be offered their special programs at the middle-class schools. The program is voluntary. Many students will be eligible for free busing. The magnet schools are Clifford, Cloud, Garfield, Hoover, Orion, and Selby Lane.

The remaining six schools will remain "neighborhood" schools. In a few years, the magnet approach will be introduced in the middle schools.

Sequoia High School District serves Redwood City and also draws students from Atherton, Woodside, East Palo Alto, Portola Valley and Belmont. The upper-income towns have very high elementary scores and parents who have high expectations for their schools and children.

Redwood City elementary schools and the high schools are encountering a problem showing up statewide: Scores are dividing along ethnic and class lines; poor (often Hispanic and Black), low scores; middle and upper-middle class (often White and Asian), high scores, with crossovers for all groups.

In one testing period at the high schools, 60 percent of white students got A's and B's vs. 38 percent of Hispanic students and 32 percent of Black students — a bipolar split that's pushing Sequoia and other districts to offer programs aimed at high and low achievers.

Schools and kids have misunderstandings and conflicts but a great effort · is being made to appreciate diverse cultures and viewpoints.

After-school care available at many public elementary schools.

Voters in 1993 turned down measures that would have raised money for schools. On the other hand, parents group raises about $30,000 annually for grants to teachers for classroom projects. Garfield Elementary, in the Fair Oaks neighborhood, is to get $900,000 over the next three years to reduce class sizes, encourage parent involvement and possibly to turn the institution into a charter school, which would give it more control over its affairs.

Plans are being made to build an elementary school in Redwood Shores, which is served by the Belmont school district. Menlo-Atherton High is to be expanded. Woodside High is to add an art-science lab.

For Silicon Valley workers, Redwood City is a short hop but San Francisco is a long drive. Two freeways in either direction. Also CalTrain. SamTrans runs the local buses. Local annoyances: trains blocking street traffic. City intends to build "separations of grade" on Jefferson Avenue and on Whipple Avenue.

Latest news on sign brouhaha: old sign to return. It reads, "Climate Best by Government Test," a reference to a favorable but old and obscure study that praised the local weather.

San Bruno

Bedroom town located just east of San Francisco International Airport. Rises from the flats to the hills. Great views. Tanforan Park one of biggest shopping malls, about 120 stores, on the Peninsula.

Added 3,544 residents in last decade, an increase of 10 percent. Population as of 1993 was 40,275 (state estimate). About 19 percent of San Bruno is over age 55, about 22 percent under 18. Kids under 5 years: 1,351 boys, 1,278 girls (1990 census).

Name probably inspired by Bruno Heceta, Spanish explorer who sought to honor his patron saint. Built along toll road, railroad junction, which gave early development a slight boost. Popular with duck hunters. Incorporated in 1914 with a population of 1,000.

Most of housing built after World War II, and styles will remind you of Fifties and Sixties. Town is aging gracefully. Older, cheaper homes will generally be found near El Camino Real. Generally, lot of care, attention.

San Bruno in 1993 counted 15,184 residential units, of which 8,964 were single homes, 484 single-family attached, 5,646 multiples, 90 mobile. One condo-apartment complex, called Shelter Creek, has about 1,300 units.

Many Bayside cities stop at Interstate 280. San Bruno extends well on the other side of this freeway. From some western streets, you can see Pacific, but most views are confined to Bay. San Francisco City jail is hidden in hills but it may soon be closed. Also in hills, cop shooting range.

Weather is a little tricky. Coast mountains are not that high near San Bruno, which allows the fog to move all the way to Bay. If driving Highway 101 on a late summer afternoon, look west toward the San Bruno ridge line. The fog will be cresting the ridge and spilling down into the lowlands, but the farther it advances, the more it falls prey to the sun. Pattern changes from neighborhood to neighborhood. Those west of Interstate 280 might get a good amount of fog. If shopping for home, talk to neighbors.

One library, 15 parks including major county park, Junipero Serra. Nearby is Crystal Springs Reservoir, pretty and nice for hiking. Annual festival, draws about 50,000 — crafts, pony rides. Municipal dog run, a place where Rover and pals can exercise and take care of business.

Skyline Community College is a big plus, day and evening classes. San Bruno owns its own cable system (43 channels), rare for a city. Shop-till-you-drop at Tanforan and Bayhill Shopping plazas, main sources of sales tax revenue for San Bruno. Tanforan is remembered for what it used to be: a race track and place where local Japanese, at start of World War II, were gathered before being shipped to internment camps.

Golden Gate National Cemetery is located in the northern section of San Bruno. Also situated in the city: the Federal Archives and Records Center and naval facilities engineers.

Crime rate low-middle. Zero homicides in 1992, one in 1991, one in 1990, zero in 1989, one in 1988, zero in 1987, two in 1986, four in 1985.

Most students attend San Bruno school district but west of Interstate 280, some are enrolled in Laguna Salada District, which has had money problems. Check with school district to find out where your child will attend school.

San Bruno schools, with exceptions, score well above the 50 percentile. Schools in Laguna Salada land about the middle.

Enrollments in San Bruno district show increasing ethnic diversity, a trend on the Peninsula. Bond issue, passed years ago, is still pumping money into the San Bruno district. District hopes to augment bond with state money and renovate all seven campuses.

Good commute. Two freeways, Skyline Boulevard, CalTrain, Sam Trans buses. If you miss a plane from this town, you're beyond help. Ask neighbors about plane noise. Airport is expanding. More money is to be allocated to insulating homes. Ask also about BART, the train system coming to San Bruno. Some people don't like route.

San Carlos

Located mid peninsula. Bay town that rises to hills. Views from hills. Peaceful. Bedroom community that has picked up some Silicon Valley-type industries. Small airport west of the freeway, away from homes.

Several attempts were made around the turn of the century to get San Carlos going as a suburb but the town did not jell until about World War I.

Subdivision in 1924 aimed for upper end of market, and San Carlos has remained an upper-middle town. Incorporated as city in 1925, hit by suburban housing after war. Between 1950 and 1960, the city increased its population by 50 percent to 21,370, then gradually filled in. Added 1,457 residents in 1980s. State estimated the 1993 population at 27,147. Census counted 25 percent over 55 years, 19 percent under 18. Kids under 5 years: 856 boys, 767 girls.

Residential units number 11,441, of which 8,059 are single homes, 519 single attached, 2,819 multiples, 44 mobiles. City in 1990 surveyed vacant land to determine future housing. Best guess: space for about 300 more units.

Crime low. One homicide each in 1993, 1992, 1991 and 1990, zero in 1989, 1988, 1987, two in 1986, none in 1985.

School rankings high, mostly 80s and 90s. Day care at all elementary schools. Educational foundation and Chickens Ball raise money for schools. Older kids move up to Carlmont (Belmont) or Sequoia (Redwood City) High schools. For more on high schools, see Redwood City profile. DARE program: cops try to persuade kids not to drink or take harmful drugs.

Elementary district in fall 1994 will change one school to a charter school. This would give staff, parents, more say over how institution is run.

Library, seniors center, dog run, 13 parks, 4 playgrounds. No beer or booze allowed in parks, except by permit (usually granted for picnics, large groups). Circle Star Theater, long an entertainment draw in the Bay Area, closed in 1993; money problems.

New supermarket, one of the largest in the county, about an acre in size. Downtown spruced up: remodelings, new facades, signs. Free parking. No-smoking ordinance.

San Carlos shares fire department with Belmont. Central fire station to be rebuilt, modernized.

The usual two freeways to San Francisco but San Carlos looks more toward Silicon Valley than the City. CalTrain to San Fran, Silicon Valley. SamTrans (buses). Not far from airport or bridges to East Bay.

City is building two overpasses beneath railroad, which will ease local congestion. Land east of freeway to be developed: offices, retail, luxury hotels, helicopter museum (maybe). Local lad who made good: slugger Barry Bonds.

San Mateo

Located next to Hillsborough, one of the richest towns in California, San Mateo is a middle-class city of 89,355 people that gives the impression that change comes gradually.

Nonetheless, San Mateo is changing. Like many Peninsula cities, it is becoming ethnically diverse, more Hispanics, Filipinos and Asians. But much of the "new" diversity — it's been going on for decades — comes from an influx of first-, second- and third-generation Americans.

Pretty city. Rises from Bay to hills. On clear days, you can see Mt. Diablo, at the edge of the Sacramento Delta.

Academic rankings generally in the 70th to 90th percentiles, with the exception of three schools landing about the 50th percentiles. San Mateo shares elementary schools with Foster City. For city's three high schools, the most recent rankings were in 70s, 80s and 90s. Hillsdale High in 1993 won a Blue Ribbon; national award for academic excellence. White House presentation.

Residents approved a bond to renovate elementary schools and build new facilities, and a parcel tax to lower elementary class sizes and improve programs. Foundation raises about $75,000 annually for schools. Oracle, computer firm, and employees tutor kids in math, sciences.

College of San Mateo, among community colleges, often ranks in the top 10 in the state in advancing transfer students to four-year colleges.

Crime low-average for a middle-class city. Three homicides in 1992, one in 1991, one in 1990, zero in 1989, three in 1988, one in 1987, four in 1986, two in 1985, reports FBI. Dress code to discourage gang colors at schools.

Good commute. San Mateo is criss-crossed by Highway 101 and Highway 92. The latter runs west to Interstate 280 and Half Moon Bay, and east to the San Mateo Bridge and the East Bay. CalTrains to San Jose or San Francisco, with stops along the way. SamTrans buses carry riders all over the county and to San Francisco and the BART station at Daly City.

Recreation plentiful. 24 parks, 22 of them with play areas for children, golf course, three libraries, performing arts center, marina, softball, bocce, soccer, baseball, football, ice skating rink, funky jazz for the kids, Charlestons for the seniors, etc. Farmers market. Bike paths. Senior and activity centers. New YMCA (gym, pool).

Thoroughbred racing at Bay Meadows, wildlife center, Bay beach and swimming at Coyote Point. Crystal Springs reservoir, miles of open space and trails, just west of the city, and more.

City scrubs off or paints over graffiti within a few days of detection. Streets clean, parks maintained, lawns mowed, shrubs trimmed. Weather balmy.

Housing stock diversified, modest, and in many instances old, the same with the population. The 1990 census placed 25 percent of the residents over age 55 and 19 percent under age 18. About 12 percent of the housing was built before 1940 and 47 percent between 1940 and 1960 — in total about 59 out of every 100 units. San Mateo now is almost built out.

The state in 1993 counted 37,410 housing units, of which 17,445 were single-family, 3,265 single-family attached, 16,686 multiples and 14 mobile homes — a good mix.

When you drive San Mateo streets, you see housing that is fairly new and of modern design, especially the townhouses, but the dominant styles, led by the two-and three-bedroom home, come out of the 25 years after World War II.

With few exceptions, these homes are well maintained and many have been remodeled. Over last 20 years, new residents have tended to be minorities.

A big difference? In some ways, yes. The school district has installed Spanish immersion and "magnet" programs to meet the diverse academic needs of the children. About 1,100 of the elementary school kids have limited command of English. The district enrolls about 9,900 children. Like almost all California schools, San Mateo's now pay more attention to helping the kids to respect cultural differences.

But in other ways, a familiar experience. Among Caucasians, according to the last census, the three largest groups are German, Italian and Irish Americans, in that order — the children and grandchildren of earlier immigrants.

In north San Mateo, between railroad tracks and Highway 101, the neighborhood has gone transitional, offering housing that meets needs of low-income residents. Day laborers, many of them Hispanic, are hired off the street.

Two shopping malls. Hillsdale is thriving — Macy's, Nordstrom, Emporium, Mervyn's.

Fashion Island, east of Highway 101, is struggling and there's talk about making it a factory outlet center. The downtown is being spruced up with redevelopment money.

Two hospitals, Mills and San Mateo County General.

One of these years, the racetrack people may say, bye, bye horses, hello houses or offices or what not — a surefire send-up to a royal argument over development.

South San Francisco

Hill and dale town. Also known as South City. Famous or notorious for its large white "South San Francisco, The Industrial City" blazoned across a hillside and visible from Highway 101. Letters are 60 feet high and made of cement. Increased population by 10 percent in last decade. The 1990 census identified 21 percent of residents as over age 55, and 24 percent under age 18. Kids under 5 years: 2,107 boys, 1,951 girls. A residential and industrial-office city. Much new office and commercial construction. Home to a See's chocolate factory. Biggest employer is Genentech (biotech). New conference center.

Used to be big cattle spread. Drovers in Central Valley would round up thousands of head of cattle, trot them up El Camino Real (outside of the freeways, the main road north-south in the county) to Baden ranch, slaughter them and feed San Francisco.

In 1890 a syndicate headed by Gustavus Swift, Philip Armour, Michael Cudahy and Nelson Morris — the Chicago boys — decided to get into West Coast meat in a big way. Bought Baden ranch, set up processing plants, stockyards and for workers erected a company town. Swift, who showed no imagination in these matters — he had named similar ventures South Omaha and South Chicago — dubbed the town South San Francisco.

Land agent for meat syndicate sold lots to employees, encouraged other businesses to settle in South City, sold their employees lots. Incorporated as city in 1908. First mayor and three of four councilmen were employed by Western Meat Company. Later on, South City became the produce market for much of the Bay Region.

In the beginning, South City had Irish, French, Italian and Chinese neighborhoods. Italian tradition is recalled annually in Italian-American games, bocce, track and more wrapped up with a dinner-dance. In recent years, many Asians, Hispanics and Filipinos have settled in South San Francisco.

The produce terminal remains but the stockyards closed in 1957. Civic leaders searched for replacements. San Francisco airport was generating businesses left and right and looking to expand. The result, a happy marriage with occasional complaints about airport noise. The feds recently put up $2 million to soundproof 200 homes and with airport expansion more money is to be spent on insulation. City has about 1,100 hotel rooms.

The new South City is better symbolized by the Oyster Point Marina Business Park — sleek, modern, futuristic, cool — than the dirty white lettering on the hillside. But the lettering has reached almost cult status — so desperate, so blatant, so tacky, so human, that it's likable.

Views from hills. Many homes built in Fifties, Sixties and before World War II. The later the homes generally the more the space. In the two-story homes, a lot of space. Some bungalows.

Residential units in 1993 totaled 19,273. Single homes accounted for 11,053 units, single-family attached 2,336, multiples 5,479, mobile homes 405. South City added about 900 residential units in the 1980s.

Some homes in need of paint and landscaping, others neat and trim.

Probably rentals mixed in with owned. But many well-cared-for lawns. Drive the neighborhoods.

Under construction but delayed because of financing difficulties: Terrabay, 700 homes and condos, a hotel and shops on south slope of Mt. Bruno. Also includes a park, a swimming pool and a fire station.

Foggy in many neighborhoods. In July it's not uncommon to see people bundled in hooded sweatshirts. Coastal hills drop in elevation, allowing the fog to penetrate to the Bay.

Crime rate fairly low. One homicide in 1992, three in 1991, one in 1990, two in 1989, two in 1988, one in 1987, four in 1986, three in 1985. Police have adopted a "zero tolerance" attitude toward juvenile crime and work closely with courts and schools. Also use foot patrols.

Many schools are hitting scores well above 60th percentile, an indication parents are putting much energy into education and schools. Child care at many elementary schools.

To cut costs, Foxridge and Serra Vista elementary schools were closed in 1992. Attendance boundaries redrawn. Junior highs (grades 7 and 8) converted to middle schools (6,7, and 8).

Parents group in 1993 raised $10,000 to save music programs. More fund raising planned.

Six parks, seven playgrounds, public swimming pool, seniors center. Softball league fields 170 teams. Youth sports. Two libraries. Golf course, marina, fishing pier. Many activities, exercise, ballet, floral design, music, cake decorating, etc. Candlestick Park (Giants, 49ers) just up the road. City butts up against San Bruno State Park.

Great commute if you work in San Fran or at the airport. BART station at Daly City. So-so commute if you have to slog to Silicon Valley. Highway 101 interchange being rebuilt, improved.

Keep it down. Noise ordinance passed in 1990.

Woodside

Located above Atherton and Redwood City, next to Portola Valley. Secluded. Prestigious. Quaint. Stable to the point of dropping 5 percent of its population in the last decade.

According to 1993 state estimate, Woodside has 5,247 residents, served by a city staff of about 15 people. The 1990 census counted 141 boys under the age of 5, and 131 girls. The census also noted that 27 percent of the residents were over 55, about 20 percent under age 18.

Horses number about 2,000, according to a 1993 informal count.

Attuned more to Silicon Valley and Stanford than San Fran. Stanford Linear Accelerator stops just short of the city limits.

Named after Woodside Store, which became center of logging activity. In 1993, the local historical association reopened the store as a museum.

Woodsy. Trees all over the place, some fairly big redwoods, second growth, and town is planting more.

After redwoods were logged, the rich in the early 1900s built estates in the Woodside hills. Gradually the town caught on as nice place to talk to the trees, relax, lead good life.

Horsey: corrals, pastures, stables, trails. Tennis courts. Deer-crossing signs. Town backs up against game refuge. Some residents dabble in vineyards.

Although some demurely gorgeous mansions hide behind walls of shrubs, a lot of the homes are modest. Paying for the location, for the company of cultivated neighbors. Big name local resident: Shirley Black, who won fame under maiden name, Shirley Temple.

Cañada Community College, located in Woodside just east of Interstate 280, adds to cultural life. Annual art fair.

Crime rate not tracked by FBI but can be safely assumed to be very low. In 1993, the city recorded its first homicide in six years, a man who lived out of town and who had been shot and left on the side of the road, newspaper reported. Crooks would have hard time finding Woodside — a real deterrent since many crimes are crimes of opportunity. Patrolled by sheriff's deputies. DARE anti-drug instruction in the schools.

Library, post office, fire station. County park. Filoli, famous estate, open for tours. In 1991, an open-space trust purchased 1,300 acres next to Woodside. Land to be preserved as habitat for wildlife.

A short drive to Silicon Valley, via Interstate 280. A long drive on same road to San Fran.

Single-home burg. Of Woodside's 1,914 residences, 1,821 or 95 percent are single homes. The rest are single-family attached, 53, multiples, 26. Very little construction. Less than a dozen homes a year.

Elementary school rankings land in the top 10 percent of state. Yes, it is a one-school district. Several years ago, it won a state "distinguished" award.

Voters in 1993 renewed a parcel tax to support education programs.

Wing of school accidentally burned down in 1993; oily rags. Construction of replacement building with science wing to begin in 1994.

Some of Woodside falls within Redwood City Elementary District. In 1993, some parents in this sector petitioned to be included in Woodside district. Denied. Older kids attend Woodside High, where they mix with a more diverse group. See Redwood City profile.

7/How Public Schools Work

SAT Scores, the UCs Local Grads Chose, Getting the Most Out of Your Child's School

SCORES MEASURE academic success but they have their shortcomings. Some students know the material but are not adept at taking tests and some tests are so poorly designed that they fail to assess what has been taught. The rankings in a previous chapter do not break out students as individuals. A basic exam tests the least the children should know, not the most. There are other legitimate criticisms of the California Assessment Program (CAP) test and indeed most tests.

Nonetheless, CAP scores do correlate to SAT scores, to other measures and with teacher observations. Schools that score high on CAP tests usually score high on the SAT and send, proportionally, a greater number of their students on to college.

When your children attend a school with high test scores, they are not assured of success. These schools have their failures. Neither can you be certain that your children will get the best teachers or the right programs. Other schools with lower scores might do better on these points. What you can be certain of is that your children are entering a setting that has proven successful for many students.

The main problem with making sense out of scores concerns what is called socioeconomics, a theory educators love, hate and widely believe.

Socioeconomics — The Bottom Line

In its crudest form, socioeconomics means rich kids score high, middle-class kids score about the middle and poor kids score low. Not all the time, not predictably by individual. Many children from poor and middle-class homes succeed in school and attend the best colleges. But as a general rule

Scholastic Aptitude Test (SAT) Scores
San Francisco

High School	Enrollment	No. Tested	Verbal	Math
Abraham Lincoln	444	231	324	462
Balboa	247	69	281	354
Burton	258	205	321	451
Galileo	359	199	280	406
Geo.Washington	655	396	357	470
International	128	71	338	449
J. Eugene McAteer	289	107	337	432
John O'Connell	88	10	288	362
Lowell	668	616	495	584
Mission	256	120	270	386
Raoul Wallenberg	175	142	370	461
Woodrow Wilson	195	105	250	330
San Francisco Avg.	4,275	2,297	368	475

San Mateo County

High School	Enrollment	No. Tested	Verbal	Math
Aragon	328	199	463	533
Burlingame	287	159	448	524
Capuchino	183	78	387	468
Carlmont	233	131	446	523
El Camino	348	117	403	501
Half Moon Bay	152	53	457	523
Hillsdale	278	159	422	535
Jefferson	347	68	351	433
Menlo-Atherton	281	204	472	524
Mills	313	194	429	543
Oceana	72	14	399	460
Pescadero	18	7	419	489
San Mateo High	236	141	461	532
Sequoia	267	102	422	480
South San Francisco	294	81	399	497
Terra Nova	239	68	430	495
Westmoor	350	88	387	496
Woodside	258	144	431	507
San Mateo Avg.	4,555	2,007	433	514
California	270,675	94,929	411	485

Source: California Dept. of Education, 1992-93 tests. SAT scores are greatly influenced by who and how many take the test. A school that has more marginal students taking the test will, by one line of reasoning, be doing a good job, but the scores are likely to be lower.

socioeconomics enjoys much statistical support.

Compare San Mateo school rankings with income by cities. Hillsborough, Atherton, Woodside, rich or well-to-do, high scores; East Palo Alto, low income or poor, low scores; Redwood City, Daly City, middle-class towns, middling scores.

Where there are differences in schools in the same district, often the higher-scoring students will be from higher-income neighborhoods. The SAT scores reflect the basic test scores.

The same pattern shows up in Alameda County. The schools in the poorer neighborhoods of Oakland score low; well-to-do Piedmont scores high. And the pattern shows up around the Bay Area, the country and in other countries. The recent federal study, "Japanese Education Today," notes a "solid correlation between poverty and poor school performance ...."

San Francisco correlations are masked somewhat by the school district's integration policy: many kids attend schools outside their neighborhoods. But the overall correlation holds: Children from Twin Peaks and Pacific Heights score higher than children from the Mission and Bayview.

Family and Culture

In its refined form, socioeconomics moves away from the buck and toward culture and family influence.

Note the chart on Page 65. The towns with the highest number of college educated are generally also the towns with the highest scores. If your mom or dad attended college, chances are you will attend college or do well at school because in a thousand ways while you were growing up they and their milieu pushed you in this direction. Emphasis on "chances are." Nothing is certain when dealing with human beings.

What if mom and dad never got beyond the third grade? Or can't even speak English?

Historically, many poor and immigrant children have succeeded at school because their parents badgered, bullied and encouraged them every step of the way and made sacrifices so they would succeed. Asian kids are the latest example of poor kids succeeding but earlier generations could point to the children of peasant Europeans.

Does it make a difference if the child is English proficient? Or the parents rich? Immigrant children unfamiliar with English will have more difficulties with literature and language-proficient courses than native-born children. They will often need extra or special help in schools.

Nonetheless, the home-school correlation retains much validity: the stronger the educational support the child receives at home, the better he or she will do at school.

So thoroughly does the California Department of Education believe in socioeconomics that it worked the theory into a mathematical model. Teachers collect data on almost all students: are they on welfare, do they have language problems (immigrants), how educated are their parents? The information is fed to computers and used to predict how students will score on tests.

California College Admissions of Public School Graduates

San Mateo County Schools

High School	UC	CSU	Com	Total
Aragon	31	23	113	167
Burlingame	40	22	73	135
Capuchino	8	15	73	96
Carlmont	42	21	98	161
El Camino	12	25	153	190
Half Moon Bay	15	22	79	116
Hillsdale	43	15	99	157
Jefferson	5	14	127	146
Menlo-Atherton	27	22	62	111
Mills	51	32	130	213
Oceana	5	6	35	46
Pescadero	0	2	1	3
San Mateo	40	21	88	149
Sequoia	16	29	83	128
South San Francisco	15	27	105	147
Terra Nova	10	10	80	100
Westmoor	10	18	139	167
Woodside	29	19	106	154

San Francisco Schools

High School	UC	CSU	Com	Total
Abraham Lincoln	29	67	193	289
Alamo Park	0	2	12	14
Balboa	2	30	77	109
Burton	29	69	44	142
Downtown	0	1	9	10
Galileo	9	45	114	168
Geo. Washington	50	104	238	392
Int'l Studies Academy	9	16	8	33
J. Eugene McAteer	9	26	6	41
John O'Connell	2	9	19	30
Lowell	206	85	152	443
Mark Twain	0	0	15	15
Mission	10	54	71	135
Raoul Wallenberg	20	34	34	88
Woodrow Wilson	9	52	52	113

Source: California Department of Education, fall 1992. The chart lists the local public high schools and shows how many students they advanced in 1992 into California public colleges and universities. The state does not track graduates enrolling in private or out-of-state colleges. Continuation schools not included. **Key:** UC (University of California system); CSU (Cal State system); Com (Community Colleges); Total (total number of graduates attending California colleges).

Role of Schools

If you carry the logic of socioeconomics too far, you come to the conclusion that schools and teachers and teaching methods don't matter: Students succeed or fail according to their family or societal backgrounds.

Nonsense. No matter how dedicated or well-intentioned the parent, if the teacher is grossly inept the child probably will learn little. If material or textbooks are out-of-date or inaccurate, what the student learns will be useless or damaging. Conversely, if the teacher is dedicated and knowledgeable, if the material is well presented and appropriate, what the child comes away with will be helpful and, to society, more likely to be beneficial.

Almost every one of us can recall a favorite teacher who worked with us and influenced our lives.

Where the Confusion Enters

When scores rise or fall, frequently the blame or credit goes to the school or the scores are treated as a reflection solely of school life.

Scores in School A go up. The principal thanks the teachers and the students for their hard work and says, we're on the right track. Scores in School B drop. The principal blames cuts in funding or a program that needs to be re-worked.

In late 1992, CAP scores for eighth graders were released showing drops from recent years. State educational leaders blamed cuts in school funding and the difficulties of educating immigrant students. The immigrant aspect was also given a money shading: if schools had more money, they could do a better job with these children.

All of this is true. If the schools are adequately funded, if class sizes are kept manageable, teachers can do a better job.

But to get a rounded picture of why scores are dropping or rising or are low or high, family background and social values have to be included.

Oakland School District has some of the lowest-scoring schools in the state and some of the highest. All the teachers are paid the same. All are recruited by the same agency and all, presumably, meet the standards of the district.

Why the difference in scores? The background of the children is different. Some neighborhoods are home to many professionals affiliated with the University of California. Academic culture strong. Scores high.

Oakland flatlands have many poor students, many welfare families. Academic push weak. Scores very low.

The flatlands also have many minority children but to define achievement by ethnicity distorts the picture. Many middle-class towns or neighborhoods have high numbers of students from the same ethnic groups. Scores are much higher, sometimes very high.

The difference: probably family stability and a host of other social influences.

UCs Chosen by Public School Graduates
San Francisco

School	Berk	Davis	Irv	UCLA	SD	SB	River	SC	Total
Balboa	1	1	0	0	0	0	0	0	2
Burton	8	16	0	2	1	0	1	1	29
Galileo	2	3	2	0	1	0	1	0	9
Lincoln	4	12	1	2	1	4	2	3	29
Lowell	73	82	4	8	6	12	1	20	206
McAteer	2	0	0	1	0	0	0	6	9
Mission	3	7	0	0	0	0	0	0	10
Wallenberg	4	9	2	0	0	0	1	4	20
Washington	8	28	0	4	1	8	0	1	50
Wilson	1	6	0	0	0	0	0	02	9

San Mateo County

School	Berk	Davis	Irv	UCLA	SD	SB	River	SC	Total
Aragon	11	11	0	4	2	2	0	1	31
Burlingame	9	14	2	5	5	2	0	3	40
Capuchino	3	2	0	1	0	0	0	2	8
Carlmont	3	14	1	9	5	5	1	4	42
El Camino	4	6	0	0	1	1	0	0	12
Half Moon Bay	2	4	0	2	0	4	1	2	5
Hillsdale	9	11	0	5	2	14	1	1	43
Jefferson	1	1	0	0	1	1	0	1	5
Menlo-Ath	8	4	0	6	3	5	0	1	27
Mills	16	15	1	8	1	2	1	7	51
Oceana	0	3	0	1	0	0	0	1	5
San Mateo	6	7	2	12	8	4	1	0	40
Sequoia	0	4	1	1	2	1	0	7	16
So San Fran.	8	1	0	2	0	0	0	4	15
Terra Nova	2	1	0	2	1	2	1	1	10
Westmoor	2	3	0	1	0	2	1	1	10
Woodside	0	6	1	0	4	8	1	9	29

Source: California Dept. of Education, fall, 1992. The chart shows the University of California choices of 1992 local public high school graduates. The state does not track graduates enrolling in private or out-of-state colleges. Continuation schools not included in list. **Key:** Berk (Berkeley), Irv (Irvine), River (Riverside), SD (San Diego), SB (Santa Barbara), SC (Santa Cruz).

Which is more important?

Background or school? Educators argue about this, many contending that regardless of socioeconomics, schools should be able to educate all students. Some schools and teachers, to their great credit, do succeed with students from academically impoverished backgrounds. Many others, however, fail. The harsh truth seems to be that without a home or social life that nourishes academics — or without large-scale social programs — success in school is difficult.

Back to Scores

If a school's scores are middling, it may still be capable of doing an excellent job, if it has dedicated teachers and sound programs. The middling scores may reflect socioeconomics, not instructional quality.

Don't judge us by our overall scores, many schools say. Judge us by our ability to deliver for your son or daughter.

This gets tricky because the children do influence one another and high-income parents often interact differently with schools than low-income parents. To some extent, the school must structure its programs to ability of the students. But schools with middling and middling-plus grades can point to many successes.

Basic Instruction-Ability Grouping

California and American schools attempt to meet the needs of students by providing a good basic education and by addressing individual and subgroup needs by special classes and ability grouping.

In the first six years in an average school, children receive some special help according to ability but for the most part they share the same class experiences and get the same instruction.

About the seventh grade, until recently, students were divided into classes for low achievers, middling students and high achievers, or low-middle and advanced — tracking. Texts, homework and expectations were different for each group. The high achievers were on the college track, the low, the vocational.

Pressured by the state, schools are curtailing this practice, but many schools retain accelerated English and math classes for advanced seventh and eighth graders. Parents can always request a transfer from one group to another (whether they can get it is another matter). The reality often is, however, that remedial and middle children can't keep pace with the high achievers.

In the last 30 years or so schools introduced into the early grades special programs aimed at low achievers or children with learning difficulties. Although they vary greatly, these programs typically pull the children out of class for instruction in small groups then return them to the regular class.

Many schools also pull out gifted (high I.Q.) students and a few cluster them in their own classes.

College Influence

The junior high divisions sharpen at high school. Colleges exercise great influence over what students are taught in high school. So many local students attend the University of California and California State University schools that public and private high schools must of necessity teach the classes demanded by these institutions.

So the typical high school will have a prep program that meets University

CSUs Chosen by Public School Graduates
San Francisco

School	Cal Poly	Chico	Hay	No. Rid	Sac	S.D.	S.F.	S.J.	Son
Balboa	1	0	0	1	0	0	26	1	1
Burton	1	1	1	0	0	0	58	7	0
Galileo	1	0	0	0	0	0	41	2	0
Lincoln	2	0	1	1	0	0	57	6	0
Lowell	7	0	0	0	2	3	48	18	3
McAteer	1	1	0	1	0	0	22	0	1
Mission	1	0	0	0	0	0	45	6	2
Wallenberg	3	1	0	0	0	0	27	2	0
Washington	2	0	1	0	0	1	75	17	3
Wilson	0	0	0	1	0	1	47	2	0

San Mateo County

School	Cal Poly	Chico	Hay	No. Rid	Sac	S.D.	S.F.	S.J.	Son
Aragon	1	2	0	0	4	3	4	4	0
Burlingame	0	2	0	0	3	3	7	2	0
Capuchino	1	0	0	0	1	3	5	3	1
Carlmont	6	2	5	0	1	3	2	2	0
El Camino	1	2	1	0	0	1	16	3	0
Half Moon Bay	3	9	0	0	0	2	3	1	4
Hillsdale	0	2	5	2	1	0	1	3	0
Jefferson	0	1	0	1	0	0	6	6	0
Menlo-Ath	3	4	2	0	0	1	2	9	0
Mills	2	1	0	1	3	0	12	8	2
Oceana	0	0	1	0	0	0	2	3	0
San Mateo	2	4	1	0	2	1	1	4	0
Sequoia	1	3	2	0	0	1	2	14	2
So San Fran.	1	0	4	0	0	1	17	4	0
Terra Nova	0	1	1	0	1	1	3	1	2
Westmoor	0	0	0	0	1	0	11	6	0
Woodside	3	3	0	0	2	3	3	3	0

Source: California Dept. of Education, fall, 1992. The chart shows the most popular choices of 1992 local public high school graduates. The chart does not include all Cal State universities. The state does not track graduates enrolling in private or out-of-state colleges. Continuation schools not included in list. **Key**: Cal Poly (San Luis Obispo), Hay (Hayward), No.Rid (Northridge), Sac (Sacramento), S.D. (San Diego), S.F. (San Francisco), S.J. (San Jose), Son (Sonoma).

of California requirements. The school also will offer general education classes in math and English but these will not be as tough as the prep courses and will not be recognized by the state universities. And usually the school will teach some trades so those inclined can secure jobs upon graduation.

Can a school with mediocre or even low basic scores field a successful college prep program? With comprehensive programs, the answer is yes.

High School Dropout Rates by District
San Francisco

District	1990	1991	1992	*No.
SF Unified	13%	12%	14%	681
Countywide	18%	19%	21%	1,111

San Mateo County

District	1990	1991	1992	*No.
Cabrillo Unified	4%	6%	4%	9
Jefferson Union	11%	11%	9%	97
La Honda-Pescadero	7%	0%	23%	5
San Mateo Union	9%	7%	14%	264
Sequoia Union	20%	22%	11%	145
So. San Francisco	17%	14%	10%	70
Countywide	15%	13%	11%	590

Source: California Dept. of Education. Percentages cover dropouts in a class that would have graduated in the year shown. *No. is the actual number of dropouts in 1992.

How "Mediocre" Schools Succeed — College Admissions

The state traces public college freshmen, age 19 and under, to their high schools. The data can mislead but it shows the strengths of the middling schools (See Chart on Page 129).

If a student attends a California State University, a community college or a University of California (Berkeley, Los Angeles, San Diego, Davis, etc.), the state generally will know where he or she attended high school in California. The chart tracks freshmen in California public colleges back to their high schools. The UCs generally restrict themselves to the top 13 percent in the state. The Cal States take the top third.

Notice Westmoor High in Daly City. In basic score rankings, it often places below the 50th percentile. Yet it sent 10 kids to the University of California, 18 to Cal State Universities, and 139 to community colleges.

Mission High, one of the lowest scoring in San Francisco, sent 10 to the UCs, 54 to Cal States, and 71 to community colleges.

These schools have a prep program in place that prepares the kids for college, even the top colleges. So if your local rankings are mediocre, even low, there's hope.

Where does the chart mislead? For starters, the Cal States and UCs run on academics, the community colleges run on academics and vocational classes. Just because a student attends a community college does not mean he or she is pursuing a bachelor's degree.

Also, students who qualify for a Cal State or a UC often take their freshman and sophomore years at a community college.

Ethnic Enrollments by School District
San Francisco

District	Cauca.	Af.Am.	Asian	Filipino	Hisp.	P.Isle	Nat.	Total
San Fran. Unified	8,601	11,234	24,057	4,917	12,254	439	380	61,882

San Mateo County

District	Cauca.	Af.Am.	Asian	Filipino	Hisp.	P.Isle	Nat.	Total
Bayshore	31	91	40	110	139	46	2	459
Belmont	1,473	55	225	41	183	8	8	1,993
Brisbane	265	27	75	59	117	3	1	547
Burlingame	1,405	20	259	38	301	14	6	2,043
Cabrillo	2,475	23	65	53	749	8	17	3,390
Hillsborough	809	6	280	19	23	3	0	1,140
Jefferson	976	755	741	2,488	2,522	171	45	7,698
Jefferson High	1,254	467	502	1,289	1,328	116	18	4,974
Laguna Salada	2,457	299	243	313	650	112	34	4,108
La Honda-Pescadero	278	0	1	0	124	0	0	403
Los Lomitas	711	23	56	7	40	4	0	841
Menlo Park	1,325	79	110	23	141	22	1	1,701
Millbrae	1,160	47	399	66	417	117	4	2,210
Portola Valley	539	8	36	0	7	0	0	590
Ravenswood	38	1,522	19	24	2,214	434	9	4,260
Redwood City	3,120	335	230	48	4,346	170	33	8,282
San Bruno	1,437	65	326	101	575	146	2	2,652
San Carlos	1,781	40	137	15	167	18	2	2,160
S. Mateo-Fost. City	5,002	417	1,535	267	2,085	323	28	9,657
San Mateo High	4,293	298	1,519	333	1,481	231	27	8,182
Sequoia	2,808	783	347	61	2,229	203	27	6,458
So. San Francisco	2,951	549	913	1,970	3,170	370	56	9,979
Woodside	375	6	21	0	33	1	0	436

Source: California Dept. of Education, 1992. Key: Af.Am. (African-American); Cauca. (Caucasian); Hisp. (Hispanics); P.Isle (Pacific Islanders); Nat. (Native American Indians & Alaskans).

Location may be a factor. Students living close to a community college may attend that college in disproportionately higher numbers.

The chart does not track private colleges. It doesn't tell us how many local students went to Stanford or Harvard or Santa Clara University or the University of San Francisco. Or public colleges out of the state.

UC-Berkeley, the only UC in the Bay Area, in recent years has aggressively pursued ethnic diversity. To a lesser extent, the other UCs and Cal States have done the same.

To attract minority students, the universities, in some instances, have modified their admission policies, a practice that has critics and supporters.

The numbers mentioned above and listed in the accompanying chart may not reflect, according to the standard admissions policy, the top 13 and 33 percent.

Finally, the chart does not tell us how the students are doing at college. At community colleges, dropouts are numerous.

The chart does confirm the influence of socioeconomics: The rich towns, the educated towns or neighborhoods send more kids to the UCs than the poorer ones. But socioeconomics does not sweep the field. Not every student from a high-scoring school goes on to college. Many students from low- and middle-income towns come through.

Dissatisfaction

If high schools can deliver on college education and train students for vocations, why are so many people dissatisfied with public schools? These schools can also cite other accomplishments: textbooks and curriculums have been improved, the dropout rate has been cut, and proficiency tests have been adopted to force high school students to meet minimum academic standards.

Yet for the last 15 years or so, the California public, despite many pleas, has refused to rally round the schools and provide funding even close to what is needed. In 1993 voters trounced a measure to fund education through vouchers but the fact that it was able to get on the ballot in the first place was interpreted to indicate great dissatisfaction with public schools.

Many children are still failing and dropping out, and the system is expensive, about $23 billion annually for kindergarten-through-12 schools. Scores are stagnant or up one year, down the next, and remain very low in many urban districts.

A U.S. Department of Education study, released in 1993, concluded that California fourth graders in reading trailed their peers in 40 states and were on the level of about Mississippi.

Employers report that many high school grads are unable to understand instructions or write competently. Colleges complain that honor high school students often need remedial math and English.

It is not the intention of this book to dwell on controversies but to explain how schools work it is necessary to look at some of the disputes.

Major Disputes

• Not enough money. Many school districts in the state have cut instructional time and staff and increased class sizes, even as enrollments rise.

Almost every year bitter fights break out in Sacramento over funding for schools. With the recession, which has decreased state revenues, the battles have become more vitriolic.

Democrats generally favor more money for schools, but few in Sacramento seem to favor another tax increase, which would probably be necessary for higher funding. Republicans contend that additional money would go for salaries, not to relieve crowding or restore programs.

In recent years, throughout the state, many school districts have asked their voters to approve parcel taxes, which require two-thirds of the votes cast. Many have won approval, many have failed.

• Private vs. public. A complex battle, it boils down to one side saying public schools are the best and fairest way to educate all children versus the other side saying public education is inefficient and will never reform until it has meaningful competition.

In 1992, Sacramento approved funding to allow 100 schools statewide to restructure their programs according to local needs — an effort at eliminating unnecessary rules.

• Teachers' pay and influence. Although school funding has not kept pace with growth or need, salaries, in large measure, have remained competitive. California teachers rank usually fourth to sixth in the nation in pay. Many teachers, however, believe the entire profession is underpaid and is not keeping pace with inflation.

Through their union, teachers exert great influence over school legislation and, often, over local school boards.

• Programs inadequately funded. Washington and Sacramento have legislated certain programs into existence and underfunded them or left their funding to local jurisdictions.

Special education in California now enrolls 10 percent of all students and these children receive 2.5 to 7 times the amount spent on "regular" students, one newspaper reported.

Proposition 13 and other measures, however, restrict the ability of school districts to raise taxes. As a result, districts are biting into regular programs to sustain the special programs.

• Class size and teaching days. Many teachers argue that class sizes, often above 30 in California, are too large. The typical California school year runs 175 teaching days. The Japanese school year is over 230 days.

• Teacher competency. Once tenured, teachers are almost impossible to fire, which opens schools to accusations of coddling incompetents.

• Educational methods. Furious arguments rage over what will work. One simmering pot: how to educate children who can't speak English. Bilingual teachers are in short supply.

• Minorities and integration. One of the touchiest topics in the state. California minorities are growing rapidly and will soon be a majority in the state. Hispanics are scoring low; many Black students are also scoring low but an impressive number have made solid advances. Many Asians score high and, for college admissions, are often not considered a "minority."

Some educators argue that what is taught in public schools fails to instill pride in the accomplishments of various cultures and ethnic groups, that too much attention is paid to European civilization, too little to Asian and African. The state recently introduced textbooks that emphasize the accomplishments of minorities and women and approach history from diverse perspectives.

Ability clustering in many school districts breaks the students out along ethnic lines, and calls attention to how the system seems to work for some groups and not for others. More money is needed for language instruction.

• Clustering children by ability or problems. Opponents argue that children labeled "low achievers" will fulfill that prophecy. The sad fact is that many programs aimed at low achievers have not worked or work poorly.

California is curtailing tracking, which might seem a reform, but it raises other questions. Many children are entering kindergarten months, sometimes years, behind "average" students and in need of immediate remedial work. The state is arguing that children widely ranging in academic ability can be educated in the same classroom and no one will suffer. There are doubters.

• Parental influence. Almost everyone agrees that schools would work better, students would score higher, if parents did a better job at home. This is a major but often muted complaint among teachers: society (family, television, social influences) is failing the schools, not the schools failing the society. The problem: how to get parents to do a better job, how to influence home life.

• Many of the above problems are tied together. If funding was adequate, pull-out programs might work better, class sizes could be lowered, allowing teachers to work better with mixed groups, and so on.

The Parent's Role

What's a parent to do? You would be foolish to ignore the socioeconomic message: To succeed in school, children need strong support from the home. Bookstores and libraries are full of books with advice on how you can work with your child. You as a parent, with a little work and discipline, can make a real difference in the quality of your child's education.

You should probably look for outside help even if your child is doing well.

This is a hard call because many children are doing well. The belief seems almost universal, however, that schools are underfunded, that programs and instruction are being weakened, and that large infusions of money will not be forthcoming.

In well-to-do neighborhoods and rich towns, parents are informally taxing themselves to raise money for schools. Poor and middle-class parents find it hard, if not impossible, to duplicate the efforts of the richer towns.

Shop for Bargains

This dumps the burden on financially struggling families who have high educational ambitions for their children. Shop for bargains: reading classes in the summer, local tutors who might work with small groups, day schools that have afternoon programs. Perhaps a private school.

The editors, as a matter of policy, do not endorse private schools over public or vice versa, but private schools, having more flexibility than public institutions, clearly have a place in the educational picture.

Choosing the Right School

In San Francisco, where choice of school is based partially on racial balance, many children attend schools outside their home neighborhoods (see Chapter 8 on San Francisco schools).

In San Mateo County, almost all public schools have attendance zones, usually the immediate neighborhood. The school comes with the neighborhood; often you have no choice. If you don't know your school, call the school district office.

Many parents mix private day care with public education. The day-care center takes the kid to the school in the morning and picks him up in the afternoon. Many public schools have installed day-care programs.

If you don't like your neighborhood school, you can request a transfer to another school in the district or to a school outside the district. But the school won't provide transportation.

Transfers to schools inside the district are easier to get than transfers outside the district. New laws supposedly make it easier to transfer children to other districts. In reality, however, some of the more popular districts, claiming lack of space, are now turning away "outside" students.

School districts dislike outside transfers because they usually lose funds. For every student enrolled, the state, with exceptions, allots a district a certain amount of money. When a student transfers out, the allotment usually goes with him or her.

If your child has a special problem that may demand your attention, speak to the school administrators about a transfer to a school close to your job.

If your child's ethnicity adds some diversity to a school or district, it might bend its rules. Never hurts to ask.

Register Early

First-come, first-served is not the policy of many school districts in California. Just because you enroll your child first does not necessarily mean that you will get your first choice of schools or teachers.

But in some districts first-come does mean first-served. Enrollment and

For Additional Reading ...

Things to Do with Kids, Bike Trails, Hikes, Trips, Tours, Restaurants, Gardens, Real Estate ...

For more on Northern California see the Book List and order blank on the pages at the end of this guide

transfer policies change from year to year in some districts, depending on the number of children enrolled and the space available. When new schools are opened, attendance boundaries are often changed.

If you are buying a home or moving into one, call the school district for the latest information or the local school. Give the school your address and ask, what school(s) will my children attend?

Even if the school district says, "there's plenty of time to register," the prudent parent will register the children right away. If a dispute arises over attendance — the school might get an unexpected influx of students — early registration might give you a leg up in any negotiations.

Persistence sometimes helps in trying for transfers. The author has seen it go both ways: school officials dig in and enforce their attendance policies; and school officials vow to enforce policy, then under pressure allow exceptions.

Does Remedial Help Work?

This is a minefield of conflicting studies. Nothing would seem more logical than to give a child special attention when he or she falters in class. Some children clearly do benefit.

But, critics argue, singling a child out for this attention often implants the idea that he is inferior, that he can't do the work without special help. Also, the teacher may lower her expectations for the pull-out group, may move them at a pace slower than they are capable of.

If your child is pulled out for remedial education, don't assume that the problem is solved. The kid may need extra help at home.

Gifted Programs

The labeling accusation, in different form, surfaces when schools implement gifted programs for very young children. By labeling one group extra smart, the rest of the children may conclude they are dumb, the argument runs. Where the gifted are clustered in their own classes (magnet programs), the fault is supposedly accentuated. On the other side, parents of these children argue that they should be allowed to learn as fast as they can.

Here's how the Gifted and Talented Education (GATE) program usually works. About the third grade, usually at the teacher's recommendation, the advanced children are given an I.Q. or achievement test. Those who score about I.Q. 132 or in the top 2 percent will be admitted to the program. This generally means they spend about three hours a week on special projects or in activities with other gifted children. Programs vary from district to district.

Tap Into the School's Gossip

Schools never release evaluations of teachers, but parents informally work out their own rankings. Join the PTA. Get to know other parents.

Although teachers are rarely dismissed, it doesn't follow that many deserve to be fired. Don't approach the schools with a chip on your shoulder. They will resent you. Schools, like private businesses, have their lackluster people but most teachers are diligent and greater efforts are being made to improve teacher quality.

If your kid gets an incompetent, request a transfer to another class. For that matter, ask for a particular teacher before the teaching assignments are made. Schools try to cooperate with parents. If you can't get your first choice, you might get your second.

The Official Rhetoric

School officials cannot say anything public against individual teachers. To do so would violate the union contract and expose the district to a lawsuit for slander. Even when a teacher is grossly incompetent, the school district will not say anything. When asked, many administrators will say teachers are "wonderful," "underpaid" and "the salt of the earth."

If the teacher is screwing up royally, get the principal behind a closed door and tell her. If she doesn't take action, union contracts usually spell out the procedure for confronting a teacher.

Year-Round Schools

Year-round schools are becoming increasingly popular as a way to handle rapidly increasing enrollments.

Schedules, called "tracks," vary from district to district but all students attend a full academic year (175-180 teaching days). Traditional holidays are observed. One group may start in summer, one in late summer and so on. A typical pattern is 12 weeks on, four weeks off. One track is always off, allowing another track to use its class space. So far, year-round education has been confined to elementary and junior high schools.

Repeating a grade

Between 1986 and 1989, about 6 percent of all California kindergartners repeated the grade, and about 4 percent of all first graders. After that, retention rates dropped, less than 1 percent of all fourth-graders repeating a grade.

Good idea or bad? Except for a few students, bad, or more precisely, ineffective, the state says now, after reviewing 60 studies,
Compared to similar students, retained children, the studies revealed, performed less effectively in "achievement, personal adjustment, self concept, and attitude toward school."

New Tests

The first round was given in 1993; the first results are to be released in 1994. Instead of testing grades 3,6,8 and 12, the new exams will be given to grades 4,5,8 and 10.

The old (CAP) tests used multiple choice and, critics contended, did not assess thinking skills. The new ones depend more on essays and supposedly will remedy the faults of the old method. The new approach, however, already has critics who say it's too subjective.

The CAP tests focused on classes and schools, not individual students. Other tests — still in use — were used to test individuals and the results were sent home to parents.

The new tests will break out students individually but possibly not in the first round.

High School Changes

Some are switching to "block" instruction. The traditional six 50 minute-classes a day is replaced by three blocks of 90 minutes. Proponents argue that the block schedule will reduce class sizes and cut teaching loads. Opponents note that it will shorten instructional time.

A Little Effort Helps

Make the open houses and conferences. Teachers are human beings: If you take an interest in what they are doing, they are more likely to take an interest in your child.

One study indicated that when parents attend open houses, their children are much more likely to take an interest in school. If you can't visit the school during the day, have the teacher phone you at evening.

8/San Francisco Integration

Court-Ordered Plan Mixes
Parental Choice with Ethnic Balance

SAN FRANCISCO SCHOOL DISTRICT, under court order, employs an enrollment system that tries to advance integration while leaving parents some influence over what schools their children will attend.

The system has many critics and although down through years changes have been made and sweeping changes promises, the basic system remains intact. Here is how it works:

Parents sign up their child for school. If the neighborhood school has space and if the child would not create a racial imbalance, as defined by the court, the child will usually be allowed to attend the school. Otherwise, the child will be bused, at public expense, to another school.

Transfers

Some schools are academically enriched and enjoy good reputations. Many parents prefer these schools over the neighborhood schools but transfers depend on space and racial balance, and other factors, including whether a child gets sick riding buses.

The district gets so many transfer requests that it has programmed a computer to sort out admissions. Once in a school, the child can stay for the natural duration, for example, kindergarten through the fifth grade. Siblings will be given preference to the school.

At the sixth grade, the child will be assigned to the neighborhood middle school, unless it is full or the child's race would upset the ethnic balance. If the parent wants another school, the petition process would be followed.

High school attendance is partially determined by scholastic achievement, mainly test scores. Lowell High is the top prep school in the district.

Within some elementary schools, high-scoring children or children with special abilities are clustered in their own classes. Middle schools and high schools have honors classes, another form of ability clustering.

This is a bare-bones description of the system. The district runs "newcomer" schools for immigrant children — a year of intensive language instruction before they are placed in "regular" school. At least one school offers a "year-round" schedule. Many schools have special programs.

Debate over Integration

Although thousands of children have thrived in this system and have gone on to college, many people blame it for the exodus of the middle class from the City, for enrollment drops and for a general decline in educational quality — charges often hard to substantiate.

To take one point, after the baby boom fizzled, enrollments declined in public and private schools up and down the state. For another, San Francisco public schools appear to have kept the confidence of the Asian community, a high-scoring group. For a third, San Francisco has a long tradition of private (mostly parochial) education.

But undeniably the system has angered and disappointed many, including the disadvantaged minorities.

The 1990 census counted 65,078 students in public elementary and secondary schools. The tally for private schools was 18,853. The percentage split was 78 vs. 22.

By comparison, only 16 percent of San Mateo County's students were enrolled in private schools and only 10 percent of Contra Costa's.

The San Francisco enrollment has a class twist. The upper-income neighborhoods sent the highest number to the private schools.

Pacing and Program

For the why, let's leave aside parental concerns about safety and reluctance to busing children out of the neighborhood. These are very important and by themselves may account for much of the opposition. But they don't illustrate the complexity of integration. Let's focus on pacing and program.

In the best of situations, these are tough challenges for educators. Children enter school with varying abilities and somehow the school and the teacher must find the pace and instructional methods to bring out the best in each student.

Where the children are close in ability, the class, generally, can move forward as a group. The teacher doesn't have to slow the fast child or rush the child who needs more time.

This was one hidden benefit of the neighborhood school. Academic achievement, many studies have shown, reflects family background. When families of similar income or education or traditions or values gathered in a neighborhood, the children received a common message at home, which often translated into cohesive — or fairly cohesive — groupings in the classroom.

A middle-class neighborhood would send its middle-class kids to the (middle-class) neighborhood school. Scores would break out: a few at the bottom, many in the middle, a few at the top. If the neighborhood were rich or well-to-do or academically proficient, scores might break out: a few at the bottom, a good grouping at the middle and a good grouping at the top.

In a poor or low-income neighborhood, the breakout might be many at the bottom, a smaller grouping at the middle, very few at the top.

If left in their own groupings, which reflected housing patterns, each school would be easy to "teach" but lacking the motivating tension of high-achieving children, the poor children might stagnate — one argument for integration.

Integration would also blend the children socially and break down prejudices. Lastly, the "poor" schools would work better because the middle- and high-income parents would be adept at capturing resources and working the system to their (and the school's) advantage.

In San Francisco and California, Caucasians and Asians tend to hit the middle and high, African-Americans and Hispanics the low (A generalization covering large numbers. There are Caucasians and Asians who score low, African-Americans and Hispanics who score high. The groupings can also be described by class: The middle class and rich score middle and high, the poor and low-income low.)

Integration brings them all together but it leaves unanswered the question of how schools should educate children of sometimes vastly different academic backgrounds.

Magnet Schools

San Francisco and many integrating school districts attempt to solve the problem with magnet schools. Load certain schools up with good and interesting programs, the idea runs, and parents won't object when their kids are bused out of their neighborhoods.

And so came the academically enriched schools, and the gifted clusters: grouping the "advanced" kids in their own classes. Also, schools that stress performing arts or science or foreign languages.

To some extent, they work. San Francisco public schools graduate students to the best colleges in the state and nation. Lowell is one of the finest high schools in the West.

But for many kids they don't work. The uncomfortable truth is that San Francisco has many children who are unprepared for school, who need intensive work far beyond the resources of the schools.

The academic rankings tell most of the story: many schools are scoring in the 10th and 20th percentiles, the lowest in the state. To be fair to San Francisco district, many traditional programs don't work either. How to educate poor children is a big problem throughout the state and nation.

The magnet approach also creates its own difficulties. Imagine your child being assigned to school with a gifted cluster, third grade. Only he doesn't get in it. He gets placed in a class with many low-achievers.

To many parents, gifted cluster means college track. If you're not on the track, you're on the road to someplace else. It's a harsh message for the parent of a third grader. The same for academically enriched schools. Great if your kid is in one; not so great if she isn't. The district, having so many low-achieving students, cannot create these schools in great numbers.

Bilingual Classes

In recent years, the district has enrolled many children who can't speak English or speak it with difficulty. On top of balancing kids by race, by neighborhood, by ability, by parents' request, there's the need to group immigrant children in their own classes so they can be taught effectively within the financial constraints of the district.

Grass is Greener

Finally, San Francisco's inability to hold on to middle-class families works against the system. So does the presence of an alternate system: the private schools. Many families, of all colors, get a few bucks and move to the suburbs. When public schools lose their middle class, they often lose their reputations because their scores drop.

Enrollment

The tensions and contradictions bubble to the surface at enrollment. Newspapers report that parents frequently lie about race for the purpose of tricking the computer into approving a transfer to a high-scoring school.

The higher-scoring schools are well-known and the district every year is bombarded with transfer petitions. Of the 11,807 requests made one recent year, the district granted 5,148.

If it had more money, the system would work much better but even with more bucks the basic problem would remain: how do you educate children of vastly different backgrounds in an integrated setting?

Lowell is the only high school in the City that accepts children based on their test scores. But to assure ethnic balance, the school district has set different admissions cutoffs. In early 1993, it was 66 (out of 69) for Chinese, 59 for Caucasian and 56 for African-Americans and Hispanics.

When Chinese parents hit the roof, the superintendent lowered the Chinese cutoff to 61, admitting 108 more students from this group but only if they came from public schools. Private-school parents went bonkers; superintendent changed his mind but vowed that for future admissions public school kids would get preference. Court actions are threatened.

Less all this be given an immigrant overlay, Chinese here generally means Chinese-American, second and third generation.

A complicated business.

Steps Parents Can Take

What's a parent to do? Well, ask plenty of questions, do your research. As for lying and manipulating ... let your conscience be your guide (To be fair to parents, they don't want to lie but they also want a good education for their kids.) If you can't get the transfer and want to stick with public schools, pay a tutor for after-school help — assuming you have the money.

If inclined, take a look at the private schools. Their reputation is elitist but many are not. All or almost all, including the religious, accept children of any race or creed, although with the religious, preference is usually given practicing believers.

In 1990, private schools in San Francisco accounted for 24 percent of all Black students advancing to a UC, 18 percent of all Asian students, 51 percent of all Hispanic, and 47 percent of all Filipinos.

San Francisco education summed up: The schools need more money. Scores certainly could be higher. But many children in the public schools are succeeding.

In 1991, San Mateo public schools, total enrollment about 79,000, sent 381 students to the University of California. San Francisco public schools, enrollment then about 62,000, sent 371 students to UC. When you throw in San Francisco private schools, the picture becomes brighter. If you get the public school you want, the system might really deliver for you and your child.

Recent San Francisco Items

• School of Arts moved from McAteer to school near San Francisco State University.

• Academic elementary school opened in Hunters Point; ties kids and families with social agencies.

• Two evening high schools were opened to attract dropouts.

• In February 1994, the superintendent, noting that three schools had failed to make progress, said the faculties at the schools would be replaced. The schools are Wilson High, Visitacion Valley Middle, and Bret Harte Elementary. Action has to be approved by the court.

9/Private Schools & Colleges

San Francisco, San Mateo County School Directories

PRIVATE SCHOOLS ARE NOT free of problems. The typical private or parochial school is funded way below its public school counterpart. In size, facilities and playing fields, and in programs, public schools usually far outstrip private schools. Private school teachers earn less than public school teachers.

By their nature, however, private schools enjoy certain advantages.

The Advantages

Public schools must accept all students, have almost no power to dismiss incompetent teachers and are at the mercy of their neighborhoods for the quality of students — the socioeconomic correlation. The unruly often cannot be expelled or effectively disciplined.

Much has been said about the ability of private schools to rid themselves of problem children and screen them out in the first place. But tuition probably does more than anything else to assure private schools quality students.

Parents who pay extra for their child's education and often agree to work closely with the school are, usually, demanding parents. The result: fewer discipline problems with the students, fewer distractions in the class, more of a willingness to learn.

When you place your child in a good private school, you are, to a large extent, buying him or her scholastic classmates. They may not be the smartest children — many private schools accept children of varying ability — but generally they will have someone at home breathing down their necks to succeed in academics.

The same attitude, a reflection of family values, is found in the high-achieving public schools. When a child in one of these schools or a private

College Admissions of Private School Graduates
San Mateo County Schools

High School	UC	CSU	Com	Total
Crystal Springs	9	0	3	12
Menlo School	54	4	2	60
Mercy	9	10	32	51
Notre Dame	11	10	9	30
Sacred Heart	11	10	14	35
SF Christian	0	1	0	1
Serra	19	19	69	103
Woodside Priory	3	0	1	4

San Francisco Schools

High School	UC	CSU	Com	Total
Bridgemont	1	2	6	9
Conv. of Sa. Ht.	16	1	0	17
Drew College Prep	2	8	7	17
Erik Erickson	0	4	0	4
Hebrew Academy	1	0	2	3
Immaculate Conception	3	23	36	52
Independent Learning	0	0	10	10
Lick-Wilmerding	34	3	2	39
Lycee-Francais	2	2	0	4
Mercy	11	24	49	84
Notre Dame	0	4	0	4
Riordan	7	20	44	71
Sacred Heart	38	47	77	162
St. Ignatius	65	48	39	152
St. Paul	1	7	8	16
SF University	34	0	2	36
Urban	5	2	1	8

Source: California Dept. of Education. The chart tracks California public colleges or universities, and high school graduates from private schools. It shows how many students from these high schools enrolled as college freshmen in fall 1992. The state does not track graduates enrolling in private colleges or out-of-state colleges. **Note**: Small or family schools not included in list. **Key:** UC (University of California system); CSU (Cal State system); Com (Community Colleges).

school turns to his left and right, he will see and later talk to children who read books and newspapers. A child in a low-achieving school, public or private, will talk to classmates who watch a lot of television and rarely read.

(These are, necessarily, broad generalizations. Much depends on whom the children pick for friends. High-achieving students certainly watch television but, studies show, much less than low-achieving students. Critics contend that even high-scoring schools are graduating students ill-prepared for college.)

The Quality of Teaching

Do private schools have better teachers than public schools? Impossible to tell. Both sectors sing the praises of their teachers. Private schools have much more freedom to dismiss teachers but this can be abused. The private schools themselves advise parents to avoid schools with excessive teacher turnover.

Although most can't pay as much as public schools, private institutions claim to attract people fed up with the limitations of public schools, particularly the restrictions on disciplining and ejecting unruly children. Some proponents argue that private schools attract teachers "who really want to teach."

Religion and Private Schools

Private schools talk in depth about religion or ethics, and many teach a specific creed.

Until recently public schools almost never talked about religion or religious figures. They now teach the history of major religions and the basic tenets of each, and they try to inculcate in the children a respect for all religions.

It's hard, if not impossible, however, for public schools to talk about values within a framework of religion or a system of ethics. Often, it's difficult for them to talk about values. Some people argue that this is major failing.

Many religious schools, Catholic and Protestant, accept students of different religions or no religion. Some schools offer these students broad courses in religion — less dogma. Ask about the program.

Money

Private-school parents pay taxes for public schools and they pay tuition. Public-school parents pay taxes but not tuition. Big difference.

Ethnic Diversity

Many private schools are integrated and the great majority of private-school principals — the editor knows no exceptions — welcome minorities. Some principals fret over tuition, believing that it keeps many poor students out of private schools. Money, the lack of it, weighs heavily on private schools. Scholarships, however, are awarded, adjustments made, family rates offered.

What's in San Francisco and San Mateo Counties

San Francisco has long had a strong tradition of private education. In its early years, the City attracted thousands Irish and Italian immigrants who built many parochial schools, many of which are still in operation.

About 22 percent of all students in San Francisco are enrolled in private schools and about 16 percent of San Mateo students.

UCs Chosen by Private School Graduates
San Francisco Schools

High School	Berk	Davis	Irv	UCLA	SD	SB	River	SC	Total
Bridgemont	0	0	0	0	0	0	0	1	1
Conv. of Sa. Ht.	2	5	0	5	0	3	0	1	16
Drew College	0	0	0	0	0	1	0	1	2
Hebrew Acad.	0	0	0	0	0	1	0	0	1
Lick-Wilmerdg	7	2	1	5	7	7	0	5	34
Lycee-Francais	0	1	0	1	0	0	0	0	2
Mercy	1	5	1	1	0	1	1	1	11
Riordan	2	1	0	1	0	3	0	0	7
Sacred Heart	6	11	2	1	0	9	0	9	38
St. Ignatius	15	27	2	4	2	12	1	2	65
St. Paul	1	0	0	0	0	0	0	0	1
SF Univ.	12	0	0	5	8	3	2	4	34
Urban	0	0	0	0	1	0	0	4	5

San Mateo County Schools

High School	Berk	Davis	Irv	UCLA	SD	SB	River	SC	Total
Crystal Spring	4	4	0	0	0	1	0	0	9
Menlo Sch.	9	9	3	6	8	9	0	10	54
Mercy	3	3	0	0	1	1	0	1	9
Notre Dame	1	7	0	0	2	0	0	1	11
Sacred Heart	3	2	1	1	0	3	0	1	11
SF Christian	0	0	0	0	0	0	0	0	0
Serra	4	10	0	0	2	2	1	0	19
Woodside Priory	1	1	1	0	0	0	0	0	3

Source: California Dept. of Education. The chart tracks the Universities of California and high school graduates from private schools. It shows how many students from these schools enrolled as UC freshmen in fall 1992. The state does not track graduates enrolling in private colleges or out-of-state colleges. **Key**: Berk (Berkeley), Irv (Irvine), River (Riverside), SD (San Diego), SB (Santa Barabara), SC (Santa Cruz).

San Mateo County has about 300 private schools, many one-family affairs, mother and father teaching their own children at home. A support network that supplies books and materials has grown up for these people.

Private schools in both counties come in great variety, Christian, Jewish, Montessori, Carden (schools with different teaching approaches), prep schools, schools that emphasize language or music, boarding and day schools, schools that allow informal dress, schools that require uniforms, boys' schools, girls' schools, schools for high achievers, schools for children with problems.

Some schools have low teacher-pupil ratios, fewer than 15 students per teacher, occasionally around 10 to 1. Public school classes usually go 25 to 30 per teacher, sometimes higher. Catholic schools are the major exceptions. Their class sizes run close to the public school ratio, and in some schools higher. Catholic schools, nonetheless, are the most numerous and most popular.

Choosing a Private School

1. Inspect the grounds, the school's buildings, ask plenty of questions. "I would make myself a real pest," advised one private school official. The good schools welcome this kind of attention.

2. Choose a school with a philosophy congenial to your own, and your child's. Carden schools emphasize structure. Montessori schools, while somewhat structured, encourage individual initiative and independence.

Ask whether the school is accredited. Private schools are free to run almost any program they like, to set any standards they like, which sounds nice but in some aspects hurts the schools. A few bad ones spoil the reputation of the good ones. To remedy this an increasing number of private schools are submitting to inspections by independent agencies such as the Western Association of Schools and Colleges and the California Association of Independent Schools. These agencies try to make sure that schools meet their own goals.

To save money some good schools do not seek accreditation.

3. Have all details about tuition carefully explained. How is it to be paid? Are there extra fees? Book costs? Is there a refund if the student is withdrawn or dropped from the school?

4. Ask about progress reports and parent conferences. How often are they scheduled?

5. Ask about entrance requirements. When must they be met? Although many schools use entrance tests, often they are employed to place the child in an academic program, not exclude him from the school.

6. For prep schools, find out what percentage of the students go on to college and to what colleges.

7. How are discipline problems handled?

8. What are the qualifications of the teachers, the teacher turnover rate?

9. How sound financially is the school? How long has it been in existence? There is nothing wrong per se with new schools. But you want a school that has the wherewithal to do the job.

10. Don't choose in haste but don't wait until the last minute. Some schools fill quickly, some fill certain classes quickly.

For San Francisco private schools, act quickly. Newspapers report that some private schools, for lack of space, are turning away students.

Lastly, don't assume that because your child attends a private school you can expect everything will go all right, that neither the school nor the student needs your attention. The quality of private schools in California varies widely. The prudent parent will keep a watchful eye, and the good schools will welcome your interest.

Adult Schools

Although rarely in the headlines, adult schools serve thousands of residents. English as a second-language, upholstery, microwave cooking, ballroom dancing, computers, cardiopulmonary resuscitation, aerobic exercise, how to invest in stocks, art, music, how to raise children — all these and much more are offered in the adult schools.

These schools and programs are run by school districts and by cities. Many schools also run adult sports programs, basketball, volleyball, tennis. Call your local school or city for a catalog.

The Colleges

Traditionally, students graduated from high school and went off to college. Now many mature adults are attending college, some to get the degree they missed, others to acquire a master's degree, many to train in a specific field.

The reasons are not hard to find. White-collar jobs pay more, and the nature of work is changing. It used to be that college equipped a person for life. No more. Changes are coming so fast to the professions that people need constant retraining throughout their careers. Some major businesses, recognizing this, have set up their own schools.

Getting the Older Students

As the public's needs have changed, so have the colleges. Many colleges now offer evening and weekend programs, especially in business degrees and business-related subjects. Some programs — an MBA — can take years, some classes only a day. The Bay Area is loaded with educational opportunities.

Here is a partial list of local colleges. As with any venture, the student should investigate before enrolling or paying a fee.

San Francisco Colleges

• Academy of Art College, 540 Powell St., San Francisco, 94108. Day and evening classes. Phone (415) 274-2200.

• City College of San Francisco, 50 Phelan Ave., San Francisco, 94112. Liberal arts. Phone (415) 239-3000.

• Golden Gate University, 536 Mission St., San Francisco, 94105. Business and law. Phone (415) 442-7000.

• John Adams Community College Center, 1860 Hayes St., San Francisco, 94117. Remedial instruction. Phone (415) 561-1900.

• John O'Connell Community College Center. Two sites: 108 Bartlett and 425 Fourth St., San Francisco. Vocational instruction. Phone (415) 550-4380.

• New College of California, 766 Valencia St., San Francisco, 94110. Humanities and public interest law. Phone (415) 626-1694.

• San Francisco State University-Downtown Center, 814 Mission St., San Francisco, 94103. Day, evening, extended education. Phone (415) 543-4250.

Community College Transfers to UCs
San Francisco

College	Berk	Davis	Irv	UCLA	SD	SB	River	SC	Total
City College	80	18	2	25	4	2	1	7	139

San Mateo County

College	Berk	Davis	Irv	UCLA	SD	SB	River	SC	Total
Cañada	11	1	0	2	3	4	2	2	25
San Mateo	38	35	2	16	8	19	1	9	128
Skyline	7	6	1	3	1	0	1	5	24

Source: California Dept. of Education. The chart shows which UCs community college transfers entered in fall, 1991. The state does not track transfers to private colleges or out-of-state colleges. Key: Berk (Berkeley), Irv (Irvine), River (Riverside), SD (San Diego), SB (Santa Barbara), SC (Santa Cruz).

Community College Transfers to CSUs
San Francisco

College	CPly	Chico	Fres	Hay	Sacto	SF	SJ	Oth	Total
City College	24	4	2	28	18	486	76	12	670

San Mateo County

College	CPly	Chico	Fres	Hay	Sacto	SF	SJ	Son	Total
Cañada	2	9	4	17	10	20	25	1	97
San Mateo	16	13	7	60	38	85	106	7	363
Skyline	6	6	1	21	9	106	29	3	188

Source: California Dept. of Education. The chart shows which California State Universities community college transfers entered in fall, 1991. The state does not track transfers to private colleges or out-of-state colleges. Key: CPly (Cal Poly San Luis Obispo), Chico (Chico State), Fres (Fresno), Hay (Hayward), Sacto (Sacramento), SF (San Francisco), SJ (San Jose), Son (Sonoma), Total (total Cal State transfers).

• San Francisco State University, 1600 Holloway Ave., San Francisco, 94132. Phone (415) 338-1111.

• University of California Extension. Many enrichment and business classes. Also classes for teachers, government workers. Downtown campus. Phone (510) 642-4111.

San Francisco's community college system has several campuses devoted to teaching English as a second language. They include:

• Alemany Community College Center, 750 Eddy St., San Francisco, 94109. Phone (415) 561-1875.

• Chinatown-North Beach Community College Center, 940 Filbert St., San Francisco, 94133. Phone (415) 561-1850.

• Downtown Community College Center, 800 Mission, San Francisco, 94103. Phone (415) 267-6500.

• Mission Community College Center, 106 Bartlett St., San Francisco, 94110. Phone (415) 550-4384.

• Southeast Community College Center, 1800 Oakdale Ave., San Francisco, 94124. Phone (415) 550-4300.

San Mateo County Colleges

• Cañada College. 4200 Farm Hill Blvd., Redwood City, 94601. Community college. Phone (415) 364-1212.

• College of San Mateo. 1700 West Hillsdale Blvd., San Mateo, 94402. Community college. Phone: (415) 574-6161.

• College of Notre Dame. 1500 Ralston Ave., Belmont, 94002. Catholic. Private, coeducational. Undergraduate and graduate programs including MBA. Phone (415) 593-1601.

• Menlo School and College. 1000 El Camino Real, Atherton. Private. Undergraduate programs include business administration , humanities, mass communication. Ph. (415) 323-6141.

• Skyline College. 3300 College Drive, San Bruno, 94066. Community college. Phone (415) 355-7000.

• Stanford University. Located in nearby Palo Alto. One of the great universities of the planet. Enrollment about 13,500. Well worth a visit even if you or yours don't stand a ghost of a chance of attending. Many Stanford concerts, lectures and events are open to the public.

Directory of Private Schools

Schools provided directory information by responding to questionnaires and phone surveys. Many schools offer family rates. Religious schools often charge higher for non-members.

San Francisco

Adda Clevenger Junior Preparatory and Theater School for Children, Mid-Sunset District, San Francisco, 94122. Ph: (415) 681-1140. Enroll: 79, K-8th. Fee: $5,985/yr.

Archbishop Riordan High School, 175 Phelan Ave., San Francisco, 94112. Ph: (415) 586-8200. Enroll: 600, Ninth-12th boys. Fee: $5,305/yr.

Big City Montessori School, 240 Industrial St., San Francisco, 94124. Ph: (415) 648-5777. Enroll: 75, Age 2-K. Fee: $4,950/yr.

Binet-Montessori School, 1715 Octavia St., San Francisco, 94109. Ph: (415) 567-4000. Enroll: 150, Pre-3rd. Fee: $525/mo.

Brandeis-Hillel Day School, 655 Brotherhood Way, San Francisco, 94132. Ph: (415) 406-1035, , K-8th. Fee: $6,250-$6,550/yr.

Bridgemont Junior High and High School, 501 Cambridge, San Francisco, 94134. Ph: (415) 333-7600. Enroll: 189, Sixth-12th. Fee: $2,125-$3,375/yr.

Cathedral School for Boys, 1275 Sacramento St., San Francisco, 94108. Ph: (415) 771-6600. Enroll: 227 Episcopal, K-8th. Fee: $7,950-$8,475/yr.

Challenge to Learning, 924 Balboa St., San Francisco, 94118. Ph: (415) 221-9200. Enroll: 30, Ungraded Special Ed. Fee: funded through school district.

Children's Day School, 333 Dolores St., San Francisco, 94110. Ph: (415) 861-5432. Enroll: 195, Pre-2nd, ages 2 through 7. Fee: $525-$545/mo.

Convent Elementary School, 2222 Broadway, San Francisco, 94115. Ph: (415) 563-2900. Enroll: 276, K-8th Girls. Fee: $8,350/yr.

Convent High School, 2222 Broadway, San Francisco, 94115. Ph: (415) 563-2900, 175, 9-12 girls. Fee: $9,800.

Convent of the Sacred Heart High School, 2222 Broadway, San Francisco, 94115. Ph: (415) 563-2900. Enroll: 175, Ninth-12th Girls. Fee: $9,800-$9,900/yr.

Cornerstone Academy, 801 Silver Ave., San Francisco, 94134. Ph: (415) 587-7256. Enroll: 750, Pre-8th. Fee: $2,800/yr. (1-8 only).

Drew College Preparatory School, 2901 California, San Francisco, 94115-2432. Ph: (415) 346-4831, fax 415-346-0720. Enroll: 135, Ninth-12th. Fee: $8,400/yr.

Ecole Notre Dame Des Victoires, 659 Pine St., San Francisco, 94108. Ph: (415) 421-0069. Enroll: 310, K-8th. Fee: $3,000/yr.

Edgewood Children's Center, 1801 Vicente St., San Francisco, 94116. Ph: (415) 681-3211. Enroll: 47 residential, 24 day treatment, Special Ed. for emotionally disturbed, ages 6-12. Fee: Referrals by schools, courts or social agencies.

Edgewood Day Treatment Program, 1733 Vicente St., San Francisco, 94116. Ph: (415) 664-7584. Enroll: 25, Special Education. Fee: Funded by local schools.

Erikson School, 130 Church St., San Francisco, 94114. Ph: (415) 252-5707. Enroll: 28, Special education. Fee: Referred and funded by local schools.

Fellowship Academy, 495 Cambridge St., San Francisco, 94134. Ph: (415) 239-0511. Enroll: 235, Pre-8th. Fee: $2,270- $2,300/yr; $395-preschool, fulltime.

French-American International School, 220 Buchanan, San Francisco, 94102. Ph: (415) 626-8564, fax 415-626-8551. Enroll: 485, PreK-12th. Fee: $6,825-$9,250/yr.

Hamlin School, 2120 Broadway, San Francisco, 94115. Ph: (415) 922-0300. Enroll: 390, K-8th Girls. Fee: $8,100-$8,450/yr.

Hebrew Academy of San Francisco, 645 14th Ave., San Francisco, 94118. Ph: (415) 752-9583. Enroll: 290, Nursery-12th. Fee: NA.

Hergl School, 1570 Greenwich St., San Francisco, 94123. Ph: (415) 474-0191. Enroll: 10, Ungraded. Fee: $75/day.

Hillwood Academic Day School, 2521 Scott St., San Francisco, 94115. Ph: (415) 931-0400. Enroll: 100, K-8th. Fee: $350/mo.

Holy Name of Jesus School, 1560 40th Ave., San Francisco, 94122. Ph: (415) 731-4077. Enroll: 580, K-8th. Fee: $180-$235/mo.

Immaculate Conception Academy, 3625-24th St., San Francisco, 94110. Ph: (415) 824-2052. Enroll: 350 , Ninth-12th Girls. Fee: $3,700/yr.

International Christian School, 42 Waller St., San Francisco, 94102. Ph: (415) 863-1691. Enroll: 200, Pre-6th. Fee: $300/pre-$220/mo K-6.

Jamestown Learning Center, 55 Farallones St., San Francisco, 94112. Ph: (415) 334-6481. Enroll: 26, Ungraded Special Ed. Fee: Referred and funded by local school districts.

Joshua Marie Cameron Academy, 100 Whitney Young Circle, San Francisco, 94124. Ph: (415) 824-4107. Enroll: 10, Ungraded Special Ed. Fee: Referral by local school district.

Katherine Delmar Burke School, 7070 California St., San Francisco, 94121. Ph: (415) 751-0177, 80, K-8th Girls. Fee: $7,200-$7,800/yr.

Katherine Michiels School, 1335 Guerrero St., San Francisco, 94110. Ph: (415) 821-1434. Enroll: 81, Infant-Grade 2. Fee: $465-$725/mo.

Kittredge School, 2355 Lake St., San Francisco, 94121. Ph: (415) 751-3050. Enroll: 110, First-8th. Fee: $6,000-$6,200/yr + $100 reg. fee.

La Mel School, 1801 Bush St., San Francisco, 94109. Ph: (415) 931-1972. Enroll: 32, Pre-12th & college prep. Fee: Varies, call school.

Lick-Wilmerding High School, 755 Ocean Ave., San Francisco, 94112. Ph: (415) 333-4021. Enroll: 350, Ninth-12th. Fee: $10,475/yr, flexible tuition $350-$9,975.

Live Oak School, 117 Diamond St., San Francisco, 94114. Ph: (415) 861-8840. Enroll: 140, K-8th. Fee: $5,500-$6,000/yr.

Lycee Francais French School, 3301 Balboa St., San Francisco, 94121. Ph: (415) 668-1833. Enroll: 425, Pre-12th. Fee: $5,950-$8,150/yr.

Maria Montessori School of the Golden Gate, 678 Portola Drive, San Francisco, 94127. Ph: (415) 731-8188. Enroll: 60, Pre-8th. Fee: $4,700/yr.

Mercy High School, 3250 19th Ave., San Francisco, 94132. Ph: (415) 334-0525. Enroll: 500, Ninth-12th Girls. Fee: $4,350/yr.

Montessori House of Children, 1187 Franklin St., San Francisco, 94109. Ph: (415) 441-7691. Enroll: 100, PreK-1st. Fee: $390/mo.

Mother Goose School Inc., 334 28th Ave., San Francisco, 94121. Ph: (415) 221-6133. Enroll: 110, Pre-1st. Fee: $600/mo. full time.

New Learning School, 888 Turk St., San Francisco, 94102. Ph: (415) 923-9900. Enroll: 50, Sixth-12th. Fee: $5,800- $6,800/yr.

Oakes Children's Center, 1348 10th Ave., San Francisco, 94122. Ph: (415) 564-2310. Enroll: 20, Ungraded Special Ed. Fee: Funded by city and state.

One Fifty Parker St. **School,** 150 Parker Ave., San Francisco, 94118. Ph: (415) 221-0294. Enroll: 60, Pre & K, extended child care. Fee: $3,105-$3,365-$3,622/yr.

Pacific Primary School, 1500 Grove St., San Francisco, 94117. Ph: (415) 346-0906. Enroll: 81, Pre & K. Fee: $7,970/yr.

Presidio Hill School, 3839 Washington St., San Francisco, 94118. Ph: (415) 751-9318. Enroll: 140, PreK-8th. Fee: $5,800-$6,200/yr.

Rivendell School, 4501 Irving St., San Francisco, 94122. Ph: (415) 566-7454. Enroll: 48, K-6th. Fee: $4,950/yr.

Sacred Heart Cathedral Preparatory, 1055 Ellis St., San Francisco, 94109. Ph: (415) 775-6626. Enroll: 1,100, Ninth-12th. Fee: $4,800/yr.

Sacred Heart Grammar School, 735 Fell St., San Francisco, 94117. Ph: (415) 621-8035. Enroll: 136, K-8th. Fee: $140/mo.

San Francisco Chinese Parents' Committee School, 843 Stockton St., San Francisco, 94108. Ph: (415) 391-5564. Enroll: 160, PreK-6th, .

San Francisco Christian School, 25 Whittier St., San Francisco, 94112. Ph: (415) 586-1117. Enroll: 255, K-12th. Fee: $2,500- $3,150/yr.

San Francisco Day School, 350 Masonic Ave., San Francisco, 94118. Ph: (415) 931-2422. Enroll: 400, K-8th. Fee: $7,375-$8,425/yr.

San Francisco Hearing and Speech Center, 1234 Divasadero St., San Francisco, 94115. Ph: (415) 921-7658. Enroll: 37, Ungraded. Fee: $87.50/day.

San Francisco Junior Academy, 66 Geneva Ave., San Francisco, 94112. Ph: (415) 585-5550. Enroll: 106, K-8th. Fee: $225- $245/mo.

San Francisco University High School, 3065 Jackson St., San Francisco, 94115. Ph: (415) 346-8400. Enroll: 385, Ninth-12th. Fee: $11,300/yr.

San Francisco Waldorf School, 2938 Washington St., San Francisco, 94118. Ph: (415) 931-2750. Enroll: 247, K-8th, $6,000-$7,000/yr.

Sand Paths Academy, 525 Bryant St., San Francisco, 94107. Ph: (415) 495-7937. Enroll: 30, Ungraded, ages 7 to 21 Special Education. Fee: Provided by Bay Area school districts.

St. Anthony's School, 299 Precita Ave., San Francisco, 94110. Ph: (415) 648-2008. Enroll: 284, K-8th. Fee: $185/mo.

St. Dominic School, 2445 Pine St., San Francisco, 94115. Ph: (415) 346-9500. Enroll: 206, K-6th. Fee: $1,250/yr.

St. Emydius School, 301 De Montfort Ave., San Francisco, 94112. Ph: (415) 333-4877. Enroll: 220, K-8th. Fee: $2,170/yr.

St. Gabriel School, 2550 41st Ave., San Francisco, 94116. Ph: (415) 566-0314. Enroll: 480, K-8th. Fee: $1,825-$1,911/yr for the 1st child.

St. Ignatius College Preparatory School, 2001-37th Ave., San Francisco, 94116. Ph: (415) 731-7500. Enroll: 1,383, Ninth-12th. Fee: $5,220/yr.

St. John's Elementary School, 925 Chenery St., San Francisco, 94131. Ph: (415) 584-8383. Enroll: 267, K-8th. Fee: $2,150/yr.

St. Monica School, 5920 Geary Boulevard, San Francisco, 94121. Ph: (415) 751-9564.

Enroll: 346, K-8th. Fee: $1,700-$2,000/yr.

St. Thomas The Apostle School, 3801 Balboa St., San Francisco, 94121. Ph: (415) 221-2711. Enroll: 270, K-8th. Fee: $1,650- $1,900/yr.

Sterne School, 2690 Jackson St., San Francisco, 94115. Ph: (415) 922-6081. Enroll: 60, Sixth-12th Special Ed. Fee: $7,250-$8,050/yr.

Stuart Hall for Boys, 2252 Broadway, San Francisco, 94115. Ph: (415) 563-2900. Enroll: 311, K-8th Boys. Fee: $8,350/yr.

Synergy School, 975 Grove St., San Francisco, 94117. Ph: (415) 567-6177. Enroll: 90, K-6th. Fee: $4,700/yr.

The Children's School of San Francisco, 420 29th Ave., San Francisco, 94121. Ph: (415) 386-1226. Enroll: 30, Pre-6th. Fee: $4,000/yr.

The Discovery Center School, 65 Ocean Ave., San Francisco, 94112. Ph: (415) 333-6609. Enroll: 380, K-8th. Fee: $4,0500/yr.

The Laurel School, 350 9th Ave., San Francisco, 94118. Ph: (415) 752-3567. Enroll: 66, Pre-8th. Fee: $6,800/yr.

The San Francisco School, 300 Gaven St., San Francisco, 94134. Ph: (415) 239-5065. Enroll: 225, Pre-8th. Fee: $5,550-$6,575/yr.

The Urban School of San Francisco, 1563 Page St., San Francisco, 94117. Ph: (415) 626-2919. Enroll: 185, Ninth-12th. Fee: $11,300/yr.

Town School, 2750 Jackson St., San Francisco, 94115. Ph: (415) 921-3747. Enroll: 400, K-8th. Fee:$7,000-$8,000/yr.

West Portal Lutheran School, 200 Sloat Boulevard, San Francisco, 94132. Ph: (415) 665-6330. Enroll: 606, PreK-8th. Fee: $2,300/yr.

Woodside International School, 1555 Irving St., San Francisco, 94122. Ph: (415) 564-1063. Enroll: 80, Sixth-12th, Fee; $7,260/yr.

Zion Lutheran School, 495 9th Ave., San Francisco, 94118. Ph: (415) 221-7500. Enroll: 225, K-8th. Fee: $2,800/yr.

San Mateo County
Atherton

Menlo School, 50 Valparaiso Ave., Atherton, 94027. Ph: (415) 688-3866. Enroll: 500, 6th-12th coed, day only. Fee: $9,800- $10,995/yr.

Sacred Heart Schools, 150 Valparaiso Ave., Atherton, 94027. Ph: (415) 322-1866. Enroll: 790, Pre-12th. Fee: $5,200-$9,600/yr.

St. Joseph's Elementary, 50 Emilie Ave., Atherton, 94027. Ph: (415) 322-9931. Enroll: 500, K-8th. Fee: $4,500-$6,100/yr.

Belmont

Acacia Montessori School, 2820 Ponce Ave., Belmont, 94002. Ph: (415) 592-4725. Enroll: 65, Pre-3rd. Fee: $475/mo full time.

Belmont Oaks Academy, 2200 Carlmont Drive, Belmont, 94002. Ph: (415) 593-6175. Enroll: 160, K-3rd. Fee: $470-$520/mo.

Charles Armstrong School, 1405 Solana Drive, Belmont, 94002. Ph: (415) 592-7570. Enroll: 193, Ungraded special ed. Fee: $9,200/yr.

Curiosity Corner, 3100 St. James Road, Belmont, 94002. Ph: (415) 592-7664. Enroll: 108, K-5th. Fee: $240/mo avg.

Gloria Dei Lutheran School, 2600 Ralston Ave., Belmont, 94002. Ph: (415) 593-3361. Enroll: 42, K-8th. Fee: $1,300- $1,900/yr.

Immaculate Heart of Mary School, 1000 Alameda de las Pulgas, Belmont, 94002. Ph: (415) 593-4265. Enroll: 295, K-8th. Fee: $1,975/yr.

Notre Dame College Preparatory, 1540 Ralston Ave., Belmont, 94002-1995. Ph: (415) 595-1913. Enroll: 350, Ninth-12th Girls. Fee: $5,414/yr.

Notre Dame Elementary, 1500 Ralston Ave., Belmont, 94002. Ph: (415) 591-2209. Enroll: 264, First-8th. Fee: $2,395/yr.

Burlingame

Hart Day School, 1151 Vancouver, Burlingame, 94010. Ph: (415) 348-0921. Enroll: 12,

Fifth-12th Special Ed. Fee: NA.

Mercy High School, 2750 Adeline Drive, Burlingame, 94010. Ph: (415) 343-3631. Enroll: 325, Ninth-12th Girls. Fee: $4,675/yr.

Our Lady of Angels Elementary, 1328 Cabrillo Ave., Burlingame, 94010. Ph: (415) 343-9200. Enroll: 310, Pre-8th. Fee: $1,976/yr.

St. Catherine of Siena Elementary, 1300 Bayswater Ave., Burlingame, 94010. Ph: (415) 344-7176. Enroll: 315, K-8th. Fee: $1,780/yr.

Colma

Holy Angels Elementary, 20 Reiner St., Colma, 94014. Ph: (415) 755-0220. Enroll: 323, K-8th. Fee: $185/mo.

Daly City

Hilldale School, 79 Florence St., Daly City, 94014. Ph: (415) 756-4737. Enroll: 136, K-8th. Fee: $3,850/yr.

Our Lady of Mercy Elementary, Seven Elmwood Drive, Daly City, 94015. Ph: (415) 756-3395. Enroll: 585, K-8th. Fee: $245/mo.

Our Lady of Perpetual Help Elementary, 80 Wellington Ave., Daly City, 94014. Ph: (415) 755-4438. Enroll: 325, K-8th. Fee: $180- $380/mo.

Rainbow School, 99 Elmwood Drive, Daly City, 94015. Ph: (415) 994-3414. Enroll: 20, Pre & K. Fee: $375/mo, K.

Young World Learning Center, 699 Serramonte Blvd., Daly City, 94015. Ph: (415) 994-6599. Enroll: 80, Pre-6th. Fee: $400/mo.

East Palo Alto

Creative Montessori Learning Center, 1425 Bay Road, East Palo Alto, 94303. Ph: (415) 325-9543. Enroll: 60, Pre-K. Fee: $200-$410/mo.

Shule-Mandela Academy, 321 Bell St., East Palo Alto, 94303. Ph: (415) 327-5848. Enroll: 40, K-8th. Fee: $300/mo.

El Granada

Wilkinson School, 750 Alhambra Ave., El Granada, 94018. Ph: (415) 726-2990. Enroll: 120, K-6th. Fee: $2,600/K-$3,600/1st-6th.

Foster City

St. Ambrose Sea Breeze School, 900 Edgewater Blvd., Foster City, 94404. Ph: (415) 574-5437. Enroll: 225, Pre & K. Fee: $135- $460/mo.

Hillsborough

Crystal Springs Uplands School, 400 Uplands Dr., Hillsborough, 94010. Ph: (415) 342-4175. Enroll: 350, Sixth-12th. Fee: $10,150/yr.

Screen Play, Family Computer Training, 2600 Ralston Ave., Hillsborough, 94010. Ph: (415) 343-5133. Enroll: 100, 3 yrs.-adult. Fee: $12.50/hr.

Screen Play, Family Computer Training, 6565 Skyline Blvd., Hillsborough, 94010. Ph: (415) 343-5133. Enroll: 75, 3 yrs.-adult. Fee: $12.50/hr.

The Nueva School, 6565 Skyline Blvd., Hillsborough, 94010. Ph: (415) 348-2272. Enroll: 305, PreK-8th. Fee: $5,500-$10,600/yr.

Menlo Park

Beechwood School, 50 Terminal Ave., Menlo Park, 94025. Ph: (415) 327-5052. Enroll: 150, PreK-8th. Fee: $120/mo.

German-American School, 275 Elliott Drive, Menlo Park, 94025. Ph: (415) 324-8617. Enroll: 90, K-8th. Fee: $400-$490/mo.

Hansel and Gretel Private School, 2050 Gordon Ave., Menlo Park, 94025. Ph: (415) 854-1894. Enroll: 21, Pre-1st. Fee: $440/mo full time.

Nativity Elementary, 1250 Laurel St., Menlo Park, 94025. Ph: (415) 325-7304. Enroll: 258, K-8th. Fee: $2,500/yr.

Phillips Brooks School, 2245 Avy Ave., Menlo Park, 94025. Ph: (415) 854-4545. Enroll: 205, Pre-6th. Fee: Call school.

St. Raymond's School, 1211 Arbor Rd., Menlo Park, 94025. Ph: (415) 322-2312. Enroll: 278, K-8th. Fee: $260/mo.

The Roberts School, 641 Coleman Ave., Menlo Park, 94025. Ph: (415) 322-3535. Enroll: 50, 2 yrs. old-K. Fee: $575/mo.

Trinity School, 2650 Sand Hill Road, Menlo Park, 94025. Ph: (415) 854-0288. Enroll: 165, Pre-6th. Fee: $6,000/yr.

Woodland School, 360 La Cuesta Drive, Menlo Park, 94028. Ph: (415) 854-9065. Enroll: 200, Pre-8th. Fee: $5,300- $5,600/yr.

Millbrae

Hoover Children's Center, One Alp Way, Millbrae, 94030. Ph: (415) 697-9444. Enroll: 100, Age 18 mo.- PreK & K. Fee: $430- $470/mo.

St. Dunstan's Elementary, 1150 Magnolia Ave., Millbrae, 94030. Ph: (415) 697-8119. Enroll: 315, K-8th. Fee: $2,150/yr.

Pacifica

Alma Heights Christian Academy, 1030 Linda Mar Blvd., Pacifica, 94044. Ph: (415) 355-1935/ 359-0555. Enroll: 261, K-12th. Fee: $180-$230/mo.

Good Shepherd School, 909 Oceana Blvd., Pacifica, 94044. Ph: (415) 359-4544. Enroll: 345, K-8th. Fee: $2,130/yr.

Portola Valley

Woodside Priory School, 302 Portola Road, Portola Valley, 94028-7897. Ph: (415) 851-8221 Fax 851-2839. Enroll: 180/coed day-boys boarding, 6th-12th. Fee: $10,430/yr. day, $21,130/yr. boarding.

Redwood City

Our Lady of Mt. Carmel School, 301 Grand St., Redwood City, 94062. Ph: (415) 366-6127. Enroll: 295, Pre-8th. Fee: $1,980/yr.

Redeemer Lutheran Elementary, 468 Grand St., Redwood City, 94062. Ph: (415) 366-3466. Enroll: 111, K-8th. Fee: $2,050-$2,750/yr.

Redwood Baptist Christian Academy, 435 Fifth Ave., Redwood City, 94063. Ph: (415) 364-1606. Enroll: 35, K-12 Ungraded. Fee: $190/mo.

Redwoods Int'l Montessori House of Children, 181 Clinton St., Redwood City, 94062. Ph: (415) 366-9859. Enroll: 24, Ungraded, ages 2-6 yrs., incl. K. Fee: Varies by program & full or part time.

Redwoods Int'l Montessori House of Children, 2000 Woodside Road, Redwood City, 94061. Ph: (415) 366-9859. Enroll: 48 , Ungraded, Ages 2 -6 yrs., incl. K. Fee: Varies by program & full or part time.

St. Pius Elementary, 1100 Woodside Road, Redwood City, 94061. Ph: (415) 368-8327. Enroll: 315, K-8th. Fee: $1,950- $4,300/yr.

The Heritage School, 1305 Middlefield Rd., Redwood City, 94063. Ph: (415) 366-3842. Enroll: 200, Pre-8th. Fee: $3,150- $3,500/yr.

Thumbelina Nursery School, 20 Horgan Ave., Redwood City, 94061. Ph: (415) 364-5165. Enroll: 60 (12 per class), Pre & K. Fee: $450 full day-$275 half day.

Wherry Academy, 820 Cassia St., Redwood City, 94063. Ph: (415) 367-6791. Enroll: 35, Kinder-12th. Fee: $395/mos for 10 mos-$3,950 yr.

San Bruno
Happy Hall School, 233 Santa Inez Ave., San Bruno, 94066. Ph: (415) 583-7370. Enroll: 128, Nursery-K. Fee: NA.

Highlands Christian Schools, 1900 Monterey, San Bruno, 94066. Ph: (415) 873-4090. Enroll: 800, Kinder-8th. Fee: Call school.

St. Robert's Elementary, 345 Oak Ave., San Bruno, 94066. Ph: (415) 583-5065. Enroll: 325, K-8th. Fee: $1,800/yr.

San Carlos
Alpha Beacon Christian School, 750 Dartmouth Ave., San Carlos, 94070. Ph: (415) 592-2811. Enroll: 305, Pre-12th. Fee: $1,200-$4,000/yr.

Edison Montessori, 750 Dartmouth Ave., San Carlos, 94070. Ph: (415) 592-4828. Enroll: 90, Pre-K. Fee: $330/mo, part time; $55/mos., full time.

St. Charles Elementary, 850 Tamarack Ave., San Carlos, 94070. Ph: (415) 593-1629. Enroll: 298, K-8th. Fee: $2,085/yr.

West Bay High School, 1482 Laurel, San Carlos, 94070. Ph: (415) 595-5022. Enroll: 88, Ninth-12th. Fee: $910- $1,390/yr.

San Mateo
Carey School, 2101 Alameda de las Pulgas, San Mateo, 94403. Ph: (415) 345-8205. Enroll: 162, Nursery-5th. Fee: Call school.

Grace Lutheran School, 2825 Alameda de las Pulgas, San Mateo, 94403. Ph: (415) 345-9082. Enroll: 66, K-6th. Fee: $1,550-$2,400/yr.

Hoover/Knolls Children's Center, 525 42nd Ave., San Mateo, 94403. Ph: (415) 341-0641. Enroll: 95, Pre . Fee: $460/mo.

Screen Play, Family Computer Training, 27 Tenth Ave., San Mateo, 94402. Ph: (415) 343-5133. Enroll: 50, 3 yrs-adult. Fee: $12.50/hr.

Serra High School, 451 West 20th Ave., San Mateo, 94403. Ph: (415) 345-8207. Enroll: 750, Ninth-12th Boys. Fee: $5,000/yr.

St. Gregory Elementary, 2701 Hacienda St., San Mateo, 94403. Ph: (415) 573-0111. Enroll: 320, K-8th. Fee: $185-$215/mo.

St. Matthews Catholic School, 900 South El Camino Real, San Mateo, 94402. Ph: (415) 343-1373. Enroll: 492, K-8th. Fee: $1,610-$1,785/yr.

St. Matthews Episcopal School, 16 Baldwin Ave., San Mateo, 94401. Ph: (415) 342-5436. Enroll: 220, Pre-8th. Fee: $3,380-$6,980/yr.

St. Timothy School, 1515 Dolan Ave., San Mateo, 94401. Ph: (415) 342-6567. Enroll: 255, K-8th. Fee: $170-$178/mo.

North Peninsula Jewish Community Day School, 525 West 42nd Ave., San Mateo , 94403. Ph: (415) 345-8900. Enroll: 110, K-5th. Fee: $4,500-$5,200/yr.

Transfiguration Nursery School, 3900 Alameda de las Pulgas, San Mateo , 94403. Ph: (415) 341-7878. Enroll: 15, K. Fee: NA.

South San Francisco
All Souls Catholic School, 479 Miller Ave., So. San Francisco, 94080. Ph: (415) 583-3562. Enroll: 315, K-8th. Fee: $1,890-$2,860/yr.

Mater Dolorosa, 1040 Miller Ave., So. San Francisco, 94080. Ph: (415) 588-8175. Enroll: 290, Kinder-8th. Fee: $200-$240/mo.

St. Veronica Elementary, 434 Alida Way, So. San Francisco, 94080. Ph: (415) 589-3909. Enroll: 335, K-8th. Fee: $2,312/yr.

10/Day Care

A List to Start You on Your Search for a Care Center in San Francisco and San Mateo County

DAY CARE OVER THE LAST 10-20 years has undergone a transformation in the Bay Region. As more mothers entered the work force, the demand for quality care rose and private enterprise moved to fill the need, followed, often begrudgingly, by public schools.

Yes, more can be done, especially in incorporating child care in work places. But compared to the 1970s, day care is much more accessible now and probably better managed. Community colleges train people who work in and run care centers. Because of well-publicized abuses in the past, many parents are more aware that day-care providers should be chosen carefully.

What Day-Care Directory Contains

Here is a list of day-care providers that serve the local towns. It is not an exhaustive list. The state licenses day-care providers according to the number of children served: over 12 children or under 12.

The following list, drawn from state sources and phone books, confines itself generally to the centers with 12 or more students.

This is not an endorsement list. McCormack's Guides does not inspect centers or in any way monitor their activities.

It is a list, as current as we could make it, to start you on your search for a day-care center.

Ask Questions

Ask plenty of questions, tour the facilities, check with other parents about the care of their children. Read a pamphlet or book on day-care centers and what to look for.

San Francisco

A and Christa Wayne DC, 135 Forest Side Ave., San Francisco, 94127. Ages: NA. Ph: (415) 759-8825.

A Child's Garden Presch., 90 Paradise Ave., San Francisco, 94131. Ages: NA. Ph: (415) 333-9306.

ABC PreSch, 426-33rd Ave., San Francisco, 94121. Ages: 3-5 yr. Ph: (415) 387-9111.

ABC's Unlimited, 6555 Geary Blvd., San Francisco, 94121. Ages: 2-5 yr. Ph: (415) 752-5533.

After School Pursuits, 2290 14th Ave., San Francisco, 94116. Ages: NA. Ph: (415) 731-5007.

Alfa Dev Ctr, 3401 Mission St., San Francisco, 94110. Ages: 0-5 yr. Ph: (415) 641-4072.

All My Children's Presch., 1995 17th Ave., San Francisco, 94116. Ages: NA. Ph: (415) 566-5740.

Alvarado After School, 625 Douglass, San Francisco, 94114. Ages: NA. Ph: (415) 285-7756.

Angela's Infant CCC, 775 7th Ave., San Francisco, 94107. Ages: NA. Ph: (415) 386-0189.

Angelina's Day Care, 649 12th Ave., San Francisco, 94118. Ages: NA. Ph: (415) 386-2077.

Au Pair Care, 1 Post St., San Francisco, 94104. Ages: NA, (800) 288-7786.

Audrey L. Smith Dev Ctr, 1050 McAllister St., San Francisco, 94115. Ages: 2-5.9 yr. Ph: (415) 346-3268.

Audrey L. Smith Dev Ctr, 1101 Masonic Ave., San Francisco, 94117. Ages: 2-5.9 yr. Ph: (415) 863-0909.

Aupair Care, 1 Post, San Francisco, 94104. Ages: NA. Ph: (415) 434-8788.

Baby Steps, 117 Lunado Wy., San Francisco, 94127. Ages: NA. Ph: (415) 239-5588.

Big City Montessori, 240 Industrial St., San Francisco, 94124. Ages: 2-6 yr. Ph: (415) 648-5777.

Binet-Montessori, 1715 Octavia St., San Francisco, 94109. Ages: 2-8 yr. Ph: (415) 567-4000.

Bippity Bop Presch., 121 Spear, San Francisco, 94105. Ages: NA. Ph: (415) 543-4595.

Caheed Infant, 1030 Oakdale Ave., San Francisco, 94124. Ages: 1 mo.-3 yr. Ph: (415) 821-1300.

California Childcare Network, 111 New Montgomery, San Francisco, 94104. Ages: NA. Ph: (415) 882-0234.

Candlelight CD Ctr, 5845 Mission St., San Francisco, 94112. Ages: 2.6-8 yr. Ph: (415) 587-1070.

Cheryl Anderson CC, 4150 Clement St., San Francisco, 94121. Ages: NA. Ph: (415) 751-8511.

Children & Language, 35 San Juan Ave. #A, San Francisco, 94112. Ages: 0-5 yr. Ph: (415) 469-0111.

Children's Comm. Ctr. for the Creative Arts, 1351 Haight St. #205, San Francisco, 94117.

Ages: NA. Ph: (415) 431-1189.

Children's Day School, 333 Dolores St., San Francisco, 94110. Ages: 2-5 yr. Ph: (415) 861-5432.

Chinatown Comm. Children's Ctr., 979 Clay St., San Francisco, 94108. Ages: NA. Ph: (415) 986-2528.

Chinatown-N. Beach YWCA, 965 Clay St., San Francisco, 94108. Ages: 5-12 yr. Ph: (415) 397-6883.

City Kids Presch. & DC, 1219 15th Ave., San Francisco, 94122. Ages: NA. Ph: (415) 759-6898.

Civic CCC, 505 Van Ness, San Francisco, 94110. Ages: NA. Ph: (415) 626-4880.

Cleo Wallace CDC, 71 Turner Terrace, San Francisco, 94107. Ages: NA. Ph: (415) 282-6300.

Coo Child Care, 777 7th Ave., San Francisco, 94118. Ages: NA. Ph: (415) 386-0184.

Cornerstone Sch00l, 1939 Lawton St., San Francisco, 94122. Ages: 2-6 yr. Ph: (415) 661-2251.

Cross Cultural Fam Ctr, 1347 Pierce, San Francisco, 94115. Ages: NA. Ph: (415) 921-7019.

Cross Cultural Fam Ctr, 1672 Eddy St., San Francisco, 94115. Ages: 2-6 yr. Ph: (415) 567-9126, or 921-7019 office.

Cross Cultural Fam Ctr, 1901 O'Farrell, San Francisco, 94115. Ages: 2-5 yr. Ph: (415) 921-7019.

Cross Cultural Fam Ctr, 741-30th Ave., San Francisco, 94121. Ages: 2-6 yr. Ph: (415) 668-6539.

Cross Cultural Fam Ctr, 750-31st Ave., San Francisco, 94121. Ages: 2-6 yr. Ph: (415) 668-7863.

Cross Cultural Fam Ctr, 80 Olive St., San Francisco, 94109. Ages: 2-5 yr. Ph: (415) 775-4046.

Davis and Jenkins CCC, 670 Head, San Francisco, 94132. Ages: NA. Ph: (415) 586-0948.

Discoverland of SF, 7777 Geary Blvd., San Francisco, 94121. Ages: 3-6 yr. Ph: (415) 752-0107.

Early Years Acad, 500 Raymond Ave., San Francisco, 94134. Ages: 2-5 yr. Ph: (415) 333-1450.

Faith Hope Pre-K CC, 495 Cambridge, San Francisco, 94134. Ages: NA. Ph: (415) 239-0511.

First Start DC, 243 Broad, San Francisco, 94112. Ages: NA. Ph: (415) 337-6721.

Friends of St. Francis Ctr, 50 Belcher St., San Francisco, 94114. Ages: 2-5.9 yr. Ph: (415) 861-1818.

Friends of Wren, 1227 Divisadero, San Francisco, 94115. Ages: NA. Ph: (415) 992-2602.

Grace Infant Ctr, 3201 Ulloa St., San Francisco, 94116. Ages: 2 mo.-2 yr. Ph: (415) 681-6606.

Happy Day PreSch, 809 Taraval St., San Francisco, 94116. Ages: 2.5-5 yr. Ph: (415) 564-7999.

Hawthorne CCC, 95 Hawthorne, San Francisco, 94105. Ages: NA. Ph: (415) 882-9157.

Holy Family, 220 Montgomery, San Francisco, 94103. Ages: 2-7 yr. Ph: (415) 398-0708.

Ideal Day Care, 1523 La Salle, San Francisco, 94124. Ages: NA. Ph: (415) 821-7269.

Infant Care State Presch. Ctr., 799 Pacific, San Francisco, 94133. Ages: NA. Ph: (415) 982-6522.

Infant Dev Ctr Presch. Prgm., 1050 Kirkham St., San Francisco, 94122. Ages: 2-5.5 yr. Ph: (415) 664-3005.

Intergenerational CDC, 1601 Lane, San Francisco, 94124. Ages: NA. Ph: (415) 822-1086.

Irene Stojkova DC, 1030 Vicente, San Francisco, 94116. Ages: NA. Ph: (415) 569-9106.

Jewish CC of SF, 3200 California, San Francisco, 94118. Ages: NA. Ph: (415) 346-6040.

Joyful Time Learning Ctr., 250 4th Ave., San Francisco, 94103. Ages: NA. Ph: (415) 387-8145.

Keep, 1570 31st Ave., San Francisco, 94122. Ages: NA. Ph: (415) 681-6067.

Keep, 220 Middlefield Dr., San Francisco, 94132. Ages: NA. Ph: (415) 664-8685.

Kiddie Korner, 2140 Pierce St., San Francisco, 94115. Ages: 2-5 yr. Ph: (415) 921-2116.

Kiddieland Play Nursery, 637 Peralta Ave., San Francisco, 94110. Ages: 2.9-6 yr. Ph: (415) 824-7061.

Kids and Toddlers Nursery Sch., 156 Noe, San Francisco, 94114. Ages: NA. Ph: (415) 664-5437.

Kids Kollege PreSch, 3939 Lawton St., San Francisco, 94122. Ages: 2-6 yr. Ph: (415) 753-1869.

Kids R First DC & Presch, 1655 46th Ave., San Francisco, 94122. Ages: NA. Ph: (415) 664-5437.

Kinderhaven, 475 Embarcadero, San Francisco, 94107. Ages: NA. Ph: (415) 391-3639.

Learning Bridge, 593-4th Ave., San Francisco, 94118. Ages: 2-6 yr. Ph: (415) 387-0412.

Little Bear School, 5300 Diamond Heights Blvd., San Francisco, 94131. Ages: NA. Ph: (415) 564-2327.

Little People's Workshop, 416 Cortland, San Francisco, 94110. Ages: NA. Ph: (415) 648-5156.

Little Rascals, 39 Whitney, San Francisco, 94131. Ages: NA. Ph: (415) 821-9070.

Little Star, 2540 Taraval St., San Francisco, 94116. Ages: 2.5-6 yr. Ph: (415) 753-3442.

Littlest Angel Prep PreSch, 32 Broad St., San Francisco, 94112. Ages: 3-5 yr. Ph: (415) 584-5437.

Love & Learn Nursery, 1419 Howard St., San Francisco, 94103. Ages: 2.5-5 yr. Ph: (415) 863-4059.

Lutheran Church of Our Savior, 1011 Garfield St., San Francisco, 94132. Ages: 2.5-5.9 yr. Ph: (415) 587-1424.

M'Eadd Preparatory DC, 1783 Revere Ave., San Francisco, 94124. Ages: NA. Ph: (415) 822-9686.

Maria Montessori, 678 Portola Dr., San Francisco, 94127. Ages: 2-4.6 yr. Ph: (415) 731-8188.

Marin Day, 2 Harrison, San Francisco, 94105. Ages: NA. Ph: (415) 777-9696.

Marin Day, 2266 California, San Francisco, 94115. Ages: 2-6 yr. Ph: (415) 775-2211.

Marsha's Family Day Care, 656 Banks, San Francisco, 94110. Ages: NA. Ph: (415) 647-1445.

Minds in Motion, 939 Irving, San Francisco, 94122. Ages: NA. Ph: (415) 731-9705.

Misrae Infant Toddler Ctr., 129 Hugo, San Francisco, 94122. Ages: NA. Ph: (415) 753-5212.

Mission CCC, 754 14th, San Francisco, 94103. Ages: NA. Ph: (415) 863-2228.

Montessori Big City Sch., 240 Industrial, San Francisco, 94124. Ages: NA. Ph: (415) 648-5777.

Montessori Children's Ctr, 755 Font Blvd., San Francisco, 94132. Ages: 2-6 yr. Ph: (415) 333-4410.

Montessori Children's House, 25 Lake St., San Francisco, 94118. Ages: 2-5.9 yr. Ph: (415) 922-9235.

Montessori House of Children, 1187 Franklin St., San Francisco, 94109. Ages: 2-6 yr. Ph: (415) 441-7691.

Mother Goose, 334-28th Ave., San Francisco, 94121. Ages: 2-8 yr. Ph: (415) 221-6133.

Multicultural PreSch, 380-A-21st Ave., San Francisco, 94121. Ages: 2.6-6 yr. Ph: (415) 386-5100.

Multicultural PreSch II, 3300 Balboa St., San Francisco, 94121. Ages: 2.6-6 yr. Ph: (415) 668-3300.

Munchkinland Childcare & Tutoring, 58 Danton, San Francisco, 94112. Ages: NA. Ph: (415) 585-1158.

Nelson Claudia, 201 Downey, San Francisco, 94117. Ages: NA. Ph: (415) 731-7724.

New Liberation DC Ctr, 1100 Divisadero St., San Francisco, 94115. Ages: 2-5 yr. Ph: (415) 567-5924.

Nihonmachi Little Friends, 1700 Sutter St., San Francisco, 94115. Ages: 4.9-11 yr. Ph: (415) 346-5064.

Nihonmachi Little Friends, 1830 Sutter St., San Francisco, 94115. Ages: 2.5-5 yr. Ph: (415) 922-4060.

Nihonmachi Little Friends, 2031 Bush St., San Francisco, 94115. Ages: 2-5 yr. Ph: (415) 922-8898.

One Fifty Parker Ave. Nursery, 150 Parker Ave., San Francisco, 94118. Ages: 2.6-6 yr. Ph: (415) 221-0294.

Pacific Primary, 1500 Grove St., San Francisco, 94117. Ages: 2.5-5.9 yr. Ph: (415) 346-0906.

Park Presidio Montessori, 788-8th Ave., San

Francisco, 94118. Ages: 2-6 yr. Ph: (415) 751-2790.

Parkside Nursery, 2425-19th Ave., San Francisco, 94116. Ages: 2-6 yr. Ph: (415) 564-6250.

Pepper Tree Family DC, 4333 23rd., San Francisco, 94114. Ages: NA. Ph: (415) 282-5650.

Potrero Hill Head Start, 824 Carolina St., San Francisco, 94107. Ages: 3-5 yr. Ph: (415) 821-6639.

Rainbow Mission Possible, 1887 Palou Ave., San Francisco, 94124. Ages: NA. Ph: (415) 821-4335.

Rainbow Montessori, 24th & Taraval, San Francisco, 94116. Ages: NA. Ph: (415) 661-9100.

Rainbow Westside Presch., 916 Laguna, San Francisco, 94115. Ages: NA. Ph: (415) 921-5329.

Royal Montessori, 1550 Eddy, San Francisco, 94115. Ages: NA. Ph: (415) 292-7970.

San Francisco School, 300 Gaven, San Francisco, 94134. Ages: 2.5-6 yr. Ph: (415) 239-5065.

Seacliff DC, 339 26th Ave., San Francisco, 94121. Ages: NA. Ph: (415) 666-3559.

Second Comm CC Ctr, 500 Clarendon Ave., San Francisco, 94131. Ages: 5-10 yr. Ph: (415) 759-1897.

SF Jewish Comm Ctr, 3200 California St., San Francisco, 94118. Ages: 2-5.6 yr. Ph: (415) 346-6040, main office.

SF Jewish Comm Ctr, 325 Arguello Blvd., San Francisco, 94118. Ages: 2-6 yr. Ph: (415) 386-4999.

SFUSD-Argonne Ctr, 750-16th Ave., San Francisco, 94118. Ages: 2-5 yr. Ph: (415) 750-8494.

SFUSD-Bret Harte Ctr, 950 Hollister Ave., San Francisco, 94124. Ages: 2-12 yr. Ph: (415) 330-1545.

SFUSD-Bryant Ctr, 1060 York St., San Francisco, 94110. Ages: 2-14 yr. Ph: (415) 695-5784.

SFUSD-Burnett Ctr, 1520 Oakdale Ave., San Francisco, 94124. Ages: 2-12 yr. Ph: (415) 695-5660.

SFUSD-Commodore Stockton Ctr, 949 Washington St., San Francisco, 94108. Ages: 2.9-11 yr. Ph: (415) 291-7932.

SFUSD-Dr. Charles R. Drew Ctr, 50 Pomona St., San Francisco, 94124. Ages: 2-14 yr. Ph: (415) 330-1546.

SFUSD-Dr. William Cobb Ctr, 2725 California St., San Francisco, 94115. Ages: 2-14 yr. Ph: (415) 749-3544.

SFUSD-Excelsior Ctr, 125 Excelsior Ave., San Francisco, 94112. Ages: 2 yr. & up. Ph: (415) 469-4753.

SFUSD-F.E.C., 824 Harrison St., San Francisco, 94107. Ages: 2.8-9 yr. Ph: (415) 543-9636.

SFUSD-Florence Martin Ctr, 1155 Page St., San Francisco, 94117. Ages: 2-5 yr. Ph: (415) 241-6333.

SFUSD-Frank McCoppin Ctr, 651-6th Ave., San Francisco, 94118. Ages: 2-14 yr. Ph: (415) 750-8495.

SFUSD-Geary Ctr, 20 Cook St., San Francisco, 94118. Ages: 2-12 yr. Ph: (415) 750-8526.

SFUSD-Grattan Ctr, 165 Grattan St., San Francisco, 94117. Ages: 2-14 yr. Ph: (415) 759-2850.

SFUSD-Harvey Milk Ctr., 20 Cook St., San Francisco, 94118. Ages: 2.9-11 yr. Ph: (415) 749-3545.

SFUSD-Jefferson Ctr, 1325-18th Ave., San Francisco, 94122. Ages: 5-12 yr. Ph: (415) 759-2795.

SFUSD-Jefferson Nursery, 1350-25th Ave., San Francisco, 94122. Ages: 2-5 yr. Ph: (415) 759-2852.

SFUSD-John McLaren Ctr, 2055 Sunnydale Ave., San Francisco, 94134. Ages: 2-12 yr. Ph: (415) 695-5347.

SFUSD-Junipero Serra, 155 Appleton St., San Francisco, 94110. Ages: 2-12 yr. Ph: (415) 285-3044.

SFUSD-Kate Kennedy, 1670 Noe St., San Francisco, 94131. Ages: 2-5 yr. Ph: (415) 695-5873.

SFUSD-Las Americas Ctr, 3200-20th St., San Francisco, 94110. Ages: 2-12 yr. Ph: (415) 695-5746.

SFUSD-Leonard R. Flynn Ctr, 3125 Army St., San Francisco, 94110. Ages: 5-12 yr. Ph: (415) 695-5782.

SFUSD-Mission Annex, 421 Bartlett St., San Francisco, 94110. Ages: 2-5 yr. Ph: (415) 695-5844.

SFUSD-Mission Main, 2950 Mission St., San Francisco, 94110. Ages: 2-5 yr. Ph: (415) 695-5844.

SFUSD-Noriega Ctr, 1775-44th Ave., San Francisco, 94122. Ages: 2-5 yr. Ph: (415) 759-2853.

SFUSD-Potrero Terrace at Star King, 1215 Carolina Dr., San Francisco, 94107. Ages: 2-12 yr. Ph: (415) 695-5793.

SFUSD-Raphael Weill Ctr, 1501 O'Farrell, San Francisco, 94115. Ages: 2-9 yr. Ph: (415) 749-3548.

SFUSD-Redding Ctr, 1421 Pine St., San Francisco, 94109. Ages: 5-14 yr. Ph: (415) 749-3549.

SFUSD-San Miguel Ctr, 300 Seneca Ave., San Francisco, 94112. Ages: 2-12 yr. Ph: (415) 469-4756.

SFUSD-Sarah B. Cooper Ctr, 940 Filbert St., San Francisco, 94133. Ages: 2-12 yr. Ph: (415) 749-3550.

SFUSD-Sunnyside, 250 Foerester St., San Francisco, 94112. Ages: 6-12 yr. Ph: (415) 469-4758.

SFUSD-Sutro Ctr, 235-12th Ave., San Francisco, 94118. Ages: 2-12 yr. Ph: (415) 750-8524.

SFUSD-Theresa S. Mahler Ctr, 990 Church St., San Francisco, 94114. Ages: 2-6 yr. Ph: (415) 695-5871.

SFUSD-Yerba Buena Ctr, 2110 Greenwich St., San Francisco, 94123. Ages: 2-12 yr. Ph: (415) 749-3551.

SFUSD-Yoey at Bessie L. Smith, 95 Gough St., San Francisco, 94102. Ages: 2-6 yr. Ph: (415) 241-6313.

Sonshine PreSch, 3535 Balboa St., San Francisco, 94121. Ages: 2-6 yr. Ph: (415) 668-0233.

St. Francis Day Care, 610 Vallejo St., San Francisco, 94133. Ages: 2.5-5 yr. Ph: (415) 989-6626.

St. James Episcopal, 4620 California St., San Francisco, 94118. Ages: 2.5-6 yr. Ph: (415) 752-8258.

St. Johns Extension Pgm., 925 Chenery, San Francisco, 94131. Ages: NA. Ph: (415) 333-5515.

St. Nicholas DC, 5200 Diamond Heights Blvd., San Francisco, 94131. Ages: 3 mo.-6 yr. Ph: (415) 550-1536.

Sts Peter and Paul-Laura Vicuna Prep, 666 Filbert St., San Francisco, 94133. Ages: 3.9-5 yr. Ph: (415) 421-5219.

Sunset Co-op Nursery, 4245 Lawton St., San Francisco, 94122. Ages: 2-5 yr. Ph: (415) 681-7659.

Telegraph Hill Nurssery, 660 Lombard St., San Francisco, 94133. Ages: 2.6-6 yr. Ph: (415) 421-6443 .

TLC Daycare, 1115 Plymouth, San Francisco, 94112. Ages: NA. Ph: (415) 239-7745.

True Sunshine PreSch, 777 Stockton St. #201, San Francisco, 94108. Ages: 2-5 yr. Ph: (415) 956-4207.

Twelve Hugs Children's Ctr., 3786 Mission, San Francisco, 94110. Ages: NA. Ph: (415) 824-2159.

Ulloa Children's Ctr, 2650-42nd Ave., San Francisco, 94116. Ages: 5-11 yr. Ph: (415) 759-8854.

Valerie's Daycare, 1151 Fitzgerald, San Francisco, 94124. Ages: NA. Ph: (415) 822-1420.

VE & VO Establishment, 21 Stanley, San Francisco, 94132. Ages: NA. Ph: (415) 469-8115.

Visitacion Valley Comm Ctr, 50 Raymond Ave., San Francisco, 94134. Ages: 2-6 yr. Ph: (415) 467-6300.

Wah Mei School, 1400 Judah St., San Francisco, 94122. Ages: 2.6-5 yr. Ph: (415) 665-4212.

West Portal CARE, 5 Lenox Way, San Francisco, 94127. Ages: 5-10 yr. Ph: (415) 753-1113.

Whitehouse Daycare, 2055 Palou Ave., San Francisco, 94124. Ages: NA. Ph: (415) 647-8857.

Wu Yee Lok Yuen CC, 855 Sacramento St., San Francisco, 94108. Ages: 2.9-5 yr. Ph: (415) 864-8396.

WuYee CC, 117 Golden Gate Ave., San Francisco, 94102. Ages: NA. Ph: (415) 864-3396.

YMCA- Chinatown, 855 Sacramento, San Francisco, 94108. Ages: 5-12 yr. Ph: (415) 982-4412.

YMCA- Hawthorne, 825 Shotwell St., San Francisco, 94110. Ages: 5-12 yr. Ph: (415) 282-0953.

YMCA-Buchanan, 1530 Buchanan St., San Francisco, 94115. Ages: 2.5-12 yr. Ph: (415) 931-9622.

YMCA-Douglas School, 4235 19th Street, San Francisco, 94114. Ages: 5-12 yrs. Ph: (415) 647-7108.

YMCA-John Swett, 727 Golden Gate Ave., San Francisco, 94102. Ages: 5-12 yr. Ph: (415) 255-4668.

YMCA-Mission, 4080 Mission St., San Francisco, 94112. Ages: 5-12 yr. Ph: (415) 586-6900.

YMCA-Mission San Francisco, 4235-19th St., San Francisco, 94114. Ages: 6-12 yr. Ph: (415) 775-9622.

YMCA-Richmond Lafayette, 4545 Anza St., San Francisco, 94118. Ages: 4.9-12 yr. Ph: (415) 668-0945.

YMCA-Richmond PreSch, 360-18th Ave., San Francisco, 94121. Ages: 2-5 yr. Ph: (415) 668-2060.

YMCA-Richmond Star of the Sea, 345-8th Ave., San Francisco, 94121. Ages: 5-12 yr. Ph: (415) 751-6796.

YMCA-Sherman, 1651 Union St., San Francisco, 94123. Ages: 5-12 yr. Ph: (415) 563-7814.

YMCA-Stonestown, 1740 Sloat Blvd., San Francisco, 94132. Ages: 2.6-5 yr. Ph: (415) 661-1692.

YMCA-Stonestown, 333 Eucalyptus Dr., San Francisco, 94132. Ages: 2-5 yr. Ph: (415) 759-9622.

YMCA-Stonestown, 400 Sargent St., San Francisco, 94132. Ages: 5-12 yr. Ph: (415) 584-7328.

YMCA-Stonestown, 50 Darien Way, San Francisco, 94127. Ages: 5-12 yr. Ph: (415) 664-9622.

YMCA-Stonestown, Robert Louis Stevenson, 2051-34th Ave., San Francisco, 94116. Ages: 5-12 yr. Ph: (415) 759-9662.

Yook Yau Ji Ga, 925 Stockton St., San Francisco, 94108. Ages: 2.5-5 yr. Ph: (415) 397-1468.

YWCA Chinatown-North Beach, 950 Powell St., San Francisco, 94108. Ages: 5-12 yr. Ph: (415) 397-6886.

YWCA Mission, 1855 Folsom St., San Francisco, 94103. Ages: 2.9-5 yr. Ph: (415) 552-6790.

YWCA Residence Club, 950 Powell St., San Francisco, 94109. Ages: 3-5 yr. Ph: (415) 397-6886.

San Mateo County
Atherton

Lion's Den, 299 Alameda de Las Pulgas, Atherton, 94063. Ages: NA. Ph: (415) 854-2946.

Selby Lane Ctr, 170 Selby Lane, Atherton, 94063. Ages: 5-12 yr. Ph: (415) 368-5506.

Sequoia YMCA-Encinal School, 195 Encinal

Ave., Atherton, 94025. Ages: 5-12 yr. Ph: (415) 368-4168.

Belmont

After School-Central, 525 Middle Road, Belmont, 94002. Ages: NA. Ph: (415) 593-4229.

Curiosity Corner, 3100 St. James Rd., Belmont, 94002. Ages: 5-12 yr. Ph: (415) 592-7664.

Extension Care Center, 1000 Alameda De Las Pulgas, Belmont, 94002. Ages: NA. Ph: (415) 591-6564.

Hugh G. Fraser, 1342 6th Ave., Belmont, 94002. Ages: NA. Ph: (415) 592-1874.

Julia Chase PreSch, 2525 Buena Vista Ave., Belmont, 94002. Ages: Call School. Ph: (415) 593-8340.

Brisbane

Camp Fire Child Care, 500 San Bruno Ave., Brisbane, 94005. Ages: NA. Ph: (415) 468-6628.

Burlingame

Burglingame Montessori, 2109 Broadway, Burlingame, 94010. Ages: NA. Ph: (415) 342-445.

Excursions in Learning, 700 Peninsula Ave., Burlingame, 94010. Ages: NA. Ph: (415) 344-5707.

Palcare, 945 California Dr., Burlingame, 94010. Ages: NA. Ph: (415) 340-1289.

Peninsula Montessori, 1151A Vancouver Ave., Burlingame, 94010. Ages: 2.5-6 yr. Ph: (415) 343-8124.

Portola DC Ctr, 2385 Trousdale Dr., Burlingame, 94010. Ages: NA. Ph: (415) 692-5096.

Portola DC Ctr, 701 Paloma Ave., Burlingame, 94010. Ages: 4.9-11 yr. Ph: (415) 375-0688.

Small World, 1801 Devereaux, Burlingame, 94010. Ages: NA. Ph: (415) 259-9910.

Stepping Stone, 1421 Palm Ave., Burlingame, 94010. Ages: 2-5 yr. Ph: (415) 343-3362.

United Methodist Co-op, 1443 Howard, Burlingame, 94010. Ages: 2-6 yr. Ph: (415) 347-6432.

YMCA-Lincoln, 1801 Devereaux Dr., Burlingame, 94010. Ages: 5-12 yr. Ph: (415) 340-9622.

Daly City

Allen R & G Family Day Care, 25 Camelot Ct., Daly City, 94015. Ages: NA. Ph: (415) 878-1110.

Bayshore CC Services, 377-87th St., Daly City, 94015. Ages: 3-6 yr. Ph: (415) 467-3997.

Camp Fire Kids Club, 151 Victoria, Daly City, 94015. Ages: NA. Ph: (415) 878-3224.

Children's Paradise Learning Ctr, 1020 Sullivan Ave., Daly City, 94015. Ages: 2.5-5 yr. Ph: (415) 991-4205.

Karrie Care, 550 Clarinada Ave., Daly City, 94015. Ages: NA. Ph: (415) 991-2483.

Latchkey Alternative Ctr, 1200 Skyline Dr., Daly City, 94015. Ages: 3-12 yr. Ph: (415) 755-8574.

Maye Family Daycare, 18 Longview Dr., Daly City, 94015. Ages: NA. Ph: (415) 755-8937.

Noah's Ark, 1595 Edgeworth Ave., Daly City, 94015. Ages: 2-6 yr. Ph: (415) 991-9222.

Rainbow School, Southgate & Elmwood, Daly City, 94015. Ages: 2.5-7 yr. Ph: (415) 994-3414.

Young World Learning Ctr, 699 Serramonte Blvd., Daly City, 94015. Ages: 2-5 yr. Ph: (415) 994-6599.

East Palo Alto

A Special Place, 2201 University, East Palo Alto, 94303. Ages: NA. Ph: (415) 326-6741.

Children's Preservation Network, 2450 Ralmar Ave., East Palo Alto, 94303. Ages: NA. Ph: (415) 323-2919.

Creative Adventures Learning Ctr, 321 Bell St., East Palo Alto, 94303. Ages: 5-12 yr. Ph: (415) 964-5022.

Creative Montessori, 1425 Bay Rd., East Palo Alto, 94303. Ages: 2-7 yr. Ph: (415) 325-9543.

Daniels DC Ctr, 2589 Gloria Way, East Palo Alto, 94303. Ages: 2-5 yr. Ph: (415) 325-4746.

Faye's Daycare, 159 Verbena Dr., East Palo Alto, 94303. Ages: NA. Ph: (415) 327-0851.

Little One's Daycare, 1043 Bradley Way, East Palo Alto, 94303. Ages: NA. Ph: (415) 473-0901.

McGowain, 1590 Ursula Way, East Palo Alto, 94303. Ages: NA. Ph: (415) 853-9891.

Ragland Day Care, 8 Camelia Ct., East Palo Alto, 94303. Ages: . Ph: (415) 853-1153.

Strickly for Kids, 2274 Pulgas Ave., East Palo Alto, 94303. Ages: NA. Ph: (415) 324-4391.

Woodlands Preschool, 1767 Woodland Ave., East Palo Alto, 94303. Ages: . Ph: (415) 322-8648.

Foster City

Foster City Children's Ctr, 1130 Balclutha Dr., Foster City, 94404. Ages: 2-6 yr. Ph: (415) 341-2041.

Kids Connection, 1970 Beach Park, Foster City, 94404. Ages: 2-9 yr. Ph: (415) 578-9696.

Kindercare, 1006 Metro Center Blvd., Foster City, 94404. Ages: 0-12 yr. Ph: (415) 573-6023.

Resource Planning Associates, 1288 E. Hillsdale, Foster City, 94404. Ages: NA. Ph: (415) 341-8233.

Half Moon Bay

Buena Vida Learning Ctr, 490 Miramontes St., Half Moon Bay, 94019. Ages: 5-12 yr. Ph: (415) 726-7412.

Coastside Center, Church & Correas sts., Half Moon Bay, 94019. Ages: 1-36 mo. Ph: (415) 726-7416.

Half Moon Bay Children's Ctr, 777 Miramontes St., Half Moon Bay, 94019. Ages: 5-6 yr. Ph: (415) 726-3273.

Holy Family Children's Ctr, 1590 S. Cabrillo Hiwy., Half Moon Bay, 94019. Ages: 2-6 yr. Ph: (415) 726-0506.

Hillsborough

Mateo Camps, 545 Eucalyptus Ave., Hillsborough, 94010. Ages: 5-12 yr. Ph: (415) 347-2737.

Menlo Park

Belle Haven CD Ctr, 100 Terminal Ave., Menlo Park, 94025. Ages: 2-6 yr. Ph: (415) 322-0158.

Half Pint Day Care, 510 Central Ave., Menlo Park, 94025. Ages: NA. Ph: (415) 328-7130.

Hansel & Gretel, 2050 Gordon Ave., Menlo Park, 94025. Ages: 2-6 yr. Ph: (415) 854-1894.

Menlo Children's Ctr, 1060 Middle Ave., Menlo Park, 94025. Ages: 2 mo.-6 yr. Ph: (415) 323-0678.

Mom's Daycare, 1036 Menlo Oaks Dr., Menlo Park, 94025. Ages: NA. Ph: (415) 325-3136.

Nativity Day Care, 1250 Laurel, Menlo Park, 94025. Ages: NA, 415321-7198, 321-7198.

Next Generation Home Day Care, 1101 Del Norte Ave., Menlo Park, 94025. Ages: NA. Ph: (415) 325-0808.

Roberts Coleman Ave. School, 641 Coleman Ave., Menlo Park, 94025. Ages: 2.6-6 yr. Ph: (415) 322-3535.

University Heights Children's Ctr, 2066 Avy Ave., Menlo Park, 94025. Ages: 2-6 yr. Ph: (415) 854-6993.

Millbrae

Hoover Children's Ctr, One Alp Way, Millbrae, 94030. Ages: 2-6 yr. Ph: (415) 697-9444.

Millbrae Montessori, 797 Santa Margarita Ave., Millbrae, 94030. Ages: 2-6 yr. Ph: (415) 588-2229.

Millbrae Nursery, 86 Center St., Millbrae, 94030. Ages: 2-6 yr. Ph: (415) 589-3028.

Peace of Mind, 1 Alp Way, Millbrae, 94030. Ages: 2 mo.- 5 yr. Ph: (415) 697-2229.

Portola DC Ctr, 1101 Helen Dr., Millbrae, 94030. Ages: NA. Ph: (415) 872-3322.

Small World, 401 Ludeman Ln., Millbrae, 94030. Ages: NA. Ph: (415) 873-4864.

Small World, 817 Murchinson, Millbrae, 94030. Ages: NA. Ph: (415) 259-7749.

These Magic Times, 450 Chadbourne Ave., Millbrae, 94030. Ages: 2-6 yr. Ph: (415) 697-2648.

Montara

Farallone View Ctr, Le Conte & Kanoff Ave., Montara, 94019. Ages: 5-12 yr. Ph: (415) 728-7419.

Pacifica

Adrienne's Ctr, 1152 Peralta Rd., Pacifica, 94044. Ages: 2-6 yr. Ph: (415) 359-1129.

Adrienne's Teaching & Learning Ctr., 1496 Adobe Dr., Pacifica, 94044. Ages: 2-9 yr. Ph: (415) 359-2089.

Convention Meeting Child Care, 290 Edgewood Dr., Pacifica, 94044. Ages: NA. Ph: (415) 355-7783.

Montessori School of Linda Mar, 1666 Higgins, Pacifica, 94044. Ages: 2-6 yr. Ph: (415) 355-7272.

Pacifica Playschool, 630 Hickey Blvd., Pacifica, 94044. Ages: 2-6 yr. Ph: (415) 359-5673.

Skyline PreSch, 2450 Skyline, Pacifica, 94044.

Ages: 2-6 yr. Ph: (415) 355-9115.

Temporary Tot Tending, 290 Edgewood, Pacifica, 94044. Ages: 0-5 yr. Ph: (415) 355-7377.

Portola Valley

New Horizons, 4575 Alpine Rd., Portola Valley, 94025. Ages: 5-11 yr. Ph: (415) 948-8265.

Redwood City

Child Development, 555 Avenue Del Ora, Redwood City, 94062. Ages: NA. Ph: (415) 364-1178.

Family Service Agency Child Care, 707 Bradford, Redwood City, 94063. Ages: NA. Ph: (415) 365-2284.

Henry Ford CD Ctr, 2498 Massachusetts Ave., Redwood City, 94063. Ages: 5-12 yr. Ph: (415) 368-1138.

Hoover Children's Ctr, 303 Twin Dolphin Dr., Redwood City, 94063. Ages: 2-6 yr. Ph: (415) 593-6824.

Messiah Lutheran, 1835 Valota Rd., Redwood City, 94061. Ages: 2.9-8 yr. Ph: (415) 369-5201.

Montessori House of Children-The Redwood International, 2000 Woodside Dr., Redwood City, 94062. Ages: NA. Ph: (415) 386-9859.

Neighborhood Kids' Corner, Clifford School, Redwood City, 94070. Ages: 4.9-12 yr. Ph: (415) 367-7034.

Neighborhood Kids' Corner, Roy Cloud School, Redwood City, 94062. Ages: 4.9-12 yr. Ph: (415) 365-6117.

Noah's Ark, 3518 Jefferson Ave., Redwood City, 94063. Ages: 2-6 yr. Ph: (415) 366-1414.

Redeemer Lutheran, 452 Grand St., Redwood City, 94062. Ages: 2.9-6 yr. Ph: (415) 366-3466.

Sequoia Ctr, 1234 Brewster Ave., Redwood City, 94062. Ages: 0-2 yr. Ph: (415) 369-5277.

Sequoia YMCA-Hawes Day Care, 909 Roosevelt, Redwood City, 94062. Ages: . Ph: (415) 365-3673.

St. Matthias DC Ctr, 533 Canyon Rd., Redwood City, 94062. Ages: 2-6 yr. Ph: (415) 367-1320.

Sunshine Garden Childcare, 3231 Fair Oaks Ave., Redwood City, 94063. Ages: NA. Ph: (415) 364-3637.

Tami's Family Day Care, 303 Redwood Ave., Redwood City, 94061. Ages: NA. Ph: (415) 366-5290.

Thumbelina Nursery, 20 Hogan St., Redwood City, 94061. Ages: 2-7 yr. Ph: (415) 364-5165.

TLC Club, 1172 McKinley, Redwood City, 94061. Ages: NA. Ph: (415) 366-3799.

San Bruno

Crayon College, 300 Piedmont Ave., San Bruno, 94066. Ages: 2-6 yr. Ph: (415) 588-4197.

Family Child Dev. Center, 525 Elm Ave., San Bruno, 94066. Ages: NA. Ph: (415) 588-8708.

Happy Hall Schools, 233 Santa Inez Ave., San Bruno, 94066. Ages: NA. Ph: (415) 583-7370.

Highlands Christian School, Skyline Blvd., San Bruno, 94066. Ages: NA. Ph: (415) 873-4090.

Highlands PreSch, 1900 Monterey Dr., San Bruno, 94066. Ages: 2-6 yr. Ph: (415) 873-4090.
Hoover Children's Ctr, 2396 Evergreen Dr., San Bruno, 94066. Ages: 2-6 yr. Ph: (415) 871-5025.
Latchkey Alternative Ctr, 400 3rd Ave., San Bruno, 94066. Ages: 3-12 yr. Ph: (415) 589-2863.
Portola DC Ctr, 300 Amador Dr., San Bruno, 94066. Ages: 18 mo.-12 yr. Ph: (415) 871-6934.
Small World, 200 Santa Helena, San Bruno, 94066. Ages: NA. Ph: (415) 583-2382.
So. San Francisco, 2551 St. Cloud Dr., San Bruno, 94066. Ages: 5-12 yr. Ph: (415) 873-3811.
Twelve Hugs Children Center, 3501 College Dr., San Bruno, 94066. Ages: NA. Ph: (415) 359-5092.
YMCA Peninsula-Crestmoor, 300 Piedmont, San Bruno, 94066. Ages: 5-12 yr. Ph: (415) 873-3273.

San Carlos

After School, Brittan Acres School #15, San Carlos, 94070. Ages: 5-11 yr. Ph: (415) 591-4599.
After School, White Oak School #1, San Carlos, 94070. Ages: 5-10 yr. Ph: (415) 591-3515.
After School-Arundel, Arundel & Phelps #15, San Carlos, 94070. Ages: 5-11 yr. Ph: (415) 593-0707.
Children's Place, 1336 Arroyo Ave., San Carlos, 94070. Ages: 2-5 yr. Ph: (415) 595-1910.
Creative Children's Day Care, 701 Terrace Rd., San Carlos, 94070. Ages: NA. Ph: (415) 365-5445.
Discovery Montessori, 2757 Melendy Dr., San Carlos, 94070. Ages: 2-12 yr. Ph: (415) 570-5038.
Edison Montessori, Dartmouth at San Carlos Ave., San Carlos, 94070. Ages: 2-5 yr. Ph: (415) 592-4828.
Kindercourt Academy, 1225 Greenwood, San Carlos, 94402. Ages: 3-6 yr. Ph: (415) 591-4882.
Kindercourt Ctr, 1025 Laurel St., San Carlos, 94070. Ages: 0-6 yr. Ph: (415) 592-7980.

San Carlos Ctr, 750 Dartmouth Ave., San Carlos, 94070. Ages: 0-36 mo. Ph: (415) 594-0670.

San Mateo

Child Care Centers-Cal, 1777 Borel Pl., San Mateo, 94402. Ages: NA. Ph: (415) 345-7715.
Crystal Springs Early Childhood Ctr, 2145 Bunker Hill Dr., San Mateo, 94402. Ages: 2-6 yr. Ph: (415) 572-1110.
Discovery Montessori, 1001 Bermuda Dr., San Mateo, 94403. Ages: 2-6 yr. Ph: (415) 570-5038.
Family Child Dev. Center, 225 Tilton Ave., San Mateo, 94401. Ages: NA. Ph: (415) 347-3177.
Family Service Agency Child Care, 225 Tilton Ave., San Mateo, 94401. Ages: NA. Ph: (415) 347-7177.
Highland Montessori, 614 Highland Ave., San Mateo, 94401. Ages: 2-6 yr. Ph: (415) 347-6450.
Hoover Children's Ctr, 1001 Bermuda Dr., San Mateo, 94403. Ages: 2-6 yr. Ph: (415) 574-7001.
Hoover Children's Ctr, 42nd Ave., San Mateo, 94401. Ages: 2-6 yr. Ph: (415) 341-0641.
Hoover-Knolls Children's Ctr, 525-42nd Ave., San Mateo, 94403. Ages: 2-6 yr. Ph: (415) 341-0641.
Hope Lutheran PreSch, 600 W. 42nd Ave., San Mateo, 94403. Ages: 2.9-6 yr. Ph: (415) 345-8438.
Intercommunal Survival School, 713 Second Ave., San Mateo, 94401. Ages: 2.5-6 yr. Ph: (415) 347-0463.
Kindercourt #2, 211 So. Delaware, San Mateo, 94402. Ages: 0-5.9 yr. Ph: (415) 344-6612.
Neighborhood Montessori, 27 10th Ave., San Mateo, 94401. Ages: NA, (415) 321-7198, 343-8482.
Peninsula Jewish Comm, 1700 Alameda de Las Pulgas, San Mateo, 94402. Ages: 18 mo.- 6 yr. Ph: (415) 341-7701 or 349-4911.
Peter Pan, 1717 Gum St., San Mateo, 94402. Ages: 2-6 yr. Ph: (415) 341-6811.
Sandra's Wee Care, 1690 Taylor, San Mateo, 94402. Ages: . Ph: (415) 570-4367.

For Additional Reading ...

Things to Do with Kids, Bike Trails, Hikes, Trips, Tours, Restaurants, Gardens, Real Estate ...

For more on Northern California see the Book List and order blank on the pages at the end of this guide

Schnurpfeil's CC, 319 E. Santa Inez, San Mateo, 94402. Ages: 2-6 yr. Ph: (415) 347-8510.
Temporary Tot Tending, 525-42nd, San Mateo, 94402. Ages: 1 mo.-5 yr. Ph: (415) 355-7377.
YMCA-Baywood, 600 Alameda de Las Pulgas, San Mateo, 94401. Ages: 5-11 yr. Ph: (415) 343-8611.
YMCA-Fiesta Garden, 1001 Bermuda, San Mateo, 94401. Ages: 5-11 yr. Ph: (415) 349-2251.
YMCA-Laurel, 316-36th Ave., San Mateo, 94403. Ages: 5-12 yr. Ph: (415) 571-7764.

South San Francisco

Buri Buri PreSch, 115 El Campo Dr., South San Francisco, 94080. Ages: 2-6 yr. Ph: (415) 952-9346.
Camp Fire Child Care, 1400 Hillsdale Blvd., South San Francisco, 94080. Ages: NA. Ph: (415) 583-5045.
Camp Fire Kids Club, 1200 Miller Ave., South San Francisco, 94080. Ages: 5-10 yr. Ph: (415) 872-1152.
Eskridge Ctr, 753 Del Monte Ave., South San Francisco, 94080. Ages: 0-6 yr. Ph: (415) 589-5683.

Friends to Parents, 375 El Dorado Way, South San Francisco, 94080. Ages: 0-4.9 yr. Ph: (415) 588-8212.
Good News Chapel Ctr, 205 W. Orange Ave., South San Francisco, 94080. Ages: 2-10 yr. Ph: (415) 589-4454.
Greens Tender Loving Care, 2455 Donegal Ave., South San Francisco, 94080. Ages: NA. Ph: (415) 737-0978.
Hillside Nursery, 1415 Hillside Blvd., South San Francisco, 94080. Ages: 2.6-9 yr. Ph: (415) 583-6854.
Leo J. Ryan Intergenerational Child Care, 1200 Miller Ave., South San Francisco, 94080. Ages: NA. Ph: (415) 952-6848.
R.W. Drake Ctr, 609 Southwood Dr., South San Francisco, 94080. Ages: 2-8 yr. Ph: (415) 871-6833.
Temporary Tot Tending, 350 Dolores Way, South San Francisco, 94080. Ages: 2-6 yr. Ph: (415) 355-7377.

Woodside

Woodside School, 3195 Woodside Rd., Woodside, 94062. Ages: 5-12 yr. Ph: (415) 851-8187.

11/Hospitals & Health Services

Insurance Q & A, Directory of Major Hospitals

GOOD HEALTH CARE. You want it. Where, how, do you get it? In the next few years, health care in this country will be radically changed. Anticipating what may be coming, and squeezed by costs and new technology, hospital and medical insurance plans are already making sweeping changes. Yet much of the old system remains in place.

This chapter will give you an overview of Northern California health care and although it won't answer all your questions — too complex a business for that — we hope that it will point you in the right directions.

For most people, health care is twined with insurance, in systems that are called "managed care." But many individuals, for a variety of reasons, do not have insurance.

This is a good place to start: with nothing, all options open. Let's use as our seeker for the best of all health care worlds — on a tight budget — a young woman, married, one child. Her choices:

No Insurance—Cash Care

The woman is self-employed or works at a small business that doesn't offer health benefits. She comes down with the flu.

When she goes into the doctor's office, she will be asked by the receptionist, how do you intend to pay? With no insurance, she pays cash (or credit card), usually right there.

She takes her prescription, goes to the pharmacy and pays full cost.

If her child or husband get sick and needs to see a doctor, the same procedure holds. Also the same for treatment of a serious illness, to secure X-rays or hospitalization. It's a cash system.

Population by Age Groups in San Francisco & San Mateo County

City or Area	≤5	5-18	19-29	30-54	55+
San Francisco	5,744	14,893	14,135	27,691	16,576
Atherton	352	1,053	982	2,481	2,230
Belmont	1,430	2,836	4,481	9,963	5,206
Brisbane	184	352	415	1,455	522
Broadmoor	245	631	546	1,336	835
Burlingame	1,455	2,932	4,554	10,162	7,435
Colma	102	178	196	417	199
Daly City	6,555	15,580	18,023	32,924	17,960
East Palo Alto	2,592	5,107	5,356	7,204	2,797
El Granada	367	815	554	2,116	526
Emerald Lake Hills	272	481	361	1,566	620
Foster City	1,530	4,427	5,042	12,560	4,470
Half Moon Bay	638	1,511	1,360	3,783	1,492
Highlands	126	492	279	1,018	684
Hillsborough	480	1,885	976	3,870	3,304
Menlo Park	1,828	3,459	4,342	10,662	7,545
Millbrae	1,075	2,906	2,954	6,893	6,345
Montara	224	452	275	1,312	266
Moss Beach	268	531	345	1,463	373
North Fair Oaks	1,431	2,776	3,384	4,524	1,554
Pacifica	2,937	6,381	6,386	15,618	5,862
Portola Valley	223	574	366	1,646	1,348
Redwood City	5,200	9,366	13,390	25,003	12,404
San Bruno	2,629	5,841	7,738	14,941	8,449
San Carlos	1,623	3,352	3,432	10,952	6,579
San Mateo	5,265	10,817	15,117	31,772	21,651
So. San Francisco	4,058	9,056	9,861	19,194	11,446
West Menlo Park	244	461	512	1,567	1,155
Woodside	272	719	505	2,122	1,366
Remainder	1,188	2,902	2,675	8,819	4,291
San Mateo County Total	44,793	97,693	114,407	247,443	137,790

Source: 1990 Census.

Medi-Cal

If an illness strikes that impoverishes the family or if the woman, through job loss or simply low wages, cannot afford cash care, the county-state health system will step in.

The woman fills out papers to qualify for Medi-Cal, the name of the system (it's known elsewhere as Medicaid), and tries to find a doctor that will treat Medi-Cal patients. Many don't; they say that the paperwork is burdensome and the reimbursement low.

How to see a doctor without seeing a bill.

A lot of health plans (perhaps yours) cover only 80% of a doctor's bill. Some even less. And only after you've paid the first $100 or a lot more.

With Kaiser Permanente, one low monthly payment covers virtually all your health care. Including well-baby care, lab tests, x-rays, and much more.

For more information, visit your personnel office or give us a call. In San Francisco, (415) 512-6000. In San Mateo County, (415) 742-2097.

For over 45 years, we've seen to the health care needs of a lot of people. But without them having to see a lot of doctor bills.

KAISER PERMANENTE

Good People. Good Medicine.

If unable to find an acceptable doctor, the woman could turn to a county hospital or clinic. There she will be treated free or at very low cost.

Drawbacks-Pluses of Medi-Cal

County hospitals and clinics, in the personal experience of one of the editors — who has relatives who work at or use county facilities — have competent doctors and medical personnel. If you keep appointments sharply, often you will be seen with little wait.

If you want immediate treatment for, say, a cold, you register and you wait until an urgent-care doctor is free. If you need a specialist, often the county facility will have one on staff, or will be able to find one at a teaching hospital or other facility. You don't choose the specialist; the county physician does.

County facilities are underfunded and, often, inconveniently located — a major drawback. Some counties, lacking clinics and hospitals, contract with adjoining counties that are equipped. You have to drive some distance for treatment. The paperwork can be demanding.

County hospitals and clinics are not 100 percent free. If you have money or an adequate income, you will be billed for service. Some county hospitals run medical plans designed for people who can pay. These people can ask for a "family" doctor and receive a higher (usually more convenient) level of care.

Let's say the woman lacks money but doesn't want to hassle with a long drive and, possibly, a long wait for treatment of a minor ailment. She can sign up for Medi-Cal to cover treatment of serious illnesses, and for the colds, etc., go to a private doctor for treatment, and pay in cash, ignoring Medi-Cal.

There are many ways to skin the cat, and much depends on circumstances. For the poor and low-income, Medi-Cal is meant to be a system of last resort.

Medicare— Veterans Hospital

If our woman were elderly, she would be eligible for Medicare, the federal insurance system, which covers 80 percent, with limitations, of medical costs or allowable charges. Many people purchase supplemental insurance to bring coverage up to 100 percent (long-term illnesses requiring hospitalization may exhaust some benefits.)

If the woman were a military veteran with a service-related illness, she could seek care at a Veteran's Administration clinic or hospital.

Managed Care

This divides into two systems, Preferred Provider Organizations (PPO) and Health Maintenance Organizations (HMO). Both are popular in California and, if your employer provides health insurance, chances are almost 100 percent you will be pointed toward, or given a choice of, one or the other.

PPOs and HMOs differ among themselves. It is beyond the scope of this book to detail the differences but you should ask if coverage can be revoked or rates increased in the event of serious illness. Also, what is covered, what is not. Cosmetic surgery might not be covered. Psychiatric visits or care might be limited. Ask also how emergency or immediate care is provided.

Preferred Provider

The insurance company approaches certain doctors, clinics, medical facilities and hospitals and tells them: We will send patients to you but you must agree to our prices — a method of controlling costs — and our rules. The young woman chooses her doctor from the list, often extensive, provided by the PPO.

The physician will have practicing privileges at certain local hospitals. The young woman's child contracts pneumonia and must be hospitalized. Dr. X is affiliated with XYZ hospital, which is also signed up with the PPO plan. The child is treated at XYZ hospital.

If the woman used an "outside" doctor or hospital, she would pay extra — the amount depending on the nature of the plan. It is important to know the doctor's affiliations because you may want your hospital care at a certain institution.

Hospitals differ. A children's hospital, for instance, will specialize in children's illnesses and load up on children's medical equipment. A general hospital will have a more rounded program. For convenience, you may want the hospital closest to your home.

If you need specialized treatment, you must, to avoid extra costs, use the PPO-affiliated specialists. The doctor will often guide your choice.

Besides the basic cost for the policy, PPO insurance might charge fees, co-payments or deductibles. A fee might be $5 or $10 a visit. With co-payments, the bill, say, comes to $100. Insurance pays $80, the woman pays $20.

Deductible example: the woman pays the first $250 or the first $2,000 of any medical costs within a year, and the insurer pays bills above $250 or $2,000. The higher the deductible, usually the lower the cost of the policy. The $2,000 deductible is really a form of catastrophic insurance.

Conversely, the higher the premium, the more the policy covers. Some policies cover everything (Dental care is usually provided through a separate insurer.)

The same for prescription medicines. You may pay for all, part, or nothing, depending on the type plan.

The PPO doctor functions as your personal physician. Often the doctor will have his or her own practice and office, conveniently located. If you need to squeeze in an appointment, the doctor usually will try to be accommodating.

Drawback: PPOs restrict choice.

Health Maintenance Organization (HMO)

The insurance company and medical provider are one and the same. All or almost all medical care is given by the HMO. The woman catches the flu. She

Top 25 Baby Names

San Francisco		San Mateo County	
Boys	**Girls**	**Boys**	**Girls**
Michael (104)	Jessica (73)	Michael (118)	Jessica (110)
Christopher (78)	Jennifer (72)	Christopher (102)	Jernnifer (75)
Daniel (72)	Elizabeth (48)	Daniel (92)	Nicole (70)
David (69)	Stephanie (41)	Andrew (85)	Amanda (53)
Kevin (68)	Michelle (40)	Matthew (85)	Elizabeth (53)
Jonathan (67)	Sarah (40)	Jonathan (83)	Ashley (52)
Alexander (61)	Ashley (36)	David (80)	Sarah (49)
Andrew (59)	Emily (35)	Kevin (76)	Samantha (48)
Anthony (59)	Katherine (31)	Nicholas (75)	Stephanie (48)
John (59)	Christina (29)	Anthony (72)	Alexandra (45)
William(57)	Jasmine (29)	Joesph (70)	Andrea (45)
James (49)	Nicole (28)	William (70)	Emily (44)
Eric (45)	Kimberly (27)	Alexcander (69)	Katherine (39)
Joseph (44)	Maria (27)	John (63)	Lauren (37)
Matthew (44)	Melissa (27)	Joshua (62)	Rachel (37)
Robert (44)	Tiffany (27)	Brandon (61)	Melissa (35)
Ryan (41)	Victoria (27)	Jose (56)	Michelle (35)
Christian (40)	Amanda (26)	Kyle (49)	Monica (35)
Jose (40)	Angela (26)	Ryan (47)	Megan (34)
Luis (40)	Anna (26)	Brian (46)	Rebecca (33)
Nicholas (39)	Vanessa (25)	Sean (45)	Christina (32)
Richard (36)	Hannah (24)	Eric (44)	Laura (32)
Justin (35)	Rebecca (24)	Robert (44)	Maria (30)
Brian (34)	Samantha (24)	Samuel (44)	Natalie (30)
Carlos (33)	Amy (23)	Christian (41)	Victoria (30)

Source: California Department of Health Services, 1992 birth records. Shown in parentheses is the number of children with the given name.

sees the HMO doctor at the HMO clinic or hospital. If she becomes pregnant, she sees an HMO obstetrician at the HMO hospital or clinic and delivers her baby there.

With HMOs you pay the complete bill if you go outside the system (with obvious exceptions; e.g., emergency care).

HMOs encourage you to pick a personal physician. The young woman wants a woman doctor; she picks one from the staff. She wants a pediatrician as her child's personal doctor; the HMO, usually, can provide one.

HMO clinics and hospitals bring many specialists and services together under one roof. You can get your eyes examined, your hearing tested, your prescriptions filled, your X-rays taken within an HMO facility (this varies), and much more.

If you need an operation or treatment beyond the capacity of your immediate HMO hospital, the surgery will be done at another HMO hospital within the system.

HMO payment plans vary but many HMO clients pay a monthly fee and a small ($5-$15) per-visit fee. Often the plan includes low-cost or reduced-cost or free prescriptions.

Drawback: Freedom of choice limited. If HMO facility is not close, the woman will have to drive to another town.

Which is Better: a PPO or an HMO?

This is a competitive field with many claims and counter claims. In recent years, PPOs have signed up many doctors and facilities — increasing the choices of members.

Kaiser Permanente, an HMO, however, remains very popular and enrolls about one out of every three Northern Californians.

If you are receiving medical insurance through your employer, you will be limited to the choices offered. In large groups, unions often have a say in what providers are chosen.

Some individuals will make their choice on price, some on convenience of facilities, others on what's covered, and so on.

Many private hospitals offer Physician Referral Services. You call the hospital, ask for the service and get a list of doctors to choose from. The doctors

will be affiliated with the hospital providing the referral. Hospitals and doctors will also tell you what insurance plans they accept for payment, and will send you brochures describing the services the hospital offers.

For Kaiser and other HMOs, call the local hospital or clinic.

A PPO will give you a list of its member doctors and facilities.

Ask plenty of questions. Shop carefully.

Common Questions

The young woman is injured in a car accident and is unconscious. Where will she be taken?

Generally, she will be taken to the closest emergency room or trauma center, where her condition will be stabilized. Her doctor will then have her admitted into a hospital. Or she will be transferred to her HMO hospital or, if indigent, to a county facility.

If her injuries are severe, she most likely will be rushed to a regional trauma center. Trauma centers have specialists and special equipment to treat serious injuries.

Both PPOs and HMOs offer urgent care and emergency care.

The young woman breaks her leg. Her personal doctor is an internist and does not set fractures. What happens?

The personal doctor refers the case to a specialist. Insurance pays the specialist's fee.

In a PPO, the woman would generally see a specialist affiliated with the PPO. In an HMO, the specialist would be employed by the HMO.

The young woman signs up for an HMO then contracts a rare disease or suffers an injury that requires treatment beyond the capability of the HMO. Will she be treated?

Often yes, but it pays to read the fine print. The HMO will contract treatment out to a facility that specializes in the needed treatment.

The young woman becomes despondent and takes to drink. Will insurance pay for her rehabilitation?

Depends on her insurance. And often her employer. Some may have drug and alcohol-rehab plans. Some plans cover psychiatry.

The woman becomes pregnant. Her doctor, who has delivered many babies, wants her to deliver at X hospital. All the woman's friends say, Y Hospital is much better, nicer, etc. The doctor is not cleared to practice at Y Hospital. Is the woman out of luck?

With a PPO, the woman must deliver at a hospital affiliated with the PPO — or pay the extra cost. If her doctor is not affiliated with that hospital, sometimes a doctor may be given courtesy practicing privileges at a hospital where he or she does not have staff membership. Check with the doctor.

With HMOs, the woman must deliver within the HMO system.

The young woman goes in for minor surgery, which turns into major surgery when the doctor forgets to remove a sponge before sewing up. Upon reviving, she does what?

The obvious answer is that she reaches for the phone and calls the nastiest lawyer in the county. But these days nothing is obvious. Some medical plans require clients to submit complaints to a panel of arbitrators, which decides damages, if any. Read the policy.

The woman's child reaches age 18. Is she covered by the family insurance?

All depends on the insurance. Some policies will cover the children while they attend college (But attendance may be defined in a certain way, full-time as opposed to part-time.) To protect your coverage, you should read the plan thoroughly.

At work, the woman gets her hand caught in a revolving door and is told she will need six months of therapy during which she can't work. Who pays?

Insurance will usually pay for the medical costs. Workers Compensation, a state plan that includes many but not all people, may compensate the woman for time lost off the job and may pay for medical costs. If you injure yourself on the job, your employer must file a report with Workers Comp.

The woman wins a vacation to Switzerland where she falls off an alp, breaks a leg, and spends three days in a Swiss hospital. Her HMO or PPO is 7,000 miles away. Who pays?

Usually the insurance company, but it is wise to check out how to obtain medical services before going on vacation. The woman may have to pay out-of-pocket and then file for reimbursement on her return home.

While working in her kitchen, the woman slips, bangs her head against the stove, gets a nasty cut and becomes woozy. She should:

Call 9-1-1, which will send an ambulance. 9-1-1 is managed by police dispatch. It's the fastest way to get an ambulance. Many insurance policies cover ambulance services. Ask.

What's the difference between a hospital, a clinic, an urgent-care center and a doctor's office?

The hospital has the most services and equipment. The center or clinic has several services and a fair amount of equipment. The office, usually, has the fewest services and the smallest amount of equipment.

Hospitals have beds. If a person must have a serious operation, she goes to a hospital. Hospitals have coronary-care and intensive-care units, emergency care and other specialized, costly treatment units. But many hospitals also run clinics for minor ailments and provide the same services as the medical centers.

Urgent care or medical centers are sometimes located in neighborhoods, which makes them more convenient for some people. The doctors treat the minor, and often not-so-minor, ailments of patients and send them to hospitals for major surgery and serious sicknesses.

Some doctors form themselves into groups to offer the public a variety of services. Some hospitals have opened neighborhood clinics or centers to attract patients. Kaiser has hospitals in some towns, and clinic-offices in other towns. The doctor in his or her office treats patients for minor ailments and uses the hospital for surgeries, major illnesses. Many illnesses that required hospitalization years ago are now treated in the office or clinic. Some hospitals offer programs outside the typical doctor-patient relationships. For example, wellness plans — advice on how to stay healthy or control stress or quit smoking.

Major Hospitals & Medical Facilities In San Francisco

California Pacific Medical Center. California Campus, 3700 California St., San Francisco, 94118. Ph: (415) 387-8700. Pacific Campus, 2333 Buchanan St., San Francisco, 94115. Ph: (415) 563-4321. Breast Health Center, Cancer Care Programs, Cardiovascular Services, Critical Care (includes Cardiopulmonary Unit, CCU, ICUs, NICUs, Pediatric ICUs), Community Services, Coming Home Hospice, Diabetes Services, Emergency Services, GI (includes Inflammatory Bowel Disease Center), Home Health Care, Immunotherapy and Infectious Diseases including HIV/AIDS, International Medicine, OB (includes High-Risk Neonatology and Perinatology), GYN, Occupational Health, Ophthalmology, Organ Transplantation, Orthopedics, Outpatient Clinics, Pediatrics, Perinatal Education and Lactation Center, Physician Referral, Plastic Surgery, Primary Care, Psychiatric Services, Rehabilitation Medicine, Senior Services, Skilled Nursing, Surgical Services (includes Ambulatory Surgery), Visiting Nurses and Hospice. 1,067 beds.

Chinese Hospital, 845 Jackson St., San Francisco, 94133. Ph: (415) 982-2400. ICU, GYN, OB, Radiology, Ophthalmology. 59 Beds.

Davies Medical Center, Castro & Duboce, San Francisco, 94114. Ph: (415) 565-6000. ICU, CCU, Emergency Care, Physical Therapy, Skilled Nursing, Radiology, Home Health Care, Cancer Treatment, Microvascular Surgery, Plastic Surgery, Hemodialysis, Rehabilitation, Sports Medicine, Fitness Evaluation, Occupational Medicine. 341 Beds.

Kaiser Permanente Medical Center—San Francisco, Geary Campus: 2425 Geary Blvd., San Francisco, 94115. Phone (415) 202-2000. French Campus: 4131 Geary Blvd., San Francisco, 94118. Ph. (415) 202-2000. Services include Emergency, Acute and Intensive Care, Cardiology and Cardiovascular Surgery, high risk OB and neonatal, Home Health, Hospice, HIV Research. Outpatient care includes Internal Medicine, OB, GYN, Pediatrics, Teen Clinic, Psychiatry and Chemical Dependency Recovery, Health Education. 620 Licensed Beds.

Medical Center of the University of California, San Francisco (UC San Francisco): Moffit-Long Hospitals, 400 Parnassus, San Francisco, 94143. Ph: (415) 476-1000. ICU, CCU, OB/GYN, family-oriented birth center for normal and high risk OB, Emergency Care, Physicians Referral, Multispecialty Ambulatory Care Center, Cardiovascular Services, Neurological and Neurosurgical services, Orthopedics, Organ Transplantation, General and Specialty Pediatric Care, Cancer Referral Service for Diagnosis and Treatment (1-800-888-8664). 560 beds.

UCSF/Mt. Zion: Integrated with the Medical Center of UC San Francisco in 1990. 1600 Divisadero St., San Francisco, 94115. Ph: 567-6600. ICU, GYN, CCU, Personalized physicians referral program (ph. 855-7777), Senior Services and senior membership program, Cancer Diagnosis and Treatment, Cardiology, Orthopedics, Urology, Emergency Care, Home Health Program, Pediatric Services including Pediatric Rehabilitation Program. 439 beds.

Saint Francis Memorial Hospital, 900 Hyde St., San Francisco, 94109. Ph: (415) 775-4321. ICU, CCU, Psychiatric Care, Physical Therapy, Skilled Nursing, Home Health

Care, Physicians Referral, Radiology, Geriatric Services, Emergency Care, Cancer Treatment, Sports Medicine, Clinical Research for AIDS and Cancer, Bothin Burn Center, San Francisco Spine Center, Women's Health Center. 365 Beds.

St. Luke's Hospital, Army & Valencia streets, San Francisco, 94110. Ph: (415) 647-8600. ICU, CCU, GYN, OB, Psychiatric Care, Physical Therapy, Skilled Nursing, Physicians Referral, Radiology, Geriatric Services, Emergency Care, Pediatric Services, Cancer Treatment. 260 Beds.

St. Mary's Hospital and Medical Center, 450 Stanyan St., San Francisco, 94117-1079. Ph: (415) 668-1000. ICU, CCU, GYN, Psychiatric Care, Physical Therapy, Skilled Nursing, Home Health Care, Physicians Referral, Chemical Dependency, Radiology, Geriatric Services, Emergency Care, Alcohol Treatment, Women's Programs, Cancer Treatment, HIV Services, Rehabilitation, Spine Center, Western Heart Institute, Ophthalmology, Cardiovascular Services, Cardiac Rehab Program, MRI, GI. 531 Beds.

San Francisco General Hospital Medical Center, 1001 Potrero Ave., San Francisco, 94110. Ph: (415) 206-8100. ICU, CCU, GYN, OB, Psychiatric Care, Physical Therapy, Trauma Center, Chemical Dependency, Radiology, Geriatric Services, Emergency Care, Pediatric Services, Cancer Treatment. 582 Beds.

Veterans Affairs Medical Center, 4150 Clement St., San Francisco, 94121. Ph: (415) 221-4810. ICU, CCU, GYN, Emergency Care, Psychiatric Care, Physical Therapy (Rehabilitation Medicine), Chemical Dependency, Alcohol Treatment, Skilled Nursing, Radiology, Eating Disorders, Home Health Care, Geriatric Services, Cancer Treatment, Dentistry, Special Programs include Treatment of Post-Traumatic Stress Disorder, Prosthetic Treatment Center, MRS/MRI. Medical and surgical services in virtually all specialties except obstetrics and pediatrics. 272 Beds. 120-bed Nursing Home Care Unit.

Major Hospitals & Medical Facilities In or Near San Mateo County

Kaiser Permanente Medical Center Redwood City, 1150 Veterans Blvd., Redwood City, 94603. Ph. (415) 780-2000. Typical Hospital Services including Neurosurgery, Physical and Occupational Therapy, Emergency Services, Hospice, Home Health Care, Substance Abuse Program, Baby Club, Teen Clinic, ICU/CCU, OB, GYN, Internal Medicine, Neurology, Psychiatry, Inpatient and Ambulatory Care Surgery, Diabetes Clinic, Health Education Department. 202 Beds.

Kaiser Permanente Medical Center, 1200 El Camino Real, South San Francisco, 94080. Ph. (415) 742-2000. Typical Hospital Services, Emergency Care, No Maternity. 127 Beds.

Mills-Peninsula Hospitals-Mills Hospital, 100 S. San Mateo Drive, San Mateo, 94401. Ph. (415) 696-4400. ICU, CCU, OB, 24-Hour Emergency Dept., Arthritis Center, Center for Rehabilitation, The Breast Center, Renal Program and Dialysis Services, Occupational Health, Physician Finder, Surgery Center, Pediatrics, Family Birth Center, Senior Focus Wellness Center, Community Health Education. 278 Beds.

Mills-Peninsula Hospitals-Peninsula Hospital, 1783 El Camino Real, Burlingame, 94010. Ph. (415) 696-5400. ICU, CCU, 24-Hour Emergency Dept., Center for Assessment and Referral, Chemical Dependency Center, Menninger San Francisco Bay Area (mental health), Surgery Center, Cardiac Services, Oncology Services, Renal Program and Dialysis Services at Mid-Peninsula Medical Building, Burlingame, Fitness Center, Physician Finder, Senior Focus, Center for Rehabilitation-Injured Worker Services, Occupational Health, Community Health Education, Pediatric speech and language program. 245 Beds.

San Mateo County General Hospital, 222 W 39th Ave., San Mateo, 94403. Ph. (415) 573-2222. ICU, GYN, Emergency Care, Pediatrics, Psychiatry, Physical Rehabilitation & Skilled Nursing affiliated with Crystal Springs Rehabilitation Center of San Mateo. 145 Beds (Additional 124 Beds at Crystal Springs).

Sequoia Hospital, 170 Alameda de las Pulgas, Redwood City, 94062. (415) 369-5811.

ICU, CCU, OB, GYN, Cardiovascular Care, Emergency Care, Psychiatric Care, Physician Referral, Pediatric Services, Physical Therapy, Acute Rehabilitation, Chemical Dependency and Alcohol Treatment, Extended Care Unit, Radiology, Home Health Care, Seniors Services, Wound Treatment Center, Maternity & Family Services, Cancer Treatment, Sleep Center, Pain Treatment Center, Orthopedic and Sports Medicine Services, Health & Wellness Services, Pulmonary Services, Diabetes Treatment, Weight Management, Occupational Health and Community Education. 438 Beds.

Seton Medical Center, 1900 Sullivan Ave., Daly City, 94015. Ph. (415) 992-4000. ICU, CCU, OB, GYN, Emergency Care, Psychiatric Care, Physician Referral, Physical Rehabilitation, Skilled Nursing, Radiology, Home Health Care, Cancer Treatment, Wound Care Center, Community Outreach and Education Programs, Level II NICU, Outpatient Surgery and Services, GI Lab, Orthopedic & Spine Care Services, San Francisco Heart Institute, Health Education, Cardiac Rehab, Physical & Occupational Therapy, Breast Health Center. 357 Beds.

Seton Medical Center, Coastside, 600 Marine Blvd., Moss Beach, 94038. Ph. (415) 728-5521. Radiology, Senior Services, Emergency Care, Physical Rehabilitation, Skilled Nursing, Home Care, Medical/Surgical Physician Referral, Outpatient Services includes Radiology, GI Lab, Physical Therapy, and Health Education Programs. 123 Beds.

Stanford University Hospital, 300 Pasteur Drive, Stanford, 94305. Ph: (415) 723-4000. ICU, CCU, OB, GYN, Emergency Care & Prompt Care, Trauma Center, Psychiatric Care, Physician Referral, Physical Therapy, Radiology, Home Health Care, Cancer Treatment, Ambulatory Surgery Center, Perinatal Education, Multiorgan Transplant Center, Comprehensive Rehabilitation Center, Helicopter Transportation. 594 Beds.

Department of Veterans Affairs Medical Center, 3801 Miranda Ave., Palo Alto, 94304. Ph: (415) 493-5000. ICU, GYN, Alcohol & Chemical Dependency, Physical Rehab, Skilled Nursing Care, Wellness Program, Home Care, Urgent Care, Psychiatry. 1,250 Beds (Palo Alto and Menlo Park facilities combined).

Key: ICU, Intensive Care Unit; CCU, Coronary Care Unit; OB, Obstetrics; GYN, Gynecology.

12/Newcomer's Guide

Answers to Frequently Asked Questions about Living in San Francisco & San Mateo County

FOR NEWCOMERS, here are some answers to frequently asked questions.

Voter Registration

You must be 18 years and a citizen. Go to the nearest post office and ask for a voter registration postcard. Fill it out and pop it into the mail box. Or register in person at most county offices, or political party headquarters, which are listed in the phone book.

For more information on voting, call the elections office in San Mateo County at (415) 312-5222 and in San Francisco at (415) 554-4398. Before every election, the county will mail you a sample ballot with the address of your polling place.

School Registration

To get into kindergarten, your child must turn five before December 3 of the year he or she enters the grade.

For first grade, your child must be six before Dec. 3. If he is six on Dec. 4, if she is a mature Jan. 6 birthday girl, speak to the school. There may be some wiggle room.

For registration, you are required to show proof of immunization for polio, diphtheria, tetanus, pertussis (whooping cough), measles, rubella, and mumps. If the kid is seven or older, you can skip mumps and pertussis.

Dog (and cat) Licensing-Spaying

For licensing, in San Francisco, (415) 554-6364. In San Mateo, (415) 363-4220.

If the public agencies don't provide spaying and neutering, they can tell you who does. Unincorporated San Mateo requires the spaying-neutering of cats. Some exceptions.

In San Mateo County, Peninsula Humane Society rescues wild animals in trouble, rounds up wild dogs and cats, and performs other services. Phone (415) 340-8200.

Driving

California has the most stringent smog requirements in the country. If your out-of-state car or truck is not equipped to meet the requirements, you pay a $300 penalty.

You have 20 days from the time you enter the state to register your vehicles. After that you pay a penalty, and face getting a ticket-fine.

For registration, go to any office of the Department of Motor Vehicles. Bring your smog certificate, your registration card and your license plates.

Registration is simple but the fees can be hefty. The basic fee is 2 percent of market value. A $10,000 car would cost $200, a $15,000 car, $300, a $20,000 car $400 — plus about $40 in miscellaneous costs. These incidentally, are annual fees.

If you are a California resident, all you need to do is complete a change-of-address form, which can be obtained by calling one of the following:

Dept. of Motor Vehicles Offices

San Francisco: 1377 Fell St., (415) 557-1179.
Daly City: 1500 Sullivan Ave., (415) 994-5700.
Redwood City: 300 Brewster Ave., (415) 368-2837.
San Mateo: 425 N. Amphlett Blvd., (415) 342-5332.

Driving Rules, Requirements and Tests

• If going for a driver's license, ask to have the booklet mailed to you or pick it up. Study it. Almost all the questions will be taken from the booklet.

• To obtain a driver's license, you must be 16 years old, pass a state-certified Driver's Education (classroom) and Driver's Training (behind-the-wheel) course, and written and driving tests at DMV.

Once you pass the test, your license is usually renewed by mail. Retesting is rare, unless your driving record is poor.

• High schools used to offer driving courses but these are rapidly disappearing due to state budget cuts. Private driving schools have moved in to fill the gap. Courses average about $250.

Teenagers older than 15 who are in driver's training can be issued a permit, which allows them to drive accompanied by an 18-year-old licensed driver.

If no driver's education program has been completed, you must be at least 17 years old to apply for a driver's license. You must pass a written test, simple eye exam and a behind-the-wheel test.

• Turning Rules. If signs don't say no, you can turn right on a red light (after making a full stop), and make a U-turn at an intersection.

• Stop for pedestrians.

• Insurance. Must have it to drive.

•New law. Out-of-state applicants must supply proof of "legal presence," which could be a certified copy of a birth certificate. Foreign applicants must supply other documents. Law is aimed at illegal immigrants.

Earthquakes

They're fun and great topics of conversation, until you get caught in a big one. Then they are not so funny. At the beginning of your phone book is some advice about what to do before, during and after a temblor. It's worth reading.

Garbage Service

The garbage fellows come once a week. Rates vary by city but figure $10-$20 a month (and going up because of recycling costs).

Besides the cans, many homes will receive recycling bins for plastics, glass and cans. Pickup weekly, usually the same day as garbage. Don't burn your garbage in the fireplace or outside. Don't burn leaves. Against the law.

Property Taxes

The average property tax rate in California is 1.25 percent. If you buy a $250,000 home this year, your property tax will be $3,125. Once the basic tax is established, it goes up about 2 percent annually in following years.

"Average" needs to be emphasized. Some jurisdictions have tacked costs on to the property tax; some have not. Some school districts, in recent years, have won approval of annual parcel taxes.

Property taxes are paid in two installments - March and November. They are generally collected automatically through impound accounts set up when you purchase a home, but check your sale documents carefully. Sometimes homeowners are billed directly.

For Additional Reading ...

Bike Trails, Wine Country, Romantic Getaways
Tours, Restaurants, Gardens, Real Estate ...

*For more on Northern California
see the Book List and order blank
on the pages at the end of this guide*

Sales Tax

Varies by county. May be raised later in 1994 to help repair damage caused by the L.A. earthquake.

San Francisco: 8.5 percent.

San Mateo: 8.25 percent.

Disclosure Laws

California requires Realtors to give detailed reports on every home sold — a good law and it recently was expanded to include earthquake fault info.

Cable TV Service

Almost all Bay Area homes are served by cable. Rates vary according to channels accessed but a basic rate is $20-$25 a month. Installation is extra.

For clear FM radio reception, often a cable connection is needed.

Phones

Pacific Bell charges $34.75 to run a line to your house. It charges extra for jack installation. If you're handy, you can do the jack wiring and installation yourself. Many homes will have the jacks in place.

The basic monthly charge is $8.35 but with taxes, access to interstate calling, and other miscellaneous items the true basic for many people is $12 to $15.

Gas and Electricity

Most homes are heated with natural gas. Pacific Gas and Electric reports that gas bills, year round, average $38.55 a month, and electric bills $62 a month.

If you are located in from the coast and shielded against the fog, almost never between May and September, and rarely between April and October, will you need to heat your home. Air conditioners are used throughout the summer but on many days they're not needed. On foggy summer days, coastal neighborhoods are often socked in with the cold stuff.

Fences

If you want to build one, check with city hall. Often there are restrictions on height.

Tipping

It's not done in the Bay Area as much as it is done in other parts of the country. Tip the newspaper delivery person, cab or limo drivers, waiters and waitresses and, at the holidays, people who perform regular personal services: yard maintenance, child care, housekeeping.

Don't tip the supermarket employee who carries bags to your car. Don't tip telephone or cable TV installers. Your garbage collector will usually be a Teamster. No beer. No money. Maybe a little cake or box of candy at Christmas. California has a liquor law that can put a person in violation for as little as one drink. If a garbage collector gets nailed for drunk driving, it will probably cost him his job. Some people give the mailman or mail lady a little holiday gift; many don't.

Smoking

In public, increasingly frowned on and, in restaurants in certain cities, forbidden. The trend is to discourage the weed.

Dress

Lawyer, executive or a professional? Wear a tie and jacket if you're a man, a two- or three-piece suit, if a woman.

For almost all social occasions, even, in some circles, weddings and funerals, the dress is casual. The person who wears a tie to a restaurant on Friday or Saturday often stands out (depends a little on the town).

Dress formal for dinner in San Francisco and the theater (but even here, many men go in sports coats, no tie; women in slacks).

13/New Housing

Homes for Sale, Homes Being Built for 1994 in San Francisco, San Mateo, Other Counties

SHOPPING FOR A new home? This chapter gives an overview of new housing underway in San Francisco, San Mateo and other nearby counties. Smaller projects are generally ignored. If you know where you want to live, drive that town or ask the local planning department what's new in housing.

Prices change. Incidentals such as landscaping fees may not be included. In the 1980s, to pay for services, cities increased fees on home construction. Usually, these fees are included in the home prices but in what is known as Mello-Roos districts, the fees are often assessed like tax payments (in addition to house payments). Nothing secret. By law developers are required to disclose all fees. But the prices listed below may not include some fees.

After rocketing in the 1980s, home prices, new and resale, stabilized and in many instances dropped. Some developers, particularly in towns with many new units, have gotten very competitive in pricing — a break for buyers.

Listed alphabetically by city and development, the following directory covers first what's available on the San Francisco Peninsula, then in other Northern California counties at time of publication. For latest information, call the developers for brochures.

San Mateo County
Daly City
Linda Vista, Yamas Construction Co., Linda Vista Drive, Daly City. Ph: (415) 467-9722. Single-family, 4 bedrooms, 3.5 bath, views, $298,000-$338,000.

South Hill Estates, Sunstream Homes, San Bruno Mt., Daly City. Ph: (415) 244-0290. Single-family detached, 4 bedrooms, 3 baths, $297,950- $324,950.
San Carlos
San Carlos Highlands, Paul C. Petersen, 201 Glasgow Lane, San Carlos. Ph: (415) 592-9922. Single-family detached, 4 bedrooms, 3 baths, 3-car garages, park, $650,00-$669,950.
San Mateo
Crystal Springs Estates, Sunstream Homes, Polhemus near Ralston at Hwy. 92 exit, San

Mateo. Ph: (415) 312-9787. Single-family detached, .25-acre lot, 3-car garage, tile roofs, 4-6 bedrooms, numerous room options available, from $699,950.

South San Francisco
Foothill Estates, Sunstream Homes, Hillside Blvd. near Chestnut, South San Francisco. Ph: (415) 244-0290. Single-family detached, 4-5 bedrooms, 3 bath, 3-car garage, to $499,950.

Sunshine Villas, Sunstream Homes, Crestwood Drive, near Hillside Blvd., South San Francisco. Ph: (415) 244-0290. Single-family detached, 4-5 bedrooms, 2.5-3 baths, 2-car and 3-car garages, $378,950-$425,950.

Alameda County
Castro Valley
Palomares Hills Canyon II, Shapell Industries, 6417 Crestwood Drive, Castro Valley. Ph: (510) 581-3607. Single-family, 3-4 bedrooms, 2-3.5 baths, den option, rec center, pool, tennis court, park, 900-acre planned community, $270,900-$372,900.

Palomares Hills Regency Series, Shapell Industries, 7594 Denison Place, Castro Valley. Ph: (510) 733-3292. Single-family,4-5 bedrooms, 3-4 baths, bonus room, clubhouse, pool, tennis courts, walking trails, park, planned community $408,900-$472,900.

Fremont
Avalon at Las Palmas, The Mission Peak Co., 40729 Mission Blvd., Fremont. Ph: (510) 770-9877. Single-family homes on large lots, 4 bedrooms, from low $400,000s.

Livermore
Danbury Park, Centex Homes, 5857 Rainflower Drive, Livermore. Ph: (510) 606-5347. Single-family detached on large homesites for family activities, large homes (1,761 to 2,365 sq. ft.), $230,000-$268,500.

Monticello, Standard Pacific, 624 Zermatt St., Livermore. Ph: (510) 447-7777. Single-family, 3-5 bedrooms, from upper $200,000s.

Windmill Springs III, McBail Homes, Livermore. Ph: (510) 449-5458. Single-family detached, 3-4 bedrooms, 2-3 baths, 2-3 car garages, from $219,950.

San Leandro
Camelia Court, Ryder Homes of Northern California, Inc., 1105 Camelia Court, San Leandro. Ph: (510) 729-0105. Single-family detached, 4 bedrooms, 2.5 baths, $224,950-$236,450.

Union City
Meridien Court, Gregory Group, Wipple Road at Ahern, Union City. Ph: (510) 429-8284. Single-family homes in a gated community, 6 models, 3-5 bedrooms, gourmet kitchens, master suites with fireplaces, teen rooms, park and pool, $286,000-$384,000.

The Bay at Ponderosa Landing, Ponderosa Homes, 31432 Marlin Ct., Union City. Ph: (510) 471-7869. Single-family detached, 4-5 bedrooms, 2-3 bath, gourmet kitchens, air-conditioning, low $300,000s.

The Village at Ponderosa Landing, Ponderosa Homes, 31417 Marlin Ct., Union City. Ph: (510) 471-2140. Single-family detached, 3-5 bedrooms, G.E. appliances, front yard landscaping, upper $200,000s.

Contra Costa County
Antioch
Almondridge West, McBail Homes, Antioch. Ph: (510) 778-3246. Single-family detached, 3-4 bedrooms, 2-2.5 baths, 1-2 stories, starts at $129,950.

Carousel, Seeno Homes, 5204 Catanzaro, Antioch. Ph: (510) 778-2987. Single-family, from the $130,000's.

Lone Tree Estates, Davidon Homes, 2713 Joshua Court, Antioch. Ph: (510) 778-3092. Single-family detached, 3-5 bedrooms, 2-3 baths, front yard landscaping, AC and Jacuzzi-brand tubs included, six floor plans, from low $200,000s.

Lone Tree Glen, Davidon Homes, 1825 Vender Court, Antioch. Ph: (510) 706-1986. Duet, 3-4 bedrooms, 2.5 baths, 2 stories, HOA with pool, spa and tot lot, from low $100,000s.

Montclair, Standard Pacific, 4513 Angel Court, Antioch. Ph: (510) 778-0220. 3-4 bedrooms executive homes, low $200,000s.

New Horizons, Seeno Homes, 5053 Woodmont, Antioch. Ph: (510) 778-0357. Single-family executive homes, from the $160,000s.

Ponderosa Glen, Ponderosa Homes, 4518 Country Hills Drive, Antioch. Ph: (510) 778-5533. Single-family detached, 3-4 bedrooms, 2.5-3 baths, two-story, up to 1,765 sq. ft., mid $100,000s.

Sterling Place, Pulte Home Corp., 538 Baker Way, Antioch. Ph: (510) 779-1116. Single-family, 3-4 bedrooms, attics, bonus space, $170,000-$215,000.

Stony Creek, Centex Homes, Antioch. Ph: (510) 779-9606. Single-family detached, 5 models, 3 single-story designs, 3-5 bedrooms, 2-3 baths to choose from, from the $130,000s.

The Terraces, Pacwest Development, 5059 Sundance Way, Antioch. Ph: (510) 754-1788. Single-family, steel-framed, 3-4 bedroom, 2-3 baths, from $140,000-$180,000.

Villas, Seeno Homes, 131 S. Villa Way, Antioch. Ph: (510) 939-0942. Condominiums, rent to own, from the $120,000s.

Brentwood

Confetti, Seeno Homes, Dainty and Minnesota, Brentwood. Ph: (510) 516-2093. Single-family new models, from the $130,000s.

Edgewood, Seeno Homes, Dainty and Minnesota, Brentwood. Ph: (510) 516-2093. Single-family, great neighborhood, from the $150,000s.

Homecoming, Garrow & Company, Homecoming Way and Hwy. 4, Brentwood. Ph: (510) 634-6982. Single-family, 3-4 bedrooms, $129,950-$160,000.

Legacy Collection, Pulte Home Corp., 267 Cheshire Drive, Brentwood. Ph: (510) 634-0432. Single-family, 3-4 bedrooms, attics, bonus space, traditional detached garages, $150,000-$190,000.

Sterling Collection, Pulte Home Corp., 19 Lambert Court, Brentwood. Ph: (510) 516-7001. Single-family, attics, 3-4 bedrooms, bonus space, $170,000-$215,000.

Concord

Canyon Creek, Seeno Homes, 2199 Bluerock Cr., Concord. Ph: (510) 686-5777. Single-family executive homes, from the $230,000s.

Pavilion Place, Standard Pacific, 1523 Allegro Ave., Concord. Ph: (510) 825-4422. Single-family, 3-4 bedrooms, from $229,000.

Danville

Bettencourt Ranch, Dame Construction Co, Inc., 4315 Mansfield Drive, Danville, 410, 736-7535. Single-family, 4 bedrooms, 3 baths, 3-car garages, gated community, pool, tennis, clubhouse, $320,000-$443,000.

Classic Collection, Hidden Valley, Davidon Homes, 1001 McCauley Road, Danville. Ph: (510) 838-1283. Single-family detached from 2,110 to 2,859 sq. ft., 3-6 bedrooms, up to 3 baths, in exclusive valley on east side of I-680, from high $300,000.

Diablo Highlands, Country Estates, Shapell Industries, 16 Stirling Drive, Danville. Ph: (510) 838-6406. Single-family detached, 4-5 bedrooms, 2.5-4.5 baths, fireplace in master suite, jet spa, custom masonry fireplaces, central vacuum system, video entry system, close to Blackhawk, tennis courts, walking paths, $467,900-$619,900.

Diablo Highlands, Country Villas II, Shapell Industries, 455 Glasgow Circle, Danville. Ph: (510) 838-6406. Single-family detached, 3-5 bedrooms, 2-3 baths, hand-set ceramic tile entries, skylights, tennis courts, private recreation center, front yard landscaping, close to Blackhawk, $274,900-$342,900.

Heritage Park Townhomes, Davidon Homes, 109 Heritage Park Drive, Danville. Ph: (510) 736-0568. Townhomes from 1,798 to 2,000 sq. ft., 3 bedrooms, 2.5 baths, 2 stories, community pool and recreation room, walking distance from Blackhawk Plaza, from mid $200,000s.

Somerset Townhomes, Dame Construction Co, Inc., 4317 Conejo Drive, Danville. Ph: (510) 736-7534. Townhouse, 3 bedroom, 2.5 baths, 1,650 sq. ft. view lot, pool and landscaping, convenient Blackhawk Shopping Center, $202,500-$235,000.

Summit Collection, Hidden Valley, Davidon Homes, 1001 McCauley Road, Danville. Ph: (510) 838-1283. Single-family detached from 3,072 to 3,778 sq. ft., 4-5 bedrooms, den, library and bonus room, in exclusive valley, from mid $500,000s.

Vista Tassajara Crown Collection, Standard Pacific, 110 Parkhaven Drive, Danville. Ph: (510) 736-1866. Single-family detached, 4 bedrooms, from mid $300,000s.

Vista Tassajara Empire Collection, Standard Pacific, 17 Lakefield Court, Danville. Ph: (510) 736-1676. Single-family detached, 4-5 bedrooms, from high $300,000s.

Oakley

County Faire, Seeno Homes, Gum Tree and Live Oak, Oakley. Ph: (510) 625-1311. Single-family, new project, from the $130,000s.

The Carriages, Hal Porter Homes, 170 Century Way, Oakley. Ph: (510) 679-1000. Single-family, 3-5 bedrooms, 2-2.5 baths, 2-3 garages, $143,000-$164,000.

Pittsburg
Peppertree, Seeno Homes, 3100 Peppermill, Pittsburg. Ph: (510) 439-3630. Townhouses, rent to own, from the $90,000s.

San Ramon
Bent Creek Parc, Ponderosa Homes, 201 Hat Creek Court, San Ramon. Ph: (510) 828-1311. Single-family detached, 3-5 bedrooms, 2-3 baths, 1,648 to 2,405 sq. ft., upper $200,000s.

Easthampton, The O'Brien Group, Alcosta Blvd., San Ramon. Ph: (800) 243-UOWN (8696). Single-family detached and duets, 3-4 bedrooms, call to be on our interest list, $200,000s.

Miravilla at Gale Ranch, Shapell Industries, 101 Grassmere Circle, San Ramon. Ph: (510) 736-2693. Clustered 2-4 Townhouses, 3-4 bedrooms, 2.5 baths, fireplaces, recreation area with pool and spa, 2-car garage, landscaping, $216,900-$246,900.

Old Ranch Estates, Davidon Homes, 1150 Timbercreek Road, San Ramon. Ph: (510) 803-9545. Single-family detached, five models from 2,503 to 3,429 sq. ft., 3-5 bedrooms, bonus room, den or library, from high $300,000s.

Portola at Gale Ranch, Shapell Industries, 2090 Goldenrod Land, San Ramon. Ph: (510) 736-8465. Single-family detached, 3-4 bedrooms, 2-3 baths, $259,000-$374,000.

The Valley at Bent Creek, Ponderosa Homes, 100 Woodland Valley Drive, San Ramon. Ph: (510) 833-9056. Single-family detached, 4-5 bedrooms, 2-3 baths, 2,252 to 2,992 sq. ft. luxury homes, low $300,000's.

Marin County
Mill Valley
Cypress Hollow, Southwest Diversified-Coscan Partners, 35 Monterey Drive, Mill Valley. Ph: (415) 381-3100. Single-family, 3-4 bedrooms, den or au pair, $729,000-$1,100,000.

Novato
Wildwood-Glen, McBail Homes, Novato. Ph: (707) 763-4333. Semi-custom single-family detached, please call sales office for information.

San Rafael
Marin Lagoon, Southwest Diversified—Coscan Partners, 5 Lagoon Court, San Rafael. Ph: (415) 491-1600. Single-family, 3-4 bedrooms, 2.5-3 baths, $380,000-$450,000.

Placer County
Rocklin
The Estates at Stanford Ranch, Benchmark Housing Group, 4531 Shenandoah Road, Rocklin. Ph: (916) 624-7195. Single-family executive homes on large lots, 2,000 to 3,000 sq. ft., 3-5 bedrooms, 3-car garages, low $200,000s to high $200,000s.

Roseville
Pebble Creek, Hal Porter Homes, 1773 Calle Campana, Roseville. Ph: (916) 771-2525. Single-family, 3-5 bedrooms, 2-2.5 baths, 2-3 car garages, $140,000-$160,000.

Sacramento County
Carmichael
Whispering Oaks, Poelman Construction Inc., 2636 Arboreta, Carmichael. Ph: (916) 485-1222. Single-family nestled among oak trees, 5 bedrooms, 3.5 baths, 3-car garages, kitchen with granite counter tops, $345,000.

Folsom
Bryncliffe, Morrison Homes, 148 Cruickshank, Folsom. Ph: (916) 983-0566. Single-family detached, 3-6 bedrooms, 2-3 baths, elegant executive homes, from mid $200,000s.

Galt
Whispering Meadows, Hal Porter Homes, 136 S. Emerald Oak Drive, Galt. Ph: (209) 745-6592. Single-family, 3-4 bedrooms, 2 baths, 2-3 car garages, $115,000-$147,000.

Sacramento
Riverlake, L & P Land & Development-Pacific-Teichert, 8144 Pocket Road., Sacramento. Ph: (916) 427-2936. Single-family, 3-4 bedrooms, 2-3 baths and halfplexes, 3 bedrooms, 2-3 baths, planned unit development, lake, $163,950- $500,000.

South Land Village Condominiums, R.J. Dronberger, 5883 Gloria Drive, Sacramento. Ph: (916) 393-4971. Condominiums, 2 bedrooms, 2 baths, fireplaces, washer & dryers, garages with openers, gated entry, pool and clubhouse, $95,950- $115,000.

El Dorado Hills
Sterling Collection at Fairchild Village, Pulte Home Corp, 3719 Winlock Place, El Dorado Hills. Ph: (916) 933-9277. Single-family 3-5 bedrooms, attics, $190,000-$220,000.

San Joaquin County
Lathrop
Summerfield, McBail Homes, Lathrop. Ph: (209) 982-1677. Single-family, 3-4 bedrooms, 2-2.5 baths, from $133,950.
Lodi
Steeplechase, Hal Porter Homes, 2030 Bluejay Way, Lodi. Ph: (916) 369-4000. Single-family, 3-4 bedrooms, 2 bath, 2-car garages, $125,000-$160,000.
Salida
Heirloom, Morrison Homes, 4508 Castle Cary Lane, Salida. Ph: (209) 545-2750. Single-family detached, 3-4 bedrooms, 2-3 baths.
Stockton
Delta Vista at Weston Ranch, Standard Pacific, Stockton. Ph: (209) 982-5555. Single-family, 3-4 bedrooms, from mid $100,000s.

Pacific Sunrise at Weston Ranch, Centex Homes, Stockton. Ph: (510) 827-8100. Single-family detached, five floor plans, 3-5 bedrooms, 2-3 baths, 3-car garages, from the low $100,000s.

WindRose at Weston Ranch, Centex Homes, 1518 William Moss Blvd., Stockton. Ph: (209) 983-8184. Single-family detached, 3-4 bedrooms, 1,079 to 1,752 sq. ft., oversized 2-car garages with workshop and laundry areas, $98,900-$133,000.
Tracy
Chantilly, Standard Pacific, 646 Shaw Court, Tracy. Ph: (209) 832-3453. Single-family, 3-4 bedrooms, from $159,000.

Circle "B" Ranch, Bright Development, Tracy Blvd and Schulte, Tracy. Ph: (209) 836-9586. Single-family, 3-4 bedrooms, 1 & 2-story, 2-4 car garages, $137,490-$163,490.

Normandy, Standard Pacific, Tracy. Ph: (209) 832-2111. Single-family, 3-4 bedrooms, from low $200,000s.

Woodfield Estates, Seeno Homes, Corral Hollow Road, Tracy. Ph: (209) 836-2988. Single-family, no Mello Roos, from the $130,000s.

Santa Clara County
Milpitas
Beresford Meadows, Shapell Industries, 281 Silverlake Court, Milpitas. Ph: (408) 942-0668. Single-family, 3-5 bedrooms, 2-3.5 baths, ornate fireplaces, bonus room opt., private recreation area with pool, $273,900-$363,900.

Hillcrest Estates, Shapell Industries, 1222 Eagle Ridge Way, Milpitas. Ph: (408) 262-1037. Single-family detached, 4-5 bedrooms, 3 baths, 3-car garages, custom cabinetry, tile roof, central vacuum system, compactor, double oven plus microwave, $268,900-$439,900.

Hillcrest Terrace, Shapell Industries, 2111 Cuesta Drive, Milpitas. Ph: (408) 263-1703. Townhouses, 2-3 bedrooms, 2.5 baths, custom wood-burning fireplace, vaulted ceilings, front yard landscaping, recreation area with pool and spa, close to park, $230,900-$287,900.

Hillcrest Villas, Shapell Industries, 2335 Cascade Street, Milpitas. Ph: (408) 946-6449. Single-family detached, 2-4 bedrooms, 2.5 baths, breakfast nook, landscaping, private recreation area with pool and spa, close to park, $258,900-$314,900.
Palo Alto
Promenade, Summerhill Homes, 2573 Park Blvd., Palo Alto. Ph: (415) 325-7895. Townhomes and condominiums, 2 bedrooms, $195,000-$250,000.
San Jose
Bordeaux, Standard Pacific, 3233 Delta Road, San Jose. Ph: (408) 270-3334. Single-family, 3-5 bedrooms, from upper $300,000s.

Crown Point at Silvercreek Valley Country Club, Pondrosa Homes, 5441 Ligurian Drive, San Jose. Ph: (510) 460-8921. Single-family detached luxury homes, 4-5 bedrooms, 2-3 baths, 2,043 to 3,052 sq. ft., high $300,000's.

Haverton, Davidson, Kavanagh & Brezzo, Branham, off Almaden Expressway, San Jose. Ph: (408) 266-3355. Luxury townhomes, 2-3 bedrooms, 2.5 baths., low $200,000s.

Hidden Glen Evergreen "The Finale", Arcadia Development, 2511 Glen Dundee Way at Tully Road, San Jose. Ph: (408) 270-1697. Single-family detached from 2,235 to 3,120 sq. ft. on 6,000 sq. ft. lots, 4-5 bedrooms, $290,000-$345,000.

MillBrook at River Oaks, The Mission Peak Co., 523 Mill River Lane, San Jose. Ph: (408) 428-9144. Luxury townhomes, 2-3 bedrooms, great location, $250,000-$300,000.

Park Almaden, Davidson, Kavanagh & Brezzo, Blossom Hill & Almaden Expressway, San Jose. Ph: (408) 997-6392. Condominiums, 1-3 bedrooms, 1-3 baths., low $100,000s.
Parkside, Alta Pacific Housing Partners II, 434-16 Camille Circle, San Jose. Ph: (408) 954-8677. Townhomes, 2-3 bedrooms, bonus rooms, decks, fireplaces, AC, $240,000-$285,000.
Rose Creek, Davidson, Kavanagh & Brezzo, Ocala & White, San Jose. Ph: (408) 259-9872. Large, detached homes, 4-5 bedrooms, 2-3 baths, mid $200,000s.
Springbrook, Davidson, Kavanagh & Brezzo, Phelan & Senter, San Jose. Ph: (408) 279-3258. Condominiums, 2-3 bedrooms, 2-2.5 baths., from low $100,000s.
Vizcaya, Davidon Homes, 2142 Vizcaya Cir. at Bascom and Curtner Aves., San Jose. Ph: (408) 371-1141. Townhomes, 3-4 bedrooms, 2.5 baths, 2 stories, from mid $300,000s.
Sunnyvale
Expressions, Summerhill Homes, California Ave. and Pajaro, Sunnyvale. Ph: (408) 739-2767. Townhomes, 2-3 bedrooms, $230,000-$300,000.
Somerset, Summerhill Homes, 366 Sunset Ave, Sunnyvale. Ph: (408) 774-9493. Single-family detached, central Sunnyvale, 2-4 bedrooms, $279,000-$350,000.
Traditions, Davidson, Kavanagh & Brezzo, Fair Oaks, off Highway 101, Sunnyvale. Ph: (408) 745-0174. Executive townhomes, 2-3 bedrooms, 2-3 baths., mid $200,000s.

Solano County
Benicia
Classic at Southampton, Southampton, 531 McCall Drive, Benicia. Ph: (707) 745-1432. Single-family, 4-5 bedrooms, 3-4 baths, workshop space in garage, family-sized kitchens, low $300,000- $385,000.
Encore, Southampton Co., Currey Court off Rose Drive, Benicia. Ph: (707) 745-2340. Single-family detached, 3-4 bedrooms, 2-3 baths, $220,000-$265,000.
Encore at Southampton, Southampton, 467 Currey Court, Benicia. Ph: (707) 745-2340. Single-family, 3-4 bedrooms, 2-3 baths, fireplace, $225,000-$275,000.
Southampton-Classic, Southampton Co., Panorama and Keary off Rose Drive, Benicia. Ph: (707) 745-1432. Single-family executive homes from 2,475 to 3,375 sq. ft., 3-6 bedrooms, 3-3.5 baths, 3-car garages, $300,000-$365,000.
Villas, Southampton Co., Columbia Circle, Benicia. Ph: (707) 747-1132. Townhomes, 2-3 bedrooms, 1-2 stories, fireplaces, some views, $155,000-$172,500.
Fairfield
Castle Rock, Centex Homes, 2423 Trevino Way, Fairfield. Ph: (707) 426-5211. Single-family, 2-3 car garages, 3-5 bedrooms, 2-3 baths, $189,500-$256,000.
Diablo Vista, Miller-Sorg Group, Cherry Valley Circle, Rancho Solano, Fairfield. Ph: (707) 428-1007. Single-family homes in country club community with panoramic views, 4 bedrooms, 2.5-3-car garages, $277,000-$317,000.
Fairway Estates, Miller-Sorg Group, Southern Hills Court, Rancho Solano, Fairfield. Ph: (707) 428-1009. Single-family in country club community, 4-5 bedrooms, 3-car garages, 3 fireplaces, $300,000-$375,000.
Festival, Seeno Homes, Gold Hill exit off 680, Fairfield. Ph: (707) 864-4245. Single-family, 3-4 bedrooms, from the $130,000s.
Green Valley Lake, Duffel Financial and Construction Co., Green Valley Road, one mile from I-80, Fairfield. Ph: (707) 864-3201. Single-family, 3-4 bedrooms, 2-3 baths, lake views, $200,000-$300,000.
LeParc, Seeno Homes, Gold Hill at Hwy. 680, Fairfield. Ph: (707) 864-8145. Single-family, new release, from the $130,000s.
Meadow Glen, Condiotti Enterprise, Inc., Hillbourne Road at Martin Road, Fairfield. Ph: (707) 447-5363. Single-family detached, 3-4 bedrooms, from $150,000.
Suisun
Parkside, Seeno Homes, Sunset at Hwy. 12, Suisun. Ph: (707) 428-5938. Townhomes, from the $120,000's.
The Villages, Seeno Homes, Hwy. 12 and Village Drive, Suisun. Ph: (707) 425-6138. Single-family, 2-4 bedrooms, walk to park, from the $130,000s.
Suisun City
Victorian Harbor, The O'Brien Group, 707 Bay Street, Suisun City. Ph: (707) 421-2550. Single-family, Victorian, porches, VA Financing, $130,000-$180,000.

Vacaville

Americana at Foxwood, O'Brien & Hicks, 844 Younsdale Drive, Vacaville. Ph: (707) 421-2550. Single-family, 3-4 bedrooms, VA financing available, $140,000-$180,000.

Farmington, Condiotti Enterprises, Inc., 145 Audrey Place, Vacaville. Ph: (707) 447-5363. Single-family detached, 3-4 bedrooms, FHA and VA financing available, $137,950-$160,950.

Fiesta at Foxwood, The O'Brien Group, Younsdale Drive, Vacaville. Ph: (800) 243-UOWN (8696). Single-family detached homes coming soon, high $100,000's.

Woodcrest, Condiotti Enterprises, Inc., 1265 Cinnabar Way, Vacaville. Ph: (707) 447-5363. Single-family detached, 3-4 bedrooms, large lots, from low $140,000.

Vallejo

Clearpointe, Centex Homes, 276 Clearpointe Drive, Vallejo. Ph: (707) 643-7731. Single-family duets, 3-4 bedrooms, 2.5 baths, attached 2-car garages, $147,000- $172,000.

Summerfield Subdivision, Napa Estates Venture, 456 Canyon Creek Drive, Vallejo. Ph: (707) 553-9020. Single-family detached, 3-4 bedrooms, $157,900-$177,900.

Sonoma County
Petaluma

Americana, The O'Brien Group, Petaluma. Ph: (800) 243-8696. Single-family detached homes coming soon., high $100,000s.

Cader Farms, Ryder Homes of Northern California, Inc., 507 Greenwich St., Petaluma. Ph: (707) 778-0811. Single-family, 3-5 bedrooms, 3 baths, $255,000-$305,000.

Cader Farms Highlands, Ryder Homes of Northern California, Inc., 507 Greenwich St., Petaluma. Ph: (707) 778-0811. Single-family detached, 4-5 bedrooms, 3 baths, mid $300,000-mid $400,000.

Graystone Creek, McBail Homes, Petaluma. Ph: (707) 762-6906. Single-family detached, 3-5 bedrooms, 2-3 baths, some 3-car garages, from $223,000.

Sequoia Estates, Young America Homes, Inc., 445 Acadia Drive, Petaluma. Ph: (707) 769-8696. Single-family, 3-5 bedrooms, 2-3 baths, $249,950-$322,950.

Sonoma Mountain, Condiotti Enterprise, Inc., off Sonoma Mountain Pkwy., Petaluma. Ph: (707) 525-1358. 3-bedroom attached duplex, from $150,000s.

Santa Rosa

Burbank Housing Dev. Corp., Burbank Housing Dev. Corp., 3432 A Mendocino Ave., Santa Rosa. Ph: (707) 526-9782. Single-family detached and townhomes, 2-4 bedrooms, $95,000-$144,000.

Kensington, Keith Development, 4709 Devonshire Place, Santa Rosa. Ph: (707) 538-0102. Single-family detached, 3-5 bedrooms, large lots, $309,950-$419,950.

Wyndham, Cobblestone Development, 2223 San Miguel Ave., Santa Rosa. Ph: (707) 546-9550. Single-family detached, 3-4 bedrooms, $189,950-$234,950.

Yolo County
Davis

Scarborough Faire at Mace Ranch, Centex Homes, 3060 Hortaleza Place, Davis. Ph: (916) 757-1075. Single-family detached, 3-4 bedrooms, 2-3 baths, $171,000-$215,000.

Dixon

Mayfair Junction, Hal Porter Homes, 1860 Rehrmann Drive, Dixon. Ph: (916) 678-4200. Single-family, 3-5 bedrooms, 2-2.5 baths, 2-3 car garages, $147,000-$169,000.

West Sacramento

Province, Seeno Homes, 3103 Canvasback, West Sacramento. Ph: (916) 371-3700. Single-family homes from the $140,000s.

Winters

The Village at Putah Creek, Creekside Village Builders, Inc. & VandenBurge-Christie Construction, East Main Street at Morgan, Winters. Ph: (800) 788-0375. Single-family, 3-4 bedrooms, 2 baths, granny flats above detached garages, lots also available, $135,950-$189,950.

Woodland

College Park, Hal Porter Homes, 243 Palm Ave., Woodland. Ph: (916) 668-4663. Single-family, 3-4 bedrooms, 2-2.5 baths, $130,000-$160,000.

Yuba City

Sawyer's Landing, Hal Porter Homes, 1953 Big Oaks Ct., Yuba City. Ph: (916) 751-0102. Single-family, 3-5 bedrooms, 2-2.5 baths, 2-3 car garages, $93,000-$124,000.

14/Fun & Games

Parks, Museums, Hiking Trails, Classes Too
— Sports & Entertainment for Adults and Children

SAN FRANCISCO AND SAN MATEO COUNTY offer lots in the way of fun and recreation — San Francisco with its fine restaurants, museums, theaters and tourist attractions and San Mateo, excelling in nature's delights: beaches, trails, forests, vistas, parks.

Both counties do quite well in the hometown diversions: baseball, softball, soccer, basketball, bowling, clubs, personal enrichment classes. One pastime, unusual in the Bay Area: plane watching. The parking lot near the Millbrae Avenue exit off Highway 101 is often filled to capacity. Inside the cars, airplane and travel buffs watch jets depart San Francisco International.

In addition to Fisherman's Wharf, and other attractions in San Francisco, a partial list of activities in the City and San Mateo would include sunbathing or fishing at ocean and Bay beaches, deep sea fishing (cod, salmon), camping under the redwoods in state and county parks, ice skating, boating, recreational auto racing, whale watching, elephant seal watching, or just taking a drive.

Some suggestions: In San Mateo County, try Highway 1 along the coast, Highway 35 on the spine of the Santa Cruz Mountains, Interstate 280 with a view of Crystal Springs Reservoir and mountains and hills, and side roads in the hills and valleys of the Santa Cruz Mountains. In San Francisco, a drive up to the Twin Peaks lookout for a gull's eye view of the City eastward and Highway 1, west of Golden Gate Park. And if the local offerings are not to your liking, Monterey is a scenic two to three hours' drive along Highway 1 and the Sierra (skiing, hiking and gambling) a few hours off.

Classes, Clubs, Shopping, Too

What the public sector lacks, the private sector provides — racquetball, golf, bowling, tennis, movies, special activity classes. Also shopping, an unsung, often maligned pursuit but one that brings pleasure to thousands.

San Francisco's Union Square is the hub of big-city shopping with Macy's, Neiman Marcus, Saks Fifth Avenue, and Gump's. A couple blocks south, Nordstrom and Emporium anchor San Francisco Center and its glitzy array of shops.

San Mateo County, too, has some delightful shopping centers: Serramonte Center and Westlake Shopping Center in Daly City, Tanforan Shopping Center in San Bruno, Fashion Island and Hillsdale Mall in San Mateo.

City Parks, Sports, the Arts

Regional parks tend to get most of the attention, but city parks can be counted in the dozens and draw many people. Bicycle and jogging trails wind their way throughout both counties.

Children's activities include soccer, swimming, ice skating, football, basketball, baseball, gymnastics, tennis, golf, surfing, dancing.

If you want to sneak in some pier fishing with the kids, try the old San Mateo Bridge. Preserved for fishing, a part of it sits under the arching shadows of the new bridge. For ocean fishing there's the Pacifica Pier or in San Francisco, the beaches off the Great Highway.

Where to Look

One flaw mars this happy picture of abundance: There is so much to do that it is sometimes hard to know just what to do. Here are suggestions that will help with the sorting out.

• Find out who is organizing activities in your neighborhood or town and in nearby towns. Usually this can be accomplished by calling or visiting the chambers of commerce, the city recreation departments and the school districts.

• Get on the mailing lists. Adult schools and recreation departments change their classes about every three months. Theaters and orchestras issue calendars every season.

• Find out the rules. Some cities provide minimal support for certain activities. You may have to sign up the players on your softball team and collect the fees and meet application deadlines.

Baseball and soccer leagues usually guarantee the younger children, no matter what their skill, two innings or two quarters of play. But other sports (football) often go by skill. Ask about playing time.

• Disregard city boundaries. If you live in Pacifica and want to take a class in San Mateo, go ahead. A person with a Foster City job might want to tackle an aerobics class in that city before hitting the freeway.

• The San Mateo Convention and Visitors' Bureau puts out maps, brochures. Write 111 Anza Blvd., Suite 410, Burlingame, 94010, or phone (415) 348-7600.

• Subscribe to a local newspaper. Almost all of them will have calendars of events, lists of local attractions and hours of operation.

Major Offerings in San Francisco

San Francisco offers a wide array of entertainment, cultural activities and recreation. Check the Sunday Chronicle's Datebook or "pink section" for detailed listing on specific events.

San Francisco Museums

Academy of Sciences. Located in Golden Gate Park. General admission $7, general; children 11-17 and seniors 65+, $4; children 6-11, $1.50; under 6, free; first Wednesday free to all. The academy contains:

• Morrison Planetarium. For information and show schedules, call (415) 750-7141.

• Laserium. Laser light shows with rock, classical and contemporary music, (415) 750-7138.

• Natural History Museum. Displays of wildlife, rocks and universe, open daily 10 a.m. to 5 p.m.

Steinhart Aquarium. Great white sharks, penguins and sea life from around the world, open daily 10 a.m. to 5 p.m. (415) 750-7145.

Ansel Adams Center. Museum of photography, open 11 a.m. to 5 p.m. Tuesday through Sunday. 250 Fourth St., (415) 495-7000.

Asian Art Museum. Art works from Asia over the centuries, open 10 a.m. to 5 p.m. Wednesday through Sunday. Adults, $5; seniors, $3; youths 12-17, $2; free under 12. Admission free from 10 a.m. to noon on first Saturday. Eighth Avenue and Kennedy Drive, Golden Gate Park, (415) 668-8921.

Cable Car Museum. In addition to photographs and memorabilia of the city's long love affair with its cable cars, there is an underground viewing room to watch the cables at work; open daily 10 a.m. to 6 p.m. April through October and 10 a.m. to 5 p.m. November through March. Washington and Mason streets. (415) 474-1887.

M.H. DeYoung Memorial Museum. American art, colonial through 20th century, as well as art of Africa, Oceania and the Americas in permanent collections; touring collections also featured. Adults, $5; seniors, $3; youths, $2; under 12, free. Open 10 a.m. to 5 p.m. Wednesday through Sunday. Open until 8:45 p.m. the first Wednesday each month, and free general admission. Eighth Avenue and Kennedy Drive, Golden Gate Park. (415) 863-3330.

Palace of the Legion of Honor. Closed for renovation until mid-1995. Rodin sculptures and medieval to post-impressionist European art in permanent collections. Clement Street and Legion of Honor Drive, Lincoln Park. (415) 863-3300.

San Francisco Museum of Modern Art. Touring and permanent collections of art and photography, open 10 a.m. to 5 p.m. Tuesday, Wednesday and

Friday, 10 a.m. to 9 p.m. Thursday, 11 a.m. to 5 p.m. Saturday and Sunday; free admission first Tuesday 10 a.m. to 5 p.m. Van Ness Avenue and McAllister Street. (415) 863-8800.

The Outdoors

Day trips, overnight camping or hikes can be accommodated at parks and beaches. San Mateo County is abundantly blessed with them.

Some telephone numbers for state parks and beaches are for the area offices rather than individual parks. Area offices are staffed during business hours. Park offices are staffed only intermittently.

Beaches

• **Bean Hollow State Beach.** 44 acres. 17.5 miles south of Half Moon Bay on Highway 1. Picnicking, fishing, nature trail. (415) 879-0832.

• **Gray Whale Cove State Beach.** 1.3 acres. 9 miles north of Half Moon Bay on Highway 1. Operated by concessionaire. Fishing. Fee, $4.

• **Half Moon Bay State Beach.** 170 acres. Half mile west of Highway 1 on Kelly Ave. Family campsites plus special sites for hikers and bicyclists. 51 developed sites for campers & trailers. Outdoor showers. Picnicking, fishing, equestrian trail, stables nearby. Trailer sanitation station. (415) 726-8820.

• **Montara State Beach.** 680 acres. 8 miles north of Half Moon Bay on Highway 1. Elevation: 0-1,920 feet. Fishing, picnicking, hiking trails. Dormitory-style hostel, operated by American Youth Hostel Assn., on grounds of Montara Point Lighthouse. (415) 728-7177 after 5 p.m.

• **Pescadero State Beach.** 638 acres. 14.5 miles south of Half Moon Bay on Highway 1. Fishing. Parking fee, $4. (415) 879-0832.

• **Pomponio State Beach.** 410 acres. 12 miles south of Half Moon Bay on Highway 1. Picnicking, fishing. (415) 879-0832.

• **San Gregorio State Beach.** 172 acres. 10.5 miles south of Half Moon Bay on Highway 1. Picnicking, fishing, food service. (415) 879-0832.

State and County Parks, Reserves

• **Angel Island.** Cycling, hiking and picnicking all on a San Francisco Bay island. Ferry leaves San Francisco weekends and holidays. Park information (415) 435-3522, ferry info (415) 435-2131.

• **Año Nuevo State Reserve.** 1,192 acres. 27 miles south of Half Moon Bay on Highway 1. Visitor center open 9 a.m. to 3 p.m. plus guided tours daily Dec. 1 to April 1 during the elephant seal season. Tours very popular. Reservations a must. Fishing, nature and hiking trails, exhibits. (415) 879-2025 or 879-0227.

• **Butano State Park.** 2,700 acres. 5 miles south of Pescadero on Cloverdale Road. Elevation: 500 feet. Family campsites plus special sites for hikers and bicyclists.

Twenty-one developed sites for trailers 24 feet long and campers 30 feet long, also 18 walk-in sites. Admission $14 per vehicle per night plus $5 per extra vehicle. Picnicking, hiking trails. (415) 879-0173.

• **Edgewood County Park.** 467 acres. 1 Old Stagecoach Road, off Edgewood Road in Redwood City. Renowned for wildflowers, views from 800-foot high ridge. Hiking, equestrian trails. (415) 589-5708.

• **Fitzgerald Marine Reserve.** Off Highway 1, Moss Beach, a couple miles north of Half Moon Bay airport. Wildlife sanctuary. Lecture tours of tidal pools at low tides. (415) 728-3584 or 342-7755 for group tours.

• **Flood County Park.** 21 acres. Bay Road off Marsh Road in Menlo Park. Group picnicking, softball fields, tennis courts, playground. Part of old Flood Estate. (415) 363-4022.

• **Huddart County Park.** 974 acres. Off Kings Mountain Road, about 2 miles west of Highway 84 near Woodside. Archery, youth group camping, day camp, group picnic areas, play fields, hiking, jogging, nature, horseback trails. (415) 851-1210.

• **Junipero Serra County Park.** 108 acres. 1801 Crystal Springs Road, San Bruno, off Interstate 280. Day camp, nature area, group picnics, playfields, hiking, jogging, nature trails. (415) 589-5708.

• **Pescadero/Memorial County Park.** 339 acres. 9500 Pescadero Road, Loma Mar, between Highways 1 and 84. Views from Mt. Ellen, redwood groves, day and overnight camping, group picnics, swimming, hiking trails. (415) 879-0212.

• **Milagra Ridge County Reserve.** 232 acres. Off Sharp Park Road, Pacifica. Trails. Hike in for ocean views.

• **McDonald County Park.** 867 acres. 13435 Pescadero Road, La Honda. About 6 miles south of Highway 84. Youth group camping, group picnics, hiking, horseback trails. (415) 879-0238.

• **Pescadero Creek County Park.** 5,973 acres. Hiking, horseback trails. (415) 363-4021.

• **Pigeon Point Lighthouse.** Quarter mile west of Highway 1 on Pigeon Point Road. About 30 miles north of Santa Cruz. Views of ocean. Hostel operated by American Youth Hostel Assn. (415) 879-0633 after 4:30 p.m.

• **Portola State Park.** 2,010 acres. On Portola State Park Road, 6.5 miles west of Highway 35 on Alpine Road. Camping, picnicking, hiking and nature trails, exhibits. Elevation: 450 feet. 52 developed sites with accommodations for trailers 21 feet long, campers 27 feet. Hike-in campsites available by reservation, also four group camps. (415) 948-9098.

• **San Bruno Mountain County Park.** 2,064 acres. 555 Guadalupe Canyon Parkway, between Brisbane and Daly City. Hiking trails only. Picnicking and day camp. (415) 355-8289 or 587-7511.

• **San Pedro Valley County Park.** 975 acres. 600 Oddstad Blvd., Pacifica. Fishing, picnicking, playground, hiking. Disabled-accessible. (415) 355-8289.

• **Wunderlich County Park.** 942 acres. 4040 Woodside Road, 2 miles southwest of Woodside. Hiking, horseback trails. Redwood forest, meadows and stands of oak and madrone. (415) 851-1210.

Other Diversions

• **Acres of Orchids.** 1450 El Camino Real, South San Francisco. Open year-round, tours daily. Flower plants by the thousands in garden patio setting of retail sales house, a laboratory. See how orchids are grown and cloned.

• **Alcatraz.** Former federal prison, now a national park. Ferries leave San Francisco seven times daily from Pier 41, Fisherman's Wharf. Carry jackets, comfortable shoes. (415) 546-2805.

• **Arts Council of San Mateo County.** 1219 Ralston Ave., Belmont. Rotating exhibits of contemporary art being produced in the Bay region. Works showcased in historic 26-room restored mansion in Belmont's Twin Pines Park. Craft gallery, special events, technical assistance to artists, volunteer program. Admission free, open 9-5 Monday-Friday, 1-4 Sunday.

• **Bay Meadows Racetrack.** Adjacent to San Mateo County Fairgrounds. Between Highway 101 on the east, El Camino Real on the west, 25th Avenue on the north and Hillsdale Boulevard on the south. 100 Live racing days per year. Thoroughbreds, Labor Day through January. Satellite wagering the rest of the year. (415) 574-RACE or 573-4516.

• **Central Park.** Between Fifth and Fourth avenues, San Mateo, off El Camino Real. A great park. Former estate of Capt. William Kohl of Alaska fur trade fame. Ornamental fence built in 1874. Baseball field. Picnic grounds, Japanese garden designed by landscape architect from Imperial Palace, Tokyo. Considered one of the finest oriental gardens in state. Nice place to take the kids on a sunny afternoon.

• **Cow Palace.** Daly City, one mile from Highway 101. Home of Grand National and Junior Grand National Livestock Exposition, world-class wrestling matches, and other sporting and music events and national exhibits and conventions. Rock music.

• **Coyote Point Beach Park & Museum.** Take Peninsula Avenue exit off Highway 101 in Burlingame and head east. Admission charge to museum $3, adults; $2, seniors; $1, ages 6 to 17; and $4 parking fee. Museum a great place for the kiddies. Exhibits on humans' ties with nature. Also an aquarium, computer games, films, giant mural. Also world's largest bee tube. Open 10-5 Tuesday through Saturday, and noon to 5 Sunday, free day first Wednesday. Phone (415) 342-7755.

• **Coyote Point Yacht Harbor**. Beach park great for picnicking, windy at times, sand lots for kiddies big and small, views of windsurfers , jets landing at San Francisco International. (415) 347-6730, marina (415) 573-2594.

• **Exploratorium**. Hands-on center focusing on physical sciences and human perception; open Wednesday 10 a.m. to 9:30 p.m., Tuesday through Sunday 10 a.m. to 5 p.m.; admission free first Wednesday. Palace of Fine Arts,

Lyon Street and Marina Boulevard, San Francisco. (415) 561-0360.

• **Filoli House & Garden.** On Cañada Road in Woodside, south of the Highway 92-Interstate 280 intersection. Tours of modified Georgian-style mansion and 17 acres of formal gardens. Guided tours every Tuesday through Thursday and most Saturdays, with reservations required. Self-guided tours, no reservation, every Friday, first Saturday and second Sunday. For tour information (415) 364-2880.

• **Fisherman's Wharf/Pier 30.** Former center of San Francisco's commercial fishing industry, now collection of restaurants and shops; historic sailing ships. Open daily.

• **San Francisco Zoo.** Tuxedo Junction penguin exhibit, gorilla world, antique carousel and primate exhibits among the features; open daily 10 a.m. to 5 p.m. with weekend tours at 1 p.m. Sloat Boulevard at 45th Avenue, San Francisco. (415) 753-7083.

• **Fort Mason.** Once the command post for all U.S. forces in the west. Theaters, restaurants, workshops, art galleries, liberty ships. Marina Boulevard at Laguna Street, San Francisco. (415) 441-5705.

• **Haas-Lilienthal House.** Elaborate gables and Queen Anne-style circular tower adorn this 106-year-old mansion. 2007 Franklin St., San Francisco. Open 11 a.m. to 4 p.m. Sunday, noon to 3 p.m. Wednesday. (415) 441-3000.

• **Mission Dolores.** Founded in 1776, built in 1791, the city's oldest building includes museum and cemetery garden. Open daily 9 a.m. to 4:30 p.m., fall and winter 9 a.m. to 4 p.m. 16th and Dolores streets, San Francisco. (415) 621-8203.

• **National Maritime Park.** Liberty ships, schooners, models and nautical history displays, bookstore, museum open daily — 10 a.m. to 5 p.m. all seasons.

Hyde Street Pier, with Balclutha and Tayer sailing vessels and a ferry boat, open daily 10 a.m. to 5 p.m., in summer 10 a.m. to 5:30 p.m. Pier 45, with World War II submarine USS Pampanito open daily 9 a.m. to 6 p.m., summer 9 a.m. to 9 p.m. Located at Taylor and Embarcadero. (415) 929-0202.

• **Old Mint.** Survivors of 1906 quake and fire. Three million dollars of gold bars, coin collection and restored Victorian rooms. Open 10 a.m. to 4 p.m.

For Additional Reading ...

Bike Trails, Wine Country, Romantic Getaways
Tours, Restaurants, Gardens, Real Estate ...

*For more on Northern California
see the Book List and order blank
on the pages at the end of this guide*

Monday-Friday, free. Fifth and Mission, San Francisco. (415) 744-6830.

• **Pier 39**. Located next to Fisherman's Wharf. Shops, restaurants, and amusements. Entertainment by jugglers and musicians. Seals frolic in waters immediately to west. (415) 981-7437.

• **Presidio Museum**. Exhibits of early San Francisco military history, Presidio and Spanish-American War, 1906 quake and fire. Lincoln Boulevard at Funston Street, San Francisco. In process of being taken over by the U.S. National Park Service. Presently closed. For information on when it will reopen, possibly in 1994, call (415) 921-8193.

• **Sanchez Adobe Historical Site.** 1000 Linda Mar Blvd., Pacifica, 1 mile east of Highway 1. Sole building of Mexican era on the Peninsula that is open to the public. Small museum contains exhibits, artifacts, furniture. 10-4 Tuesday through Thursday, 1-5 Saturday and Sunday. (415) 359-1462.

• **San Jose Sharks**. Professional ice hockey team, playing home games at San Jose Arena. For information, phone (800) 755-5050.

• **San Mateo County Historical Museum.** On the grounds of the College of San Mateo, 1700 West Hillsdale Blvd., San Mateo. The story of the county told through exhibits, diorama, models. Carriage collection, special rotating exhibits. Tours, films by appointment. 9:30-4:30 Monday-Thursday, 12:30-4:30 Sunday. (415) 574-6441.

• **Shelldance Nursery.** 2000 Highway 1, Pacifica. One of the most extensive collections of bromeliads in USA, over 500 species, and also orchids. One-hour tours, by appointment only, can be tailored for children or adults or botany classes. No admission charge, can accommodate up to 60. Hours 9 a.m. to 4 p.m. Monday-Saturday. (415) 355-4845.

• **Strybing Arboretum**. Possibly world's largest greenhouse; home to more than 6,000 plant and tree species, open weekdays 8 a.m. to 4:30 p.m., weekends and holidays 10 a.m. to 5 p.m. Ninth Avenue at Lincoln Way, San Francisco. (415) 661-1316.

• **Sunset Magazine & Gardens.** Middlefield and Willow roads, Menlo Park. Tour the gardens and test kitchens of Sunset magazine at the magazine's headquarters. Open weekdays from 9 a.m. to 4 p.m., tours at 10:30 a.m. and 2:30 p.m. Reservations required for groups of 15 or more. (415) 324-5479.

• **Treasure Island Museum**. Features include exhibits on Golden Gate International Exposition of 1939 and China Clipper flying boats, and history of American sea service in the Pacific. Building 1, Treasure Island, open daily 10 a.m. to 3:30 p.m. Admission free. Exit off Bay Bridge. (415) 395-5067.

• **Whale watching.** Migration off California coast from December through March. Whales visible from many places along coast, but best place to view is from boat. Several tours embark from Pillar Point Harbor in Half Moon Bay. Capt. John's Fishing Trips, (415) 728-3377; Huck Finn Fishing Trips, (415) 726-7133; Oceanic Society, (415) 474-3385.

15/Regional Recreation

Things to Do, Places to See in Northern California — from the Bay Region to the Sierra Nevada

WHERE TO PLAY, where to spend the weekend? Northern California offers many amusements. Here is a list, by county or region, of the major ones outside Alameda County. Always call ahead. Some places are open seasonally, some only a few days weekly. Some require reservations. A few are free, most charge.

Alameda County

• **Children's Fairyland.** Off Grand Avenue at the north end of Lake Merritt in downtown Oakland. Mother Goose, Alice in Wonderland, Cheshire Cat, etc. Merry-go-round, ferris wheel. Puppets, clowns, slides, mazes. (510) 832-3609.

• **Crown Memorial State Beach.** One of the few beaches on the Bay, 383 acres in city of Alameda. Day camps, turfed play areas, 2.5 miles of beach. Estuary and reserve, wading, sunbathing, swimming, fishing. I-880 to downtown Oakland. Webster Street to end. (510) 521-6887.

• **Dunsmuir House and Gardens.** Gothic house and garden, 2960 Peralta Court, Oakland. Exit 106th Ave. from Interstate 580. (510) 562-0328.

• **East Bay Regional Park District.** Covers Alameda and Contra Costa counties. Parks, lakes, hiking trails, botanical gardens, Victorian farms, estuaries, wilderness areas. Fishing, swimming, boating, golfing, much more. For brochures, maps, (510) 635-0135.

• **Golden Gate Fields Racetrack.** Thoroughbred racing, January to June. In Albany, I-80 to Gilman St. (510) 526-3020.

• **Lawrence Hall of Science.** Science museum for adults and children. Hands-on fun, computers rabbits, snakes, brain games, astronomy, Nobel medals, classes, all fortified by strong connection to UC-Berkeley. Often features robotic, life-sized dinosaurs and whales. Store sells science toys. Located in Berkeley Hills. Highway 24 to Fish Ranch Road, to Grizzly Peak Road, left on Centennial Drive. Also can be reached from rear of university. (510) 642-5132.

• **Magnes Memorial Museum.** Art and artifacts of Jewish culture. Library, history, tours. 2911 Russell St., Berkeley. Ph. (510) 549-6950.

• **McConaghy House,** 18701 Hesperian Blvd., Hayward, next to Kennedy Park. Furnished Victorian farmhouse. Tours. (510) 276-3010.

• **Meek Estate.** Renovated and furnished five-story Victorian. Ballroom, library, solarium, bedrooms. Picnic grounds. Hampton and Boston Roads, Hayward. (510) 581-0223.

• **Mission San Jose.** 43300 Mission Blvd., Fremont. Built in 1797, destroyed in 1868 earthquake, restored. Picturesque building. Slide show, artifacts, history of Ohlone Indian. (510) 657-1797.

• **Navy-Marine Corps Museum.** Treasure Island in San Francisco Bay. Navy and Marine Corps paintings, memorabilia. Call (415) 395-5067.

• **Oakland Museum.** Located at 1000 Oak St. in downtown. California art, history and natural history. First class. (510) 834-2413.

• **Paramount Theatre,** 2025 Broadway, Oakland. "Art Deco" at its finest. Parquet floors, gold ceiling, sculptures. (510) 465-6400.

• **Steam locomotive rides.** Sunol. Abandoned line overhauled and put in service with rides for public. Leaves from hamlet of Sunol, off I-680 south of Pleasanton. (510) 862-9063.

• **University of California, Berkeley.** Bookstores, libraries, museums, lectures, concerts, ballet. University Avenue off I-80 and go east. For performances, call (510) 642-9988. For tours, (510) 642-3734. Sports tickets, (510) 642-5150.

• **Western Aerospace Museum.** 8260 Boeing St., Oakland Airport. Vintage planes, some military. Memorabilia. Model planes. Exhibits. (510) 638-7100.

Contra Costa County

• **Behring Auto Museum.** Over 200 vintage vehicles. Run by UC Berkeley. Sycamore Valley Road east off Interstate 680, to Blackhawk Plaza Circle. (510) 736-2280.

• **Concord Pavilion.** Outdoor pavilion that books top national talent, 2000 Kirker Pass Road. For tickets (510) 67-MUSIC

• **Delta.** Fishing (sturgeon, striped bass, catfish), hunting, boating, water skiing, swimming, houseboating. Highway 4 to Stockton or the Antioch Bridge up to Isleton or Highway 12 to Rio Vista. In summer, farmers set up vegetable stands and, for a fee, allow city slickers to pick berries and other goodies.

• **East Brother Light Station.** Bed-and-breakfast in a restored Victorian on a small island, just north of the Richmond-San Rafael Bridge. Great Bay views. Antiques. Museum. Lighthouse. Also, day trips. Boat leaves from Point San Pablo. (510) 233-2385.

• **John Muir Home** and Martinez Adobe, a relic from the ranchero days, located one behind the other in Martinez. Muir was conservationist, co-founder of Sierra Club. Alhambra Avenue just off Hwy. 4. (510) 228-8860.

• **Lindsay Junior Museum,** Walnut Creek. Natural history museum specializing in feathery, furry and scaly residents of Contra Costa. Also, a hospital for injured wildlife. In Larkey Park. Buena Vista and First avenues. (510) 935-1978.

• **Mt. Diablo State Park.** Recreation cornucopia, 18,000 acres, trails, views, caves, rock climbing, fossils embedded in rocks, camping and picnicking, bobcats, mountain lions, foxes, coyotes. Drive to summit, 3,849 feet. From Walnut Creek, take Northgate Road; from Danville, Diablo Road. (510) 837-2525.

• **Regional Center for the Arts.** Musicals, drama, comedy, concerts. 1676 N. California Blvd., downtown Walnut Creek. (510) 943-7469.

• **St. Mary's College,** Moraga. Beautiful church. Gallery, art works. Picnic grounds. College football and basketball. Highway 24 to Lafayette to Moraga Road to St. Mary's Road. (510) 376-4411.

• **Shadelands Ranch Museum.** Walnut Creek. Restored ranch that shows how Contra Costans lived and worked. 2660 Ygnacio Valley Road. (510) 935-7871.

• **Tao House.** Danville home of playwright Eugene O'Neill. Here he brooded and wrote, "The Iceman Cometh," "Moon for the Misbegotten," "Long Day's Journey into Night." Occasional tours. (510) 228-8860.

Marin County

• **Angel Island.** Off Tiburon. A park. West Coast Ellis Island. Chinese immigrants were detained here. Picnic grounds. Trails. Beaches. Views. Ferry from Tiburon. Park (415) 435-1915. Ferry (415) 546-2896.

• **Bay Area Discovery Museum,** Sausalito, 557 East Fort Baker Road. Live fish, murals of Bay habitats, pretend salmon fishing, science corner, boat making, story telling, drafting table, photo dark room and more. (415) 332-7674.

• **Bay Model Visitors' Center.** 2100 Bridgeway in Sausalito. How the rivers and estuary and currents of the Bay interact. A model. Natural history exhibits. (415) 332-3870.

• **Golden Gate Bridge.** You can't walk across the Bay Bridge or the San Rafael. You can the Golden Gate. It's worth it.

• **Marin Civic Center, San Rafael.** What Marin County inspired in Frank Lloyd Wright. Public building. Drop in any time. Take Civic Center Drive or San Pedro Road off of Highway 101. Tours. (415) 499-6104

• **Marin Headlands,** the land just west of Golden Gate Bridge. Spectacular vistas of San Francisco, the Golden Gate, the Pacific. Artillery fortifications. Take Sausalito exit closest to bridge, pick up Bunker Road. Information (415) 331-1540 or 556-0560.

• **Mt. Tamalpais.** See Farallones, Sierra, Richmond, Oakland, San Fran. Many trails to top. Highway 101 to Shoreline Highway (just north of Sausalito), to Panoramic Highway off Route 1. (415) 388-2070.

SAN JOSE
MUSEUM
OF ART

The View From Within: Japanese-American Art from the
Internment Camps, 1942 - 1945
January 15 - April 10,1994

Sam Hernandez: Abstract Imagist
February 5 - April 3, 1994

In the Spirit of Nature
February 5 - April 3, 1994

Squeak Carnwath
April 23 - July 4, 1994

Rupert Garcia: Aspects of Resistance
May 7 - September 4, 1994

ABODE: Sanctuary for the Familia(r)
May 7 - September 4, 1994

American Art 1900 - 1940: A History Reconsidered
Works from the Collection of the
Whitney Museum of American Art
Arshile Gorky • Marsden Hartley • Edward Hopper •
Gaston Lachaise • Georgia O'Keeffe
Opens May 7, 1994

The Whitney collaboration is sponsored in part by
The Redevelopment Agency, City of San Jose,
Knight Foundation, Applied Materials, Comerica Bank,
Deloitte & Touche, Pacific Telesis Foundation
and San Jose Mercury News

Call (408) 294-2787 to receive more information
San Jose Museum of Art • 110 S. Market • San Jose, CA • 95113

• **Muir Woods.** Giant coast redwoods. Highway 101 to Shoreline Highway to Panoramic Highway. (415) 388-2595.

• **Point Reyes.** The Pacific Coast. One big park. Lighthouse. Trails. Earthquake country, where the San Andreas Fault goes to sea. (415) 663-1092. Off Highway 1.

• **Marin Museum of American Indian.** 2200 Novato Blvd., Novato. Artifacts, exhibits. (415) 897-4064.

Napa County

• **Lake Berryessa.** Lake-reservoir located in eastern part of the county, off of Highway 128. Boating, water sports. Scenic drive.

• **Wine Country.** Napa is synonymous with wine and the wineries have gone to great lengths to welcome visitors with tours and tastings and, lately, with entertainment, such as jazz festivals. Many restaurants. Spas that tap into mineral springs. For day's tour, take Highway 29 out of Vallejo, go to Calistoga, return on Silverado Trail.

• **Wine Train.** From Napa to St. Helena and back. Old train activated to tour the valley in style. Dine and sip (wine) on board. Features many local vintages. (800) 427-4124.

Santa Clara County

• **Barbie Hall of Fame**, 460 Waverly St., Palo Alto. Barbie dolls from around the world. (415) 326-5841.

• **Children's Discovery Museum**, 180 Woz Way, San Jose. Hands-on exhibits; technology, science, humanities and arts. (408) 298-5437.

• **Great America.** Located in the city of Santa Clara, off Great America Parkway. First-class amusement park. Over 100 attractions, many of spine-tingling. Games. Musical reviews. (408) 988-1800.

• **Lick Observatory.** Atop Mt. Hamilton, southeast of San Jose, one of the most powerful observatories in the world. Scenic. Tours. (408) 274-5061.

• **Mission Santa Clara de Asis.** At Santa Clara University campus. Rebuilt mission. While there, tour the university, a pretty campus. (408) 554-4023.

• **Rosicrucian Museum.** Park and Naglee Avenues, San Jose. Egyptian, Babylonian and Assyrian artifacts, including tools, jars and jewelry. Also mummies, a walk-in tomb and exhibits about early discoveries in math and written language. Next to the museum are a planetarium and science museum. (408) 287-2807.

• **San Jose Flea Market.** 12000 Berryessa Road, between Highway 101 and Interstate 680, San Jose. One of the great bazaars of the West Coast. Open Wednesdays through Sundays. Draws 50,000 to 75,000 on weekends. Also includes farmers' markets and kiddie amusements. (408) 453-1110.

• **San Jose Historical Museum.** 635 Phelan St., San Jose. Old Santa Clara County recreated at Kelley Park — an Indian acorn granary, the Pacific Hotel, a candy store, an electric tower, a 1920s gas station, a dental building, more. Memorabilia. Exhibits on Costanoan Indians. Nearby: a petting zoo, and Japanese Friendship Park, six acres of waterfalls, stone bridges, bonsai plants. (408) 287-2290.

• **Stanford University.** Palo Alto. Beautiful campus. Spanish architecture. Hoover Tower (views). Several museums. Tours. (415) 723-2560.

• **The Tech** (Tech Museum of Innovation), 145 West San Carlos St., San Jose. How integrated chip works. Robots, biotechnology. (408) 279-7150.

• **Triton Museum**, 1505 Warburton Ave., Santa Clara. Folk, contemporary, classic art. Pastoral scenes and wildlife of the early valley. (408) 247-3754.

• **Villa Montalvo.** Located just outside Saratoga on Saratoga-Los Gatos Road. Italian Renaissance villa. Shows and programs on cultural subjects. The grounds, 175 acres, are maintained as a public arboretum. (408) 741-3421.

• **Winchester Mystery House.** 525 South Winchester Blvd., San Jose. Heiress of the shooting Winchesters pumped about $5 million into this four-story, eccentric, 160-room house. Rifle collection. Garden. Cafe. Tours. (408) 247-2101.

• **Musical and Cultural Events**
Four "must" mailing lists for music and culture buffs:

• Flint Center, De Anza College, 21250 Stevens Creek Blvd., Cupertino. (408) 864-8816.

• San Jose Center for the Performing Arts. Almaden Boulevard and Park Avenue. (408) 277-3900.

• Shoreline Amphitheater at Mountain View. (415) 967-4040.

• Stanford University, Palo Alto. (415) 723-2300.

Sacramento County

• **Capitol Mall.** Daily tours of the Capitol, a beautiful building. When Legislature is in session, public can view the action. Tour info: (916) 324-0333

• **Sutter's Fort.** Reconstructed adobe fort in the downtown, 27th and L streets. Where John Sutter built his fort. (916) 324-0539.

• **Stanford Home.** Near Capitol Mall at 8th and N streets. Tours. (916) 324-0575.

• **Governor's Mansion**. Representation of the state's Victorian architecture when it was constructed in 1877, this building at 16th and H streets now houses artifacts from state's history. (916) 323-3047.

• **Old Sacramento**. A hands-on history lesson of the gold rush, with buildings reconstructed to original Wild West specifications. Located in downtown, near the river. Among the attractions:

• **Sacramento History Museum**. A five-gallery exhibit of the city's history. One exhibit shows gold extracted from Mother Lode. (916) 264-7057.

• **B.F. Hastings Building**. In 1860 this was the end of the line for the Pony Express. Also served for sessions of the state Supreme Court. Alta Telegraph Company, operating in the building, sent the first transcontinental telegraph.

• **Big Four Building**. Where Leland Stanford, Charles Crocker, Mark Hopkins and Collis Huntington founded Central Pacific Railroad and laid plans to make it transcontinental. Art gallery, research library, re-created hardware store from 1800s featured.

• **Lady Adams Building**. Built from the wood of the ship "Lady Adams" in 1852, this building was the only one to survive a devastating fire that year.

• **Old Eagle Theater**, Front and J streets. Replica of California's first theater, established in 1849, houses slide show and theatrical production. (916) 446-6761.

• **Old Sacramento Schoolhouse**. Replica of one-room schoolhouse.

• **Delta King**. Riverboat, paddlewheeler.

• **The Globe**. Before the Panama Canal, many gold seekers and immigrants rounded the horn — Cape Horn — to reach California. The Globe is a re-creation of the type ship that made the perilous journey.

• **Railroad Museum**, About 20 restored locomotives and cars, including one that gives "passengers" impression the train is moving. Nearby are the Central Pacific Passenger Depot and the Central Pacific Freight Depot. During spring and summer, rides on a steam train. (916) 323-9280.

• **Crocker Art Museum**. What happened when a California millionaire visited Europe: 700 paintings and 1,000 drawings in a mansion remodeled in the Italianate style. (916) 264-5423.

• **Towe Ford Museum**. Edward Towe has been buying Fords for decades and houses most of his collection at 2200 Front St. (916) 442-6802.

• **Waterworld USA.** 14-acre water park. Giant water slide, surfing on machine-generated waves, swimming pools, 1600 Exposition Blvd., Sacramento. (916) 924-0556.

Solano County

• **Anheuser-Busch Brewery**, Fairfield. See how beer is brewed. Tours. Just south of Interstate 80 on Busch Boulevard. (707) 429-7595.

• **Benicia**. Used to be state capital. Historic buildings, restaurants, arsenal where U.S. Grant once served. I-680 to Highway 780, exit at Second Street, turn left.

• **Marine World-Africa USA**, Vallejo. Major theme park. Lions, tigers, elephants, seals, whales and dolphins. Feed and pet some. Restaurants. Kind of place where you spend a day or two. I-80 to Highway 37, go west. (707) 643-6722.

• **Nut Tree**, Vacaville. Restaurant, shops, train ride, airport. Musical events. Just across freeway from major outlet mall. Interstate 80 to Nut Tree Road. (707) 448-1818.

• **Wooz,** Vacaville. Small amusement park built around a large maze. Fun house, video arcade, other games. Off Interstate 80. (707) 446-5588.

Sonoma County

• **Armstrong Redwoods**. Grove of giants. Located outside Guerneville. Armstrong Woods Road from Highway 116. (707) 869-2015.

• **Farm Trails**. Pick what you eat straight from vine or tree. About 165 farms and wineries have formed into a "farm trails" group. For free map, call (707) 586-3276.

• **Fort Ross**. What Russians built when they lived in California. A detailed restoration. Interesting. Just off Highway 1, above Jenner. State park. Info. (707) 847-3286.

• **Glen Ellen**. Where Jack London, California's favorite son, wrote and lived. Ruins of London mansion, the Wolf House. Above city of Sonoma, off Highway 12, in Sonoma Valley wine country. Jack London State Historic Park. (707) 938-5216.

• **Luther Burbank Home and Gardens**. Perhaps the most famous green thumb in the history of California, Burbank made everything grow. Santa Rosa and Sonoma avenues in downtown Santa Rosa. (707) 524-5445.

• **Mt. St. Helena**. Views, trails, hiking, geologically interesting. Highest mountain in the Bay Area, 4,343 feet. Looks like volcano but isn't. Take Highway 29 to Robert Louis Stevenson State Park. (707) 942-4575.

• **Petaluma Downtown**. Good collection of Victorians, some with iron fronts, an effort at fireproofing and prefabrication. Start on Petaluma Boulevard north. (707) 762-2785.

• **Russian River**. A nice drive in winter, nicer in summer, when the river is dammed to raise the level for canoeing and swimming. Canoe rentals, public beaches along river. On Highway 101, about 5 miles above Santa Rosa you'll see the signs.

• **Sonoma Coast.** Highway 1. Start at Bodega Bay or Jenner. Rugged. Great views. To see seals, stroll beach at Goat Rock near Jenner. Restaurants, resorts along route.

• **Sonoma Mission.** The last mission built on El Camino Real, the King's Highway. Nicely restored. Downtown City of Sonoma. (707) 938-9560.

• **Sonoma Plaza.** Where Mariano Vallejo quartered and trained his soldiers and ran his vast estate. Bear Flag Rebellion began here. Restored barracks. Mission close by and, within a half mile, the home of Vallejo. Also close by, restaurants, other historical buildings. Highway 12 to middle of City of Sonoma. (707) 938-1519.

• **Whale Watching.** Migrating south between November and February, the California Grey Whale often passes within a half mile of shore. Same on return trip in a few months. Can be seen from Bodega Head State Park, Salt Point State Park, and bluffs of state beach along Sonoma coast. (707) 847-3221.

• **Wine Country.** For the quick tour, drive Highway 12 south to north, or travel the Redwood Highway north of Santa Rosa. Wineries are all along both routes. Also in Alexander and Dry Creek Valleys, the Russian River area.

Miscellaneous

• **Yosemite.** I-580, to Route 120. Nature showing off. Reservations, (209) 252-4848.

• **Lake Tahoe.** Go east on Highway 50 or Interstate 80. Resorts, skiing, gambling, swimming, boating, fishing, more. Visitors Bureau (800) 288-2463. Ch of Comm. (916) 541-5255.

• **Santa Cruz Beach Boardwalk.** Amusement park on the Pacific. Last wooden roller-coaster on the west coast, a new high-tech roller coaster, other rides, arcades, concessions, beach. Highway 17 or Highway 1 south, follow signs. (408) 423-5590.

• **Roaring Camp** and Big Trees Narrow Gauge Railroad. Ride steam engine through virgin redwood forests to the top of Bear Mountain. Visit-shop 1880s-style logging town. Felton, near Santa Cruz. Highway 17. (408) 335-4484.

• **Monterey Bay Aquarium.** Aquatic displays. Nearly 7,000 species. Three-story exhibit with kelp forest. On Pacific. 886 Cannery Row, Monterey. (408) 648-4888.

Skiing
For road info. call 800-427-ROAD

• **Alpine Meadows.** Six miles west of Tahoe City. Over 100 runs on 2,000 acres. 12 lifts. Instruction. Equipment rentals, repairs. Child care. (916) 583-4232.

• **Boreal Ridge.** Tahoe-Reno. 380 acres. Seven lifts. Ph. (916) 426-3666.

• **Diamond Peak.** Tahoe-Reno. Five lifts on 655 acres. Ph. (702) 831-3211.

• **Heavenly.** Tahoe-Reno. 68 runs on 700 acres. Snowboarding. Restaurant, cocktails, cafeteria, ski school, shops. Child care. (702) 586-7000.

• **Homewood.** Tahoe-Reno. 10 lifts on 1,260 acres. (916) 525-2900.

• **Kirkwood.** Tahoe-Reno. 11 lifts on 2,000 acres. (209) 916) 258-3000

• **Northstar-at-Tahoe.** 53 runs on 1,700 acres. 11 lifts. Ski, snowboard instruction. Child care. (916) 562-1010

• **Sierra Ski Ranch.** Tahoe-Reno. 13 miles west of the Y on Highway 50. 40 runs on 2,000 acres. 8 lifts. (916) 659-7475.

• **Squaw Valley.** More than 4,000 acres. 33 lifts. Ice skating. Bungee jumping. Cross country skiing. Snowboarding. In summer, mountain biking, concerts, golf, tennis. Ski schools. Rentals. Child care. (1-800) 545-4350.

• **Sugar Bowl.** Reno-Tahoe. 8 lifts on 1,000 acres. (916) 426-3847.

• **Badger Pass, Yosemite.** 88 acres of skiing, five lifts. Base elevation is 7200 feet, summit is 8100 feet. Lessons. Child care. (209) 372-1330

• **Dodge Ridge, near Sonora.** 27 runs on 550 acres. 11 lifts. Child care. (209) 965-3474

16/Jobs & the Economy

Which Jobs Are In, Which Ones Are Out, Salary Sampler, Trends, Unemployment Rates

BOTH SAN FRANCISCO and San Mateo counties have diverse economies and are weathering the doldrums better than other counties. But the hard economic times are taking a toll.

San Francisco, by one recent count, lost over 30,000 jobs in the 1990s. The business community blames, in part, the city's taxes on small businesses and on payroll for driving jobs away.

On the bright side, both San Mateo and San Francisco have more jobs than job seekers. Each imports "labor" from outside county. Freeway construction will provide some jobs over the next five years. About $600 million is to be

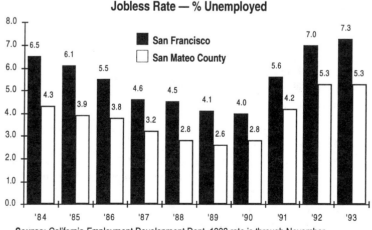

Jobless Rate — % Unemployed

San Francisco
San Mateo County

Source: California Employment Development Dept. 1993 rate is through November.

Job Outlook by Industry for San Francisco

Job Sector	1990	1997*	Change
Non-agricultural employment	573,100	582,100	8,900
Mining & Construction	15,700	15,500	-200
Manufacturing	39,100	37,000	-2,100
Non-durable goods	32,500	31,500	-1,000
Food processing	5,000	4,800	-200
Apparel	14,100	14,200	100
Printing & pub.	9,400	9,200	-200
Other non-durables	4,000	3,300	-700
Durable goods	6,600	5,500	-1,100
Primary & fab. metals	1,500	1,100	-400
Transportation equip.	1,000	800	-200
Other durables	4,100	3,600	-500
Transport & public util.	38,500	37,000	-1,500
Transportation	20,400	20,000	400
Comm. & util.	18,100	17,000	-1,100
Wholesale trade	29,800	27,300	-2,500
Retail Trade Total	78,900	81,500	2,600
Department stores	7,900	7,700	-200
Food stores	8,400	8,900	500
Apparel stores	9,500	9,800	300
Restaurants & bars	32,300	32,700	400
Other retail trade	20,800	22,400	1,600
Finance, insurance & real estate	75,800	71,600	-4,200
Finance	46,000	42,700	-3,300
Insurance	19,300	18,100	-1,200
Real Estate	10,500	10,800	300
Services Total	202,500	220,300	17,800
Hotels & motels	18,300	19,000	700
Bus. services	53,300	62,300	9,00
Health services	25,400	27,200	1,800
Legal services	20,800	22,800	2,000
Social services & membership	22400	23,900	1,500
Engr., mgmnt, archt, & related	30,200	31,800	1,600
Other services	32,100	33,300	1,200
Government Total	92,800	91,800	-1,000
Federal government	28,600	26,500	-2,100
State and local	64,200	65,300	1,100

Source: California Economic Development Department. **Key:** *Projected.

spent on Embarcadero repairs.

San Francisco city hall, in its 1993 jobs survey, said demand was going up for professional services (engineering, law, accounting), and for home health workers, computer engineers, exterminators, physical therapists, nurses, dentists and security guards. On the down escalator: tellers, postal workers, clerks, carpenters, metal workers, messengers.

Job Outlook by Industry for San Mateo County

Job Sector	1989	1996*	Change
Non-agricultural employment	294,800	324,200	29,400
Mining & Construction	14,200	16,300	2,100
Manufacturing	35,400	34,500	-900
Non-durable goods	14,100	15,000	900
Food & kindred prod.	2,800	2,700	-100
Printing & pub.	4,600	5,000	400
Chemicals & allied prod.	3,600	4,100	500
Other non-durables	3,100	3,200	100
Durable goods	21,300	19,500	-1,800
Primary & fab. metals	5,900	5,000	-900
Electrical & elect. equip.	5,700	5,300	-400
Instruments	4,000	3,900	-100
Other durables	5,700	5,300	-400
Transport & public util.	34,500	38,800	4,300
Transportation	29,900	34,300	4,400
Trucking & warehousing	2,700	2,900	200
Air transportation	23,300	27,200	3,900
Other transportation	3,900	4,200	300
Comm. & util.	4,600	4,500	-100
Wholesale trade	24,00	23,700	-300
Retail Trade Total	55,000	60,800	5,800
Dept & apparel stores	10,700	11,200	500
Food stores	6,800	7,600	800
Auto dealers & ser. sta.	5,000	5,200	200
Restaurants & bars	18,500	20,800	2,300
Other retail trade	14,000	16,000	2,000
Finance, insurance, & real estate	22,100	23,900	1,800
Finance	10,000	11,200	1,200
Insurance	5,800	6,000	200
Real Estate	6,300	6,700	400
Services Total	78,300	94,000	15,700
Hotels & motels	5,900	7,300	1,400
Bus. services	19,700	24,500	4,800
Health services	15,700	18,500	2,800
Engnrng, acctng, res. & mgmt.	10,800	14,500	3,700
Other services	20,200	22,300	2,100
Government Total	31,300	32,200	900
Federal government	6,400	6,000	-400
State and local	24,900	26,200	1,300

Source: California Economic Development Department. **Key:** *Projected.

The passenger count is up at San Francisco Airport, the mainstay of the San Mateo economy. Tourism, a major part of the San Francisco economy, is thriving.

The accompanying tables, based on estimates from the Employment Development Dept., will give some idea of what fields are growing.

What They Earn — Northern California

Position	Annual Salary
Accountant, school district	$31,224
Accounting Clerk, exper.	$24,000-$27,040
Administrative Assistant	$18,720 -$25,000
Analyst, budget, public ag.	$39,276-$47,364
Appliance Repair	$19,200
Assembler	$18,000-$20,000
Assistant Controller	$42,000
Baker, union, apprentice	$17,472
Bank Teller, experienced	$19,656-$22,800
Bartender, no experience	$8,840-$14,560
Bookkeeper	$20,000
Cable Installer, experienced	$31,491-$39,936
Canvasser, trainee	$13,520
Carpenter, journeyman	$52,000
Carpenter Helper	$16,640-$24,960
Carpet Cleaners	$10,400-$18,720
Chemist, analyst	$36,048-$42,852
Clerical, entry	$13,520
Clerical, experienced	$18,720-$24,960
Computer Analyst	to $55,000
Copy Machine Operator	$12,480
Counselor, career	$27,372-$32,964
Credit Analyst	$25,300
Customer Service Rep	$23,520
Dental Assistant	$27,040-$31,200
Dispatcher	to $25,000
Driver, warehouse	$20,000
Drycleaning Counter Worker	$12,480
Electronics Assembler	$13,000-$21,840
Guard	$8,840-16,640
Health Spa Fitness Worker	$20,000
House cleaner	$14,560
Industrial Waste Inspector, city	$34,116-$41,484
Instructional Media Technician	$20,363
Landscape Supervisor	$29,000
Legal Secretary, exper.	to $36,000
Librarian, govt.	$32,496-$39,480
Loan Processor	$24,960
Locksmith-Security Tech Trainee	$14,560-$18,720
Mailroom Clerk	$16,640
Medical Assistant, no experience	$12,480-$14,560
Medical Office, Billing	$24,000
Medical Transcriptionist	$31,200
Nurse,LVN,	$26,484-$33,816

What They Earn — Northern California

Position	Annual Salary
Office Assistant	$12,480
Office Machine Servicer, exper.	$16,640-$21,320
Operating Engineer, experienced	$27,040-$54,080
Order Entry Clerk	$14,560-18,720
Paralegal Specialist, experienced	$19,200-$28,800
Pest Control Technician	$22,443
Physical Therapist	$34,296-$51,504
Police Officer, suburban city	$38,784-$47,604
Production Worker	$16,557
Programer "C"	$40,000-$60,000
Restaurant Cook-Banquets	to $35,000
Retail Clerk	$12,480
Secretary, exper. Public Ag.	$28,267-$34,694
Security Guard, exper.	$16,640
Sheet Metal Worker	$16,640
Software Engineer	to $70,000
Switchboard Operator-Receptionist	$14,560-$17,680
Teacher, California average pay	$41,700
Teacher, Pleasanton	$52,126
Teacher, West Sacramento	$42,905
Teachers-Aides	$10,920-$17,160
Training & Placement Specialist	$14,500-$18,000
Truck Driver, experienced	to $28,080
Utility worker, transit agency	$17,680-$23,566
X-ray Technologist	to $62,400

Source: Help-wanted advertising in 1993 and early 1994. Government surveys.

Employment in Selected Cities

City	Civilian Labor Force	Number Employed	Unemployment Number	Percent
Burlingame	14,867	14,339	528	3.6
Daly City	49,731	46,324	3,407	6.9
Menlo Park	14,351	13,764	587	4.1
Pacifica	21,287	20,382	905	4.3
Redwood City	36,486	34,720	1,766	4.8
San Bruno	21,275	20,164	1,111	5.2
San Carlos	14,800	14,343	457	3.1
San Francisco	396,500	368,700	27,800	7.0
San Mateo City	48,352	45,751	2,601	5.4
S. San Francisco	28,614	26,713	1,901	6.6
San Mateo County	354,600	335,800	18,800	5.3

Source: California Employment Development Dept., June 1993. Summary of 1992 data. Note: Data partially based on 1990 census and are not seasonally adjusted.

Grocery Prices

Item	High	Low	Avg.
Apple Juice, frozen, cheapest, 12 oz.	$1.49	$1.19	$1.31
Apple Pie, Mrs. Smith's, 26 oz.	$3.99	$3.15	$3.53
Apples, Red Delicious, 1 lb.	$0.79	$0.69	$0.76
Aspirin, cheapest, 100 pills	$1.79	$1.49	$1.62
Baby Food, Gerber, bananas, 4 oz jar	$0.43	$0.41	$0.42
Baby Food, Gerber, spinach, 4 oz jar	$0.43	$0.37	$0.40
Bacon, Armour, 1 lb.	$2.28	$1.69	$1.95
Bananas, 1 lb.	$0.49	$0.34	$0.44
Beef, chuck roast, 1 lb.	$3.49	$2.88	$3.12
Beef, ground round, 1 lb.	$3.79	$1.78	$2.48
Beer, Budweiser, 6-pack, cans	$3.99	$3.69	$3.89
Beer, Coors, 6-pack, cans	$4.25	$3.99	$4.08
Bleach, Clorox, 1 gal.	$1.19	$1.19	$1.19
Bread, sourdough, Colombo, 1 lb	$1.79	$1.67	$1.74
Bread, white, cheapest, 1 lb.	$2.07	$0.69	$1.15
Broccoli, bunch	$1.29	$0.99	$1.09
Butter, Challenge, 1 lb.	$1.99	$1.65	$1.80
Cabbage, 1 lb.	$0.45	$0.25	$0.33
Cantaloupe, 1 lb.	$0.49	$0.29	$0.37
Carrots, fresh, 1 lb.	$0.39	$0.34	$0.36
Cat food, 9 Lives, 5.5 oz.	$0.39	$0.33	$0.36
Charcoal, Kingsford, 10 lbs.	$3.99	$3.29	$3.62
Cheese, Swiss, 1 lb.	$4.19	$3.59	$3.86
Chicken, fryer, 1 lb.	$1.04	$0.88	$0.97
Chili, Dennison, 15 oz. can	$1.73	$0.99	$1.32
Cigarettes, Marlboro Lights, carton	$19.49	$18.99	$19.22
Coca Cola, six-pack, 12 oz. cans	$2.49	$2.25	$2.36
Coffee, Folgers, 1 lb. 10 oz.	$3.65	$3.59	$3.61
Cookies, Oreo, 1 lb.	$2.99	$2.64	$2.84
Corn Flakes, Kellogg, 18 oz.	$2.39	$1.99	$2.12
Diapers, Pampers, box of 36	$8.39	$8.19	$8.29
Dishwashing liquid, Joy, 22 oz.	$1.69	$1.43	$1.54
Eggs, large, Grade AA, doz.	$1.59	$0.99	$1.39
Flour, Gold Medal, 5 lbs.	$1.39	$0.99	$1.16
Frozen Yogurt, Dreyers, half gal.	$4.59	$4.29	$4.39
Gin, Beefeater, 750 ml.	$13.99	$12.88	$13.58
Grapefruit, 1 lb.	$0.69	$0.45	$0.53
Grapenuts, Post, 24 oz.	$4.69	$3.79	$4.09
Ice Cream, Store Brand, vanilla half gal.	$3.89	$2.09	$2.72
Ketchup, Del Monte, 32 oz.	$1.99	$1.79	$1.88
Ketchup, Heinz, 28 oz.	$1.99	$1.99	$1.99
Lamb, leg of, 1 lb.*	$3.49	$2.99	$3.24

Grocery Prices

Item	High	Low	Avg.
Laundry Detergent, Tide, 42 oz.	$3.79	$2.99	$3.36
Lettuce, Iceberg, head	$0.99	$0.79	$0.89
Margarine, Imperial, whipped, 1-lb. tub	$1.55	$0.59	$0.94
Mayonnaise, Best Foods, 1 qt.	$2.59	$2.42	$2.53
Milk, skim, half gallon	$1.39	$1.35	$1.37
Milk, whole, half gallon	$1.40	$1.39	$1.39
Mixed vegetables, frozen, 10 oz.	$0.77	$0.59	$0.70
Mushrooms, 1 lb.	$2.59	$2.39	$2.46
Olive Oil, cheapest, 17 oz.	$3.19	$2.49	$2.86
Onions, 1 lb.	$0.55	$0.39	$0.48
Orange juice, frozen, cheapest, 12 oz.	$1.59	$0.69	$1.09
Oranges, fresh, 1 lb.	$0.99	$0.69	$0.81
Peanuts, cocktail, Planter's, 12 oz.	$2.99	$2.39	$2.72
Peas, frozen, 10 oz.	$1.19	$0.59	$0.82
Pork, chops, 1 lb.	$4.99	$2.98	$3.65
Potato Chips, Eagle, 6.5 oz	$1.59	$1.39	$1.51
Potatoes, 5 lbs.	$1.59	$1.49	$1.52
Raisins, bulk, 1 lb.*	$1.49	$1.49	$1.49
Red Snapper, fresh, 1 lb.	$3.88	$2.99	$3.45
Rice, Hinode, 5 lbs.	$2.39	$2.29	$2.34
Seven-Up, 6-pack, cans	$2.25	$1.59	$1.91
Soap, bar, Ivory, 4-pack	$1.49	$1.15	$1.27
Soup, Campbell, Chicken Noodle, 10.5 oz. can	$0.99	$0.64	$0.83
Soy Sauce, Kikkoman, 20 oz.	$2.49	$1.99	$2.29
Spaghetti, cheapest, 1 lb.	$0.59	$0.49	$0.53
Sugar, cheapest, 5 lbs.	$1.79	$1.69	$1.76
Toilet Tissue, 4-roll pack, cheapest	$0.99	$0.99	$0.99
Tomatoes, Beefsteak	$1.69	$0.89	$1.22
Toothpaste, Crest, 6.4 oz.	$2.39	$2.25	$2.31
Tortillas, cheapest, 14 oz.	$0.63	$0.43	$0.54
Tuna, Starkist, 6.125 oz	$1.79	$0.87	$1.45
Turkey, ground, 1 lb.	$2.99	$2.59	$2.82
Turkey, whole, hen, 1 lb.	$1.19	$0.89	$1.09
Vegetable Oil, Wesson, 24 oz.	$1.89	$1.45	$1.63
Whiskey, Cutty Sark, 750 ml.	$15.88	$14.88	$15.52
Whiskey, Johnnie Walker Red, 750 ml.	$16.88	$15.88	$16.25
Wine, Burgundy, Gallo, 1.5 liter	$5.79	$3.99	$4.89
Wine, Chablis, Gallo, 1.5 liter	$4.88	$3.88	$4.25

Source: Survey of three major supermarkets in fall and winter, 1993. Prices are highest, lowest and average of those found at the three stores. Asterisk (*) indicates items were carried by only two stores.

17/Commuting

Miles to Bay Bridge, Carpooling, CalTrain, Choice of Buses to, within San Francisco, San Mateo County

ALTHOUGH TRAFFIC IN DOWNTOWN SAN FRANCISCO is a mess, the City and, to a lesser extent, San Mateo County have to be considered good commutes — compared to other counties.

Before the 1989 earthquake, freeways frequently jammed during peak hours. The quake made matters worse: The Embarcadero freeway, badly damaged, was demolished in 1991, wiping out a main road to Chinatown, North Beach, Fisherman's Wharf and a good portion of the financial district. A boulevard of some sort is to replace within about five years. Several other freeway access-exit ramps have been torn down, channeling traffic to fewer ramps.

The earthquake also forced the closure of Interstate 280, from Highway 101 north to SOMA (south of Market). Since then, it has been reopened but in 1994 and 1995 the 280-101 interchange will be rebuilt.

Caltrans has mapped out detours but warns that delays should be expected.

With so much kaput, why is San Francisco still a good commute? Because it's a small city that has an extensive bus-street car system, the MUNI. Because

---

DRIVE CAUTIOUSLY ON FRIDAY

The worst day of the week to drive? Fridays, says State Office of Traffic Safety, reporting on a 1992 study.

Fridays accounted for 35,902 injury accidents. Thursdays were second with 31,558. The safest day of the week, Sundays, 26,716.

To be really safe, drive during what appears to be the safest hour of the week, Wednesday from 4 to 5 a.m. (140 accidents).

BART IS YOUR TICKET TO THE BAY AREA

The easiest way to tour the Bay Area is to pick up a BART ticket and step aboard.

Our clean, comfortable trains run every day until midnight and kids 4 and under ride FREE!

Here are just a few places of interest you careach on BART:

■ **SHOPPING** - BART is the perfect shopping companion because we stop where you shop. BART serves over 2000 stores and retail centers

■ **RESTAURANTS** - BART is easily accessible to thousands of fine restaurants throughout the greater Bay Area. Then leave the driving to us!

■ **SPORTS EVENTS** - Don't hassle with fighting the traffic to the Oakland Coliseum or other sporting events. Take BART and you'll have even more fun!

■ **PERFORMING ARTS** - From the San Francisco Opera House to the Orpheum Theatre, BART gives you a front row seat.

■ **AIR TRAVEL** - Save money on parking by taking BART right to the Oakland Coleseum/ Airport station plus a short shuttle.

BART is your ticket to everything from the major financial districts to museums and historical sites.

For more information, please call - **(510)464-6000**

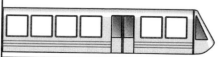

Driving Miles to Bay Bridge

City	Hwy 101	I-280
Atherton	31	31
Belmont	22	25
Brisbane	7	NA
Burlingame	15	18
Colma	NA	11
Daly City	NA	7
East Palo Alto	31	NA
Foster City	21	NA
Half Moon Bay	NA	NA
Hillsborough	NA	21
Menlo Park	30	36
Millbrae	14	17
Pacifica	NA	10
Portola Valley	NA	36
Redwood City	25	31
San Bruno	11	14
San Carlos	24	29
San Mateo	18	25
South San Francisco	9	11
Woodside	27	33

Note: These are approximate distances from the west end of the Bay Bridge near downtown San Francisco to the first available exit to each city. Highway 101 and Interstate 280 merge in San Francisco and share a common route to the bridge. **Key:** NA, not applicable. Either exits were not available or the freeway was judged to be too distant for a reasonable estimate.

BART (rail transit) picked up some of the load.

The MUNI catches a lot of flak and in 1993 residents voted to require public officials to take mass transit twice a week — so they would see the problems first hand. But MUNI also carries 750,000 riders daily.

If San Franciscans were bereft of buses, cabs, street cars and cable cars, if they were reduced to bicycles, skates and shoe leather, chances are that the great majority would arrive home before most of the suburban commuters. This is one benefit of living in a geographically small city — roughly eight miles by eight miles.

The San Mateo Advantages

San Mateo residents, many of whom work in San Francisco, have it tougher but again, compared to other Bay Area counties, they come off OK.

The northern towns are within a few minutes drive or bus or train ride to downtown San Francisco. No bridges — the great bottlenecks for commuters from the East and North Bays — separate San Mateo cities from San Francisco. Highway 101 feeds straight into the downtown.

BART's end of the line is in Daly City. Many residents of Pacifica, South San Francisco and Daly City are within a short drive or bus ride to the BART station, another straight shot to the downtown.

CalTrain runs trains up the Peninsula from Gilroy, in southern Santa Clara County, to downtown San Fran, stopping blocks from the financial district.

SamTrans, the public bus agency serving San Mateo County, makes connections with MUNI (the San Francisco bus system) and runs express buses into the downtown.

Finally, many San Mateo residents don't work in downtown San Francisco. The International Airport, one of the largest employers in the region, is located in San Mateo County, a short drive for most residents. The same for the hundreds of firms that feed into the airport's economy, the hotels, the office complexes, the warehouses, the shippers.

Southern San Mateo County is oriented toward Silicon Valley (roughly Palo Alto to Cupertino and including parts of San Jose). Santa Clara County has traffic jams but it also has many freeways, and the great bulk of industry is located within a half-hour drive of Redwood City.

All this will be cold comfort on the days you're stuck in traffic but for those thinking about settling in either San Francisco or San Mateo counties, the commute, compared to other places, has to be considered a plus. And it's something that with planning and experimenting often can be improved.

Means of Transportation to Work
San Francisco

City or Town	HM	WK	BK	MC	MV	BS	TC	BA	RR
San Francisco	4	10	1	1	50	24	3	5	*0

San Mateo County

City or Town	HM	WK	BK	MC	MV	BS	TC	BA	RR
Atherton	9	9	1	0	76	1	*0	0	3
Belmont	3	3	*0	*0	89	2	0	*0	3
Brisbane	1	3	1	1	90	3	0	*0	1
Broadmoor	2	3	0	*0	85	2	1	6	0
Burlingame	3	3	1	*0	85	2	*0	*0	5
Colma	3	5	0	0	77	11	0	4	0
Daly City	1	2	*0	*0	77	10	*0	8	*0
East Palo Alto	2	2	2	*0	86	7	0	0	1
El Granada	5	1	0	0	91	2	0	0	0
Emerald Lake Hills	5	1	*0	*0	92	1	0	*0	1
Foster City	3	1	*0	*0	91	2	0	0	2
Half Moon Bay	5	2	*0	0	89	1	0	*0	*0
Highlands	3	1	*0	*0	94	1	0	1	1
Hillsborough	7	1	*0	0	86	1	*0	*0	2
Menlo Park	4	3	5	1	83	1	0	*0	2
Millbrae	3	3	*0	*0	89	2	0	1	2
Montara	6	1	0	0	88	2	0	2	1
Moss Beach	4	1	0	*0	91	2	0	1	0
North Fair Oaks	4	5	3	*0	79	6	0	*0	2
Pacifica	2	2	*0	*0	87	5	*0	3	*0
Portola Valley	7	4	1	0	86	0	0	0	2
Redwood City	3	3	1	1	88	2	0	*0	2
San Bruno	2	2	1	1	88	2	*0	2	2
San Carlos	3	2	1	1	89	1	0	*0	3
San Mateo	2	3	1	*0	86	4	0	*0	3
South San Francisco	1	2	*0	1	86	4	0	4	1
West Menlo Park	3	4	1	0	88	1	0	0	4
Woodside	13	3	1	0	82	0	0	0	1
San Mateo County	3	3	1	*0	87	4	*0	2	2

Source: 1990 Census. Figures are percent of population, rounded to the nearest whole number.
Key: HM (work at home); WK (walk); BK (bike); MC (motorcycle); MV (motor vehicle including car, truck or van); BS (bus); TC (trolley or street car); BA (BART), RR(train, railroad). *Less than 0.5 percent.

Time-saving Strategies

• Buy a good map book and keep it in the car. The editors favor Thomas Guides. Sooner than later you will find yourself jammed on the freeway and in desperate need of an alternate route. They're out there. Many downtown streets

in San Francisco are one-way and for obscure historical reasons many streets—east and west, north and south — take a sharp turn at Market Street, confusing everything. If you travel the downtown frequently, a map is a necessity.

El Camino Real runs the length of San Mateo County. Parts of it are so tacky that the road has become a local joke. But if Highway 101 or Highway 280 are jammed, never mind looks. Take El Camino Real.

• Listen to traffic reports on the radio. Helicopters and planes give immediate news of jams. Avoid trouble before you get on the road.

• Buy SamTrans and MUNI (bus) passes and $20 BART tickets. They save delays and fumbling for the right change when you're in a hurry.

• Join a car pool. RIDES will help you find people to share a ride — free. RIDES works with thousands of commuters each month and sets up pools going everywhere in the Bay Area. If you want to start a vanpool, RIDES will help you find passengers, lease a van and get you on the road. Typically, passengers share the van expenses, and the driver gets a free commute and personal use of the van. Poolers can use the commuter express lanes on highways around the Bay. For information call RIDES at 1 (800) 755-POOL.

• Avoid peak hours. If you can leave for work — it gets earlier every year — about 6:30 a.m. and hit the freeway home before 4 p.m., your kids might not greet you, "Hey, stranger."

• Take public transportation. Yes, the car is flexible, so handy, so private. But if other, easier, cheaper ways of commuting are at hand, why ignore them?

Bus, Train, Light Rail, Street Car and Cable

• SamTrans. The bus system serving San Mateo County and the Peninsula. Also connects with BART, CalTrain, MUNI, Santa Clara County Transit and AC Transit. SamTrans serves the major shopping centers and civic centers.

Express buses to San Francisco. For information and individual time-tables, call 1 (800) 660-4BUS.

• San Francisco Municipal Railway, popularly known as The MUNI. Runs almost all the street public transit in San Francisco, diesel buses, electric buses, cable cars. Lines to almost all neighborhoods in the City. MUNI says that 95 percent of San Francisco residences are within two blocks of a MUNI stop. Carries 245 million passengers a year. Express buses along more popular routes. Beefed-up service during commute hours. For information, schedules, discount passes, (415) 673-MUNI.

———

ALONE ON THE ROAD

According to a recent study, about 65 percent of all commuters in the Bay Area drive alone to work. For San Mateo residents, the number is 69 percent. Of San Franciscans, paragons of mass transit use, only 41 percent drive to the job. Rest take mostly MUNI and BART.

SAN JOSE INTERNATIONAL AIRPORT

How To Make Connections In Silicon Valley.

San Jose International is served by these airlines: Alaska American • America West • Delta • Mexicana • Morris Air Northwest • Reno Air • Skywest • Southwest • TWA United/United Express

SAN JOSE
CAPITAL OF SILICON VALLEY

SAN JOSE INTERNATIONAL AIRPORT
City of San Jose
1661 Airport Boulevard, Suite C-205
San Jose, CA 95110-1285 (408) 277-4759

• CalTrain. The old Southern Pacific route, now employed for commute service by the Peninsula Corridor Joint Powers Board, an agency with representatives from San Francisco, San Mateo and Santa Clara counties. Trains from Gilroy to San Francisco. Stops at Morgan Hill, San Jose, Santa Clara, Sunnyvale, Mountain View, Palo Alto, Menlo Park, Redwood City, San Carlos, Belmont, San Mateo, Burlingame, Millbrae, San Bruno, South San Francisco and downtown San Francisco (4th Street, about 12 blocks south of Market). Bus service at stations. For schedules and more information, phone 1 (800) 660-4287.

• BART. From downtown San Francisco, through the Mission District, then a dogleg west to Daly City, the last stop. A short ride to downtown San Francisco. Morning riders from Daly City, first to board, usually get a seat. For info, schedules (510 464-6000). BART also serves Alameda and Contra Costa counties and is being extended south to San Francisco International Airport.

Other Transit Systems.

• AC Transit. Serves Alameda County and parts of Contra Costa. Express buses to San Francisco. (510) 839-2882.

• Golden Gate Transit. Buses from San Francisco to Marin and Sonoma counties. Ferries from San Francisco to Sausalito and Larkspur in Marin County. For bus and ferry info, (415) 332-6600.

• Santa Clara County Transportation Agency. Serves Silicon Valley and Santa Clara County. (408) 321-2300 or 1 (800) 894-9908.

Parking

San Francisco gives its residents preferred parking on 40 percent of the City's streets. If your car has a sticker, it won't be ticketed. The stickers are coded to individual neighborhoods. Sticker applicants must show proof of residence (driver's license, utility bill, lease-rental agreement) and the vehicle's registration. For more info, (415) 554-5000.

STIFF FINES

Motor vehicle fines have risen sharply over the past decade, the result, some believe, of the state's shortage of revenue.

Rather than or unable to impose taxes, the legislature is raising money through the back door: fines and fees.

In San Mateo County, if you solo drive a carpool lane, the fine is $271. Parking illegally in a handicapped slot will cost you $325. Failing to stop for a red light or stop sign, $104. Speeding fines range from $50 to $271.

Parking in a San Francisco bus zone will cost you $250.

If you can't pay the fine, go to court. The judge will often lower the amount or put you on installment payments or both.

Transit with
a View

***Golden Gate Bus & Ferry System
serving Sonoma,
Marin and San Francisco.***

Be part of Golden Gate Transit's
POLLUTION SOLUTION!

For fare and schedule information, please call:
415-453-2100 (Marin); 707-544-1323 (Sonoma). TDD: 415-257-4554. ♿

18/Weather

Pacific High, Summer Fog, Rainy & Dry Months, No Snow, Mild Winters, the Best Time to Swim

SAN MATEO AND SAN FRANCISCO weather can be described as delightful — with one big exception. In spring and summer fog often envelops the ocean towns and neighborhoods and, in some places, penetrates to the Bay.

If you like fog and brisk air ... no problem. If you don't, you may find balmy winters a fair swap but the bottom line is that some people just plain don't like the fog.

Other than that, summers are rarely excessively hot, rarely humid, and winters are rarely cold. Rain confines itself to the winter months, and winds blow pollution elsewhere.

Although erratic, the weather follows broad patterns, easily understood, and worthwhile understanding. It will help you decide when to hold picnics, when to eat in, when to visit the coast.

Five actors star in the weather extravaganza: the sun, the Pacific, the Golden Gate, the Central Valley and the Mountains.

The Sun

In the spring and summer, the sun moves north bringing a mass of air called the Pacific High. The Pacific High blocks storms from the California coast and dispatches winds to the coast.

In the fall, the sun moves south, taking the Pacific High with it. The winds slough off for a while, then in bluster the storms. Toward spring, the storms abate as the Pacific High settles in.

When should you have a picnic? Rarely will the summer disappoint you with rain, and if it does, the rain will be miniscule. But in some neighborhoods and towns the fog may seem like rain.

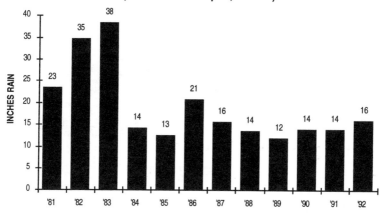

Total Annual Rainfall
(San Francisco Airport, 1981-92)

Source: National Weather Service. Rainfall is measured from July 1 to June 30 of following year; 1992 figure is 1991-1992.

The Pacific

Speeding across the Pacific, the spring and summer winds pick up moisture and, approaching the coast at an angle, strip the warm water from the surface and bring up the frigid.

Cold water exposed to warm wet air makes a wonderfully thick fog. In summer, the Sunset and Richmond districts in San Francisco, Monterey, Half Moon Bay and Pacifica, among others, often look like they are buried in mountains of cotton.

The Golden Gate and the Mountains

This fog would love to scoot inland to the Bay neighborhoods — Bayview, Potrero Hill, Mission, Noe Valley and others — and Bay towns such as San Mateo, Redwood City, Burlingame and Foster City.

But the coastal hills and mountains stop or greatly impede its progress —

Average Daily Temperature

Location	Ja	Fb	Mr	Ap	My	Ju	Jy	Au	Sp	Oc	No	Dc
Half Mn. Bay	52	53	53	53	55	57	59	60	60	58	54	52
Redwd. City	50	53	55	58	63	67	69	69	68	63	54	50
S.F. Airport	50	53	54	56	59	62	63	64	65	62	55	53
San Jose	50	54	55	58	63	67	70	69	69	63	55	50
San Fran.	51	55	55	55	57	59	60	61	63	62	60	53

Source: National Weather Service.

except where there are openings. Of the half dozen or so major gaps, the biggest is that marvelous work of nature, the Golden Gate.

The fog shoots through the Golden Gate in the spring and summer, visually delighting motorists on the Bay Bridge, banging into the East Bay hills, and easing down toward San Jose, where it takes the edge off the summer temperatures.

For most of San Mateo County, the Santa Cruz Mountains hold back the fog — one major reason why the weather delights. The fog takes the edge off the summer heat yet leaves the Bay towns basking in the sun.

Where the mountains or hills dip or flatten out, the fog penetrates. The Golden Gate Park, flat, ushers fog into Haight Ashbury and parts of the downtown. The Alemany Gap, near Lake Merced, allows some fog into Hunters Point.

In San Mateo County, the hills dip at Daly City and just north of Daly City. In July and August, it's not unusual for residents of Daly City, Colma and South San Francisco to bundle up in sweaters and jackets.

The hills dip to a lesser extent about the middle of Crystal Springs, near the City of San Mateo, which will get some of the cooler ocean air. South San Francisco and Brisbane are located side by side. Brisbane is tucked behind San Bruno Mountain. South San Francisco is more exposed to ocean winds so it will get more fog.

The sun dances in here. On many days it burns the fog away by 2 or 3 in the afternoon. But come night, the cold and the fog often assert themselves.

The radio tower atop Mt. Sutro by day appeals visually to no one. At night the hills for a few hours will hold back the fog, and all of a sudden, surrender. Great clouds will billow around the tower and down into the valleys, and the upper antennas, with their guy wires, will seem like the masts of a sailing ship making its way across the heavens.

The Central Valley

Also known as the San Joaquin Valley. Located about 75 miles inland, the Central Valley is influenced more by continental weather than coastal. In the summer, this means heat.

Hot air rises, pulling in cold air like a vacuum. The Central Valley sucks in the coastal air through the Golden Gate and openings in the East Bay hills, until the Valley cools. Then the Valley says to the coast: no more cool air.

With the suction gone, the inland pull on the ocean fog drops off, often breaking down the fog-producing apparatus and clearing San Francisco and the coastline. Coast residents enjoy days of sunshine. Meanwhile, lacking the cooling air, the Valley heats up again, creating the vacuum that pulls in the fog.

This cha-cha-cha between coast and inland valley gave rise to the Bay Region's boast of "natural air conditioning." In hot weather, nature works to bring in cool air; in cool weather, she works to bring in heat.

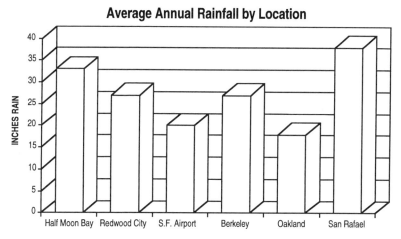

Average Annual Rainfall by Location

Source: National Weather Service

The Mountains and Pacific Again

In the winter, great banks of tule fog often form in the Central Valley and chill the air. The Pacific in the winter holds the heat better than the land and, when not raining, often settles balmy weather along coast and Bay cities — another major reason why San Francisco and San Mateo enjoy a mild climate. Recall that cold moves toward heat, much as if heat were a suction vacuum. The Central Valley fog would like to move into the Bay but is blocked by the mountain range running up the East Bay. Occasionally, however, Central Valley fog will penetrate through its openings, foremost the Carquinez Strait near Vallejo, and work down into the Bay — a perilous time for shipping.

Coastal fog often forms well above the Pacific and, pushed by the wind, generally moves at a good clip. In thick coastal fog, you will have to slow down but you can see the tail lights of a car 50 to 75 yards ahead. In valley or tule fog, you sometimes can barely make out your hood ornament. This winter fog blossoms at shoe level when cold air pulls moisture from the earth. When you read of 50- and 75-car pileups in the Central Valley, tule fog is to blame. Dust storms are another culprit in the Valley.

Within the Bay, tule fog, before radar, was often responsible for shipping accidents, including the 1901 sinking of the liner, Rio de Janeiro, 130 lives lost.

On rare days, tule fog will settle over San Francisco Airport, making takeoffs and landings risky. On the ocean side of the county, Half Moon Bay Airport will be basking in the sun.

Mountains and Rain

Besides blocking the fog, the hills also greatly decide how much rain falls in a particular location. Many storms travel south to north, so a valley that opens to the south (San Lorenzo-Santa Cruz) will receive more rain than one that opens to the North (Santa Clara-San Jose.)

When storm clouds rise to pass over a hill, they cool and drop much of their rain. Some towns in the Bay Region will be deluged during a storm, while a few miles away another town will escape with showers.

That basically is how the weather works in the Bay Area but, unfortunately for regularity's sake, the actors often forget their lines or are upstaged by minor stars.

Weather Tidbits: The 'Stick

Why the Giants want to move. Candlestick Park, present home of the Giants, lies at the junction of two windstreams that shoot through the Alemany Gap in the hills. The result: eddies and vacuums that do circus tricks with fly balls. But the summer fog and winds disappear about September. The 49ers often play in winter sunshine.

Swimming

September and October are the best months to swim in the Pacific. The upwelling of the cold water has stopped. Often the fog has departed. Sunshine glows upon the water and the coast. Almost every year the summer ends with hot spells in September and October.

Sunshine

Like sunshine? You're in the right place. Records show that during daylight hours the sun shines in New York City 60 percent of the time; in Boston, 57 percent; in Detroit 53 percent; and in Seattle, 43 percent.

Atop Mt. Tamalpais the sun shines 73 percent of the year. San Jose averages 63 percent. San Mateo and San Francisco ... well, it depends on where you're located. But 60 percent plus is a realistic figure.

Humidity

When hot spells arrive, the air usually has little moisture — dry heat. When the air is moist (the fog), the temperatures drop.

Redwood Drizzle

If you are planning a redwoods excursion to Big Basin or Muir Woods in the summer, bring a jacket and an umbrella. Redwoods are creatures of the fog, need it to thrive. Where you find a good redwood stand, you will, in summer, often find cold thick fog.

When fog passes through a redwood grove, the trees strip the moisture right out of the air. In some parts of the Bay Region redwood-fog drip has been measured at 10 inches annually.

One of the editors recalls attending a summer picnic in a redwood grove. We arrived about 11 a.m. to find the air cold and the drip heavy enough to soak our clothes. Parents bundled up children, plastic tablecloths were used as rain jackets. Two hours later, we were playing softball under a hot sun.

Scorchers

• During the summer and fall, the Pacific High will occasionally loop a strong wind down from Washington through the Sierra and the hot valleys, where it loses its moisture, and into the Bay Area.

Extremely dry, these northeasters, which are now called "Diablos," will tighten the skin on your face, cause wood shingle roofs to crackle and turn the countryside into tinder.

The October 1991 fire that destroyed 2,500 homes and apartments in the Berkeley-Oakland hills and killed 25 was caused by a Diablo.

On Sept. 27, 1923, a northeaster fire roared down upon North Berkeley, destroying homes, libraries, students' clubs, hotels and boarding homes — 584 buildings in all.

If you buy in the hills or brushy areas, take a look at fire-resistant shingles and fire prevention tactics.

Storms

Rain is rain, generally welcome all the time in dry California. But some rains are more welcome than others.

Storms from the vicinity of Hawaii turn Sierra slopes to slush and, in the upper elevations, deposit soft snow that sinks under the weight of skis.

Alaskan storms bring snow to the lower mountains and deposit a fine powder, ideal for skiing. Some Alaskan storms occasionally bless the Bay Region with snow on the mountain tops. The air will be crystal clear, with a shiver of cold. The East Bay hills, green for the winter, will overnight don a lovely mantle of white.

When your home is visited by a field mouse or two, you will know winter has truly arrived. The furry creatures are happy to bask in the sun but when the chill creeps into their nests, they seek the equivalent of Palm Springs: the closest house.

Shore Alert!

Every year the ocean reaches out and sweeps someone away. The water is cold, the waves treacherous. Take care.

19/Crime

Putting Crime in Perspective — the Numbers, How to Weigh Them, Taking Precautions

IF YOU'RE RENTING AN APARTMENT OR BUYING a house, keep in mind that although vandals, muggers and murderers can strike anywhere, they do most of their damage in sections where the poor reside.

Which is not to say that the middle class and rich are universally good. The Savings and Loans thieves, generally silvered at birth, ruined many and did the country harm. The rich and middle class have their violent and their murderers.

Nor is it to say that the poor are universally criminal. The great majority of poor and low-income people obey the law and live good lives, and in many countries the connection between poverty and crime is weak. After World War II, almost all Japanese were impoverished but social values kept crime low.

In this country, however, violent crime is most likely to be committed by the down-and-out, the abused, the addicted, the demented and the aimless, especially if they are young. These persons, because of their backgrounds and actions, are likely to be poor and live in low-income neighborhoods.

It needs to be emphasized, however, that urban life these days demands caution. San Francisco in 1993 posted 132 violent deaths, its highest count in 17 years. Always be wary.

In its annual reports, the FBI correlates crimes by age, by sex, and by other categories. Women are more peaceful than men. In homicides, the chances are about 10 to 1 he did it, says FBI.

The old are more law-abiding than the young. The FBI reports that in 1991 persons age 12 through 29 accounted for 61 percent of all arrests.

Proximity and Opportunity

Many crimes are crimes of proximity and easy opportunity (which is why

Crime Statistics by City
San Mateo County

City	Population	Rate	Homicides
Belmont	25,023	28	0
Burlingame	27,797	51	2
Daly City	95,743	40	2
East Palo Alto	24,322	72	39
Foster City	29,223	29	1
Hillsborough	11,063	7	0
Menlo Park	29,082	49	1
Millbrae	21,171	31	0
Pacifica	39,070	31	0
Redwood City	68,529	50	3
San Bruno	40,409	48	0
San Carlos	27,140	34	1
San Mateo	88,664	43	3
So. San Francisco	56,331	43	1

Crime in San Francisco & Other Bay Area Cities

City	Population	Rate	Homicides
Berkeley	106,543	127	12
Concord	115,489	64	5
Hayward	115,644	69	5
Novato	49,354	38	3
Oakland	386,086	125	165
Palo Alto	57,978	60	1
San Francisco	**750,885**	**102**	**117**
San Jose	811,342	49	43
San Rafael	50,204	58	0
Santa Rosa	117,527	61	2
Sunnyvale	121,588	40	2
Vallejo	113,259	85	13
Walnut Creek	62,821	46	0

Crime in Other Cities

City	Population	Rate	Homicides
Honolulu	875,297	61	31
Los Angeles	3,615,355	94	1,094
New York	7,375,097	85	1,195
Sacramento	383,102	100	45
Seattle	544,940	120	60
Washington, D.C.	589,000	114	443

Source: Annual 1993 FBI crime report which uses 1992 data, including population estimates based on the 1990 census. Rate is all reported crimes per 1,000 residents. Homicides include murders and non-negligent manslaughter. The FBI does not rank unincorporated towns or cities below 10,000 population.

precautions and safeguards help; they discourage the often easily discouraged.) When the violent and the criminal strike, they generally attack or rob their neighbors, often their friends and relatives, studies have shown.

Between rich and the poor, crime moves across a spectrum. In middle-class towns, crime rates are middling. Within these communities, the poorer sections will often be afflicted with higher crime than the others.

Washington, D.C., is notorious for its crime. Yet, according to the Washington Post, police studies show that the neighborhoods that have suffered high crime for decades are the ones that now suffer the most; and that crime in middle- and upper-income neighborhoods is no more serious than it has been in times past. (But the violence in the poorer neighborhoods has worsened, mainly because of drugs and easy access to guns. And the middle class and rich neighborhoods may be taking stronger precautions than before. It's not just location.)

Bay Area Pattern

The same pattern holds in the Bay Area. East Oakland, high crime; Oakland hills, low. In Contra Costa County, flatlands of Richmond, high crime; the El Sobrante section of Richmond (middle class), generally low; Orinda (rich), very low.

San Mateo County has several cities where in the course of a year 2, 3 or 4 homicides will occur, possibly making residents uneasy and more attentive to precautions.

In 1992, San Mateo County counted about 55 homicides. Of these, 39 occurred in the city of East Palo Alto. Figures for 1993 are not yet available but overall homicides are expected to drop sharply because East Palo Alto, by beefing up its police and installing new programs, cut its homicides to six.

In San Francisco, the Tenderloin, one of the poorest neighborhoods, gets singled out for having severe crime. Other trouble spots include the Bayview district, the Mission and the neighborhoods with some of the housing projects.

Twin Peaks and Pacific Heights are considered much safer. The same generally for the neighborhoods on the west side of the city.

How safe is the street you're thinking about moving onto? For a rough measure in San Mateo County, take a look at the school rankings. As most children attend school in their immediate neighborhoods, the rankings reflect the social climate. Very low rankings indicate trouble; many kids not learning, drifting, a bad sign.

In San Francisco, rankings are somewhat helpful but can also mislead. Many children attend schools outside their immediate neighborhoods.

Common Sense

Drive the streets. Bars on windows and doors, too many bums, men drinking outside liquor stores, prostitutes openly plying their trade — could be trouble. Here again, though, a little qualifier: Many homes in "safe" neighborhoods have gated doors. Goes with the territory in a big city. Talk to the neighbors.

In San Francisco, in part because of the homeless, quality of life in recent elections has been a big issue.

Is any town or neighborhood 100 percent safe? As long as human beings roam the earth, the answer is no. The "safest" place will still be prey to the random element.

Blackhawk, a gated community and one of the richest in the Bay Area, stills calls out sheriff's deputies; domestic disputes.

It's tempting to say, pick the safest place possible. But the reality is that your income will limit your choices. We can't all live in Blackhawk or Pacific Heights or Twin Peaks.

There's a flip side to crime that's rarely advertised. Felons lower housing prices. The worse the crime generally the cheaper the house. Many cities, however, have transition neighborhoods, where crime is a problem but not rampant, and housing is cheap or the location in other ways is attractive. Often the commute to the job center is short.

Choose your address with care. Take precautions: alarms, neighborhood watches, good locks, watchdogs. Call 9-1-1 if you're suspicious of anything.

San Francisco notes:

• Preliminary reports for 1993 indicate that overall crime was down. Also down were rape, aggravated assault, burglary and car theft.

Homicides were up. Eight people were killed when gunman shot up high-rise office, then killed self. Young man was shot to death at Fisherman's Wharf while trying to stop a street robbery. A teen gang, on a rampage, killed two people. Community activist was shot and killed in Western Addition; cross fire. City shocked by incidents.

• Matrix program installed. Police roust homeless, seize some of their possessions, move them along, encourage them to go to shelters. Some people say this is illegal. Courts will decide matter.

• Housing projects in 1993 got bad press. Residents at several said they were terrorized. Some projects to be torn down and rebuilt, it is hoped, in a style that discourages crime.

Subject Index

Advertisers' Index

Order McCormack's Guides
and Other Books by Phone or Mail

To order by mail, fill out the form on the opposite page and mail to McCormack's Guides, P.O. Box 190, Martinez, CA 94553. Make checks payable to McCormack's Guides. To order by phone, call toll free 1-800-222-3602 and tell our service representatives the titles you wish to order. MasterCard and Visa accepted.

  1-800-222-3602

McCormack's Guides Editions for 1994

McCormack's Guides provides information about schools (both public and private), demographics, crime, weather, home prices, jobs, recreation, day care, health care and other areas of interest to newcomers and parents of school-age children.

G1 **Alameda County '94.** Don McCormack and Allen Kanda. Alameda County. Profiles on more than 16 cities and towns including Berkeley, Oakland, Pleasanton, Fremont, among others. $6.95

G2 **Contra Costa & Solano '94.** Don McCormack and Allen Kanda. Contra Costa and Solano counties. Information on 33-plus towns and cities in Contra Costa, eight in Solano County. $6.95

G3 **Marin, Napa & Sonoma '94.** Don McCormack and Allen Kanda. Marin, Napa and Sonoma counties. Profiles on 17 towns and cities in Marin, seven in Napa and 17-plus in Sonoma County. $6.95

G4 **Sacramento County '94.** Don McCormack and Allen Kanda. Sacramento County and parts of Yolo, Placer and El Dorado counties in the Greater Sacramento Metropolitan area. More than 20 communities profiled. $6.95

G5 **Santa Clara County '94.** Don McCormack and Allen Kanda. Santa Clara County. Profiles on more than 15 cities and towns including San Jose, Cupertino, Palo Alto, Sunnyvale, among others. $6.95

G6 **San Francisco & San Mateo County '94.** Don McCormack and Allen Kanda. San Francisco and San Mateo County. Information on more than 45 neighborhoods in San Francisco and more than 20 communities in San Mateo County. $6.95

G7 **Orange County '94.** Don McCormack and Allen Kanda. Orange County. Information on more than 39 cities and towns including Anaheim, Costa Mesa, Huntington Beach, Yorba Linda, Westminster, among others. $6.95

G8 **San Diego County '94.** Don McCormack and Allen Kanda. San Diego County. Some 22 towns and cities profiled, including San Diego, Carlsbad, Santee, among others. $6.95

Other Books Available by Mail Through McCormack's Guides

B1 **Bargain Hunting in the Bay Area.** Sally Socolich. Discount places, where to find the bargains. Revised and updated. $11.95

B2 **A.M-P.M.** Popular guide to restaurants, clubs, shops, and attractions of Northern California. $9.95

B3 **Zagat Survey.** Capsule descriptions of restaurants in Bay Area, Monterey and wine country. $9.95

B4 **Best Restaurants of San Francisco.** Patricia Unterman, restaurant critic for San Francisco Chronicle. $10.95

B5 **Perfect Places Hotels.** Lynn Broadwill and Jan Brenner. Banquet halls, special locations for parties, weddings and functions. $19.95

B6 **50 Romantic Getaways for Two in Northern California.** Bill Gleeson. Inns, hotels, places to tune up relationships. Photos. $14.95

B7 **Greater Bay Area Golf Guide.** Golf courses, descriptions, in Northern California, including Sacramento, Tahoe and Reno. $9.95

B8 **Best Hikes for Children in the South Bay.** Bill and Kevin McMillan. Where to walk with the kiddies. Also includes San Francisco and Oakland. $12.95

B9 **San Francisco with Kids.** Frommer's. Attractions for kids around the Bay Area. Family entertainment. $17.00

B10 **Great Outdoor Getaways to Bay Area and Beyond.** Tom Stienstra. Parks, rivers, lakes, camping and fishing spots. $16.95

B11 **Disneyland and Southern California,** Kim Wiley. Tips on getting the most out of Disneyland. Places to take kids. $9.99

B12 **Glorious Gardens to Visit in Northern California.** Priscilla Dunhill and Sue Freedman. Profiles of and directions to 65 gardens from Mendocino to Carmel. $16.00

B13 **Visiting Eden: The Public Gardens of Northern California.** Joan C. Turner. $18.95

B14 **Golden Gate Gardening.** Pam Pearce. Complete gardening guide for Northern California. $24.95

B15 **The Missions of California.** Stanley Young. Locations, descriptions. $16.95

B16 **San Francisco Bay Area Job Bank.** Profiles of local employers, list of industry associations and publications. $15.95

B17 **Fodor's San Francisco.** All-round guide to Bay Area and wine country. Updated. $13.00

B18 **Historic San Francisco.** Rand Richards. A concise history and guide. $14.95

B19 **San Francisco Access.** Another good general guide to Bay Area, Northern California. Updated. Maps. $18.00

B20 **Dog Lover's Companion.** Places and parks that cater to man's and woman's best friend. $12.95

B21 **Peace of Mind in Earthquake Country.** Peter Yanev. How to prepare for and what to do in an earthquake. $14.95

B22 **Bay Area Bike Rides.** Ray Hasler. Scenic roads for cyclists. $9.95

B23 **Touring the San Francisco Bay Area by Bicycle.** 34 rides of the region. Maps. $10.95

B24 **Touring the Wine Country by Bicycle.** Pedal and sip rides of Napa, Sonoma, Sierra and coast. Maps. $10.95

B25 **College in California.** Surveys public and private colleges of California. Financial aid, how to apply. More. Updated. $24.95

B26 **Buying and Selling a Home in California.** Dian Hymer. Advice from a real estate agent. $16.95

B27 **Parents Guide to School Selection in Santa Clara and San Mateo Counties.** Nancy Gill. Info on private and public schools. $14.95

Please add shipping charge of $2 for first book, $1.50 per book thereafter. California buyers add 8.25% sales tax to cover price.

VISA MasterCard   **1-800-222-3602**

Code (G1, B1, etc.)	First Word of Title	Price

Name/Company _____   Tax _____

Address _____   Subtotal _____

City/State/Zip _____   Shipping _____

Phone: _____   Total _____